CONSERVATIVE
REFORMERS

CONSERVATIVE REFORMERS

The Republican Freshmen and the Lessons of the 104th Congress

NICOL C. RAE

M.E. Sharpe
Armonk, New York
London, England

Library of Congress Cataloging-in-Publication Data

Rae, Nicol C., 1960–
Conservative reformers : the Republican Freshmen and
the lessons of the 104th Congress / by Nicol C. Rae
p.   cm.
Includes bibliographical references and index.
ISBN 0-7656-0128-1 (alk. paper). —
ISBN 0-7656-0129-X (pbk. : alk. paper)
1. Republican Party (U.S. : 1854–   )   2. United States. Congress—
Elections, 1994.   3. United States—Politics and government—1993–
4. Conservatism—United States.   I. Title.
JK2356.R23   1998
324.2734′09′049—DC21   98-13252
CIP

Printed in the United States of America

The paper used in this publication meets the minimum requirements of
American National Standard for Information Sciences—
Permanence of Paper for Printed Library Materials,
ANSI Z 39.48-1984.

♾

BM (c)   10   9   8   7   6   5   4   3   2   1
BM (p)   10   9   8   7   6   5   4   3   2   1

Contents

List of Tables and Figures

Tables

Figures

Preface

In November 1994 the Republican Party won control of the U.S. House of Representatives for the first time in forty years. This new Republican Congress claimed the 1994 election as a mandate for dramatic change in American politics in terms of both public policy and institutional reform, and the role of "guardians" of that mandate fell naturally on the seventy-three Republican House freshmen whose election had made the Republican majority possible. The House Republican freshman class was distinctive both in terms of its large size and the unusual degree of attention and influence that the freshmen received.

This book is about those Republican freshmen and their impact on the American political system. It has three major themes.

The first theme is the extent to which the Republican freshmen were able to fulfill the popular demand for reform of Congress and end the long-term erosion in Congress's power and authority within the American political system. Part of the explanation for the electoral success of the freshmen in 1994 and the high level of public recognition that they subsequently achieved lay in their claim to be political "outsiders" who would reform a Congress that had become increasingly "corrupt" under Democratic rule. While the Republicans did achieve a great deal in terms of reforming Congress's internal procedures, their defeat at the hands of President Bill Clinton in the 1995–96 budget battle confirmed the prevailing rule of present-day conflict between the executive and legislative branches of the American federal government; the president generally has the upper hand because Congress as a legislative body is ill adapted to the mass electronic environment in which modern American political conflict and debate take place.

The second theme of the book is the contrast between the influence of the freshman Republicans in the House and the more limited impact of their Senate counterparts. The eleven freshman Republicans in the Senate during the 104th Congress received relatively little attention, but they did effect some potentially significant institutional changes in that body. Moreover, the comparison between the experiences of the freshmen Republicans on either side of Capitol Hill does provide some interesting insights into the persistent differences between the institutional norms and culture of the contemporary House and Senate.

The third and final theme is that the story of the Republican freshmen in the 104th Congress provides us with an excellent demonstration of American government in action and the constraints on change within the modern political system. In effect, the experiences of the freshmen are a perfect late twentieth-century illustration of the precepts set out by James Madison in the 1780s in *The Federalist #10* and *#51*. A new popular majority is elected to control of the branch of government closest to the people, the House of Representatives, reflecting widespread popular demands for change and reform in Washington. To a considerable extent the new majority is able to fulfill its mandate by confirming the shift in the direction of American public policy toward economic and social conservatism, and by implementing significant institutional reforms of Congress. As the Republican program began to encounter significant popular resistance, however, the constitutional checks provided by the other branches of the federal government—the U.S. Senate and the presidency—arrested the "Republican revolution." Furthermore, as the 104th Congress began to approach reelection in 1996, some of the most characteristic behavior of the pre-1994 Democratic Congresses—preoccupation with reelection, obsessive fund raising, and assiduous attention to state and district interests—began to reassert itself among the 1994 Republican freshmen. The Republicans effected significant change in Washington, but many of the fundamentals of the preceding era remained in place. And while most of the freshmen accommodated themselves to this situation, for many of them it was a painful and sobering experience.

The book is divided into seven chapters. Chapter 1 places the election of the Republican freshmen in the context of the long-term erosion of public confidence in Congress that contributed to their triumph in 1994. Chapter 2 analyzes the 1994 election campaign and results, including a discussion of the motives that inspired the successful freshmen to run in 1994, and the role played in the Republican victory by Newt Gingrich and the Contract with America. Chapter 3 examines the first phase of the "Republican revolution" in 1995: the procedural reforms in the House and the passage of almost all the items in the Contract through that body in less than one hundred days. Chapter 4 is an account of the freshman Republicans' brutal encounter with political reality—the budget battle and government shutdowns of 1995–96. Chapter 5 looks at the largely uncovered story of the Republican freshmen in the Senate and discusses their impact while contrasting their experiences with those of the House freshmen. Chapter 6 looks at the Republicans' successful strategy to salvage control of Congress in 1996 after defeat in the budget battle and the increasing accommodation of the freshmen to the "ways of Washington" as reelection day approached. Finally, chapter 7 wraps up the story of the freshmen and assesses how much difference they actually made in American government.

This book stems from a long-standing scholarly interest in Republican Party politics and the operations of Congress. When the Republicans unexpectedly seized control of the House in November 1994, the opportunity to experience firsthand the impact of the new majority on what had appeared to be an utterly ossified institution was too good to miss. I had the good fortune to be selected as an American Political Science Association Congressional Fellow in 1995–96, which enabled me to work on Capitol Hill as a congressional aide and view the 104th Congress at close quarters. In the course of my fellowship I conducted in-depth interviews with twenty-seven freshman Republican House members (37 percent of the class) and five freshman Republican senators (45 percent of the class). I also interviewed eight senior House members, the chair of the Senate Republican Conference and his staff director, and four senior Senate staffers. I would like to take this opportunity to thank especially Congressman George Radanovich and Senator Thad Cochran for allowing me to work in their offices during my fellowship and for indulging my all too frequent absences from my desk in pursuit of their House and Senate colleagues. This is also the proper place to thank all those members and staffers who consented to be interviewed, for their valuable time and their unique insights into the legislative process and the role of the freshman members during the 104th Congress. This book could not have been written without them.

Of course, I owe an immense debt of gratitude to the American Political Science Association for awarding me a congressional fellowship, providing the best possible congressional orientation program, and for consistent support and encouragement during my year in Washington. Particular thanks are due to APSA Executive Director Cathy Rudder, the Academic Director of the Congressional Fellowship program Chris Deering, Administrative Director Kay Sterling, and her assistant Matt Linke. All were consistently helpful and ensured that I got the most out of my experience on the Hill.

I am further indebted to my fellow congressional fellows in 1995–96 for their advice and assistance in the conduct of my research. From an excellent group, special thanks are due to Jonathan Mott, Dimitra Kessindes, Bob Franklin, Carl Walton, and Daniel Stid for their insights and their friendship.

At the office of Congressman Radanovich, I am very grateful to Ian Houston, Marko Radielovic, Lisa Ford, David Johanson, and John McCamman, who allowed me to work at close quarters with the freshman Republicans, and who endured my academic curiosity and idiosyncrasies during an especially trying four-month period at the culmination of the 1995–96 budget battle. In Senator Cochran's office, I owe a special debt to a notable "refugee" from political science, Joe Westphal, who tolerated the extracurricular activities of his temporary assistant on "sunbelt issues" with great patience, and also for his hospitality and many personal kindnesses. Thanks are also due to Doris Wagley, Kay Webber, and Fred Pagan, who did their utmost to make my time on the Senate side as comfortable and rewarding as possible.

My time in the Washington, D.C. metropolitan area was made additionally pleasant by the excellent company and friendship of Elena Pell, who represents all that is best about that much maligned part of the world. My final debt of thanks in Washington is due to Stephanie Griffith and Ben Wagner, who allowed me to occupy their apartment for ten months and did everything to make sure that the move to Washington was accomplished as smoothly and easily as possible.

Over the longer term I have continued to benefit from the wisdom and encouragement of Byron Shafer, my best sounding board for ideas on Congress and any other aspect of modern American government. David Mayhew's work has been the benchmark for my studies of Congress since my student days, and I continue to benefit from his generosity and support. Ron Peters and his colleagues at the Carl Albert Center at the University of Oklahoma have consistently produced some of the finest scholarship on the American Congress, and I am grateful for their encouragement and interest in my work over the years. Finally, among the small and sometimes beleaguered community of political scientists that study the Republican Party, Jack Pitney and Bill Connelly stand out for their support and collegiality, and for producing the definitive work on the Republican Party in the House during the last decade of Democratic rule.

My colleagues in the Political Science Department at Florida International University continue to provide the conviviality, intellectual stimulation, and reassurance that are essential to scholarship. They are also to be commended for never forgetting that the study of political science neglects the real world of politics at the cost of its own relevance as an academic discipline. Particular mention should be made of John Stack, Dario Moreno, Mary Volcansek, Chris Warren, Kevin Hill, Ron Cox, and Joel Gottlieb for having given me the benefit of their friendship and advice over the years. Moreover, as departmental chairs, Professors Gottlieb, Volcansek, Warren, and Stack have also been wonderfully supportive of a sometimes impetuous and irascible colleague. Our newest addition, Colton Campbell, is a rapidly rising scholar of Congress who adds further strength and depth to an increasingly formidable team. Elsewhere at FIU, historian Darden Asbury Pyron has been a loyal friend whose prodigious intellectual energy and general zest for life never ceases to astonish. Dean Arthur Herriot and Provost James Mau must be acknowledged for helping to arrange a last-minute sabbatical that allowed me to accept the offer of a congressional fellowship. Dorinda Mosby and Mery Mejia provided invaluable secretarial assistance and regarded my professorial antics with their usual bemused tolerance. Finally, I am particularly indebted to my excellent teaching assistant, Barbara Herrera, and other graduate students in political science at FIU with whom I have enjoyed many stimulating exchanges of ideas on Congress and other topics. Of this group especial thanks are in order to Lourdes Cue, Diane Dick, Sean Foreman, and Francois Illas.

At M.E. Sharpe, Patricia Kolb has been a patient and indulgent editor whose enthusiasm for this project has never flagged and who has helped to sustain my spirits at difficult times. Steven Martin and Elizabeth Granda responded promptly and effectively to my queries on the production of the manuscript.

At times when doubts have circled and inspiration has been lacking, I have been particularly grateful for the consistent support of dear friends and family. Among the former I remain particularly indebted to

Miguell and Elena Del Campillo, Allan and Chris Mackenzie, and John Loza, whose loyalty and commitment have never flagged in good times or bad. My mother, Lily Rae, continues to be a tower of strength and source of unyielding love, and while my father, John Nicol Rae, did not live to see me embark on this project, without his encouragement and example I could never have enjoyed the privilege of working in and writing about the Congress of the United States.

Despite the help of all these fine people, this book, including the errors and misjudgments therein, is my sole responsibility. I have attempted to present an objective assessment of a particular group of political actors at a fascinating juncture in American politics and government. Only the reader can judge whether or not I have succeeded.

CONSERVATIVE
REFORMERS

1

The Trouble with Congress

"Congress isn't working." This simple statement reflected an overwhelming consensus among the American public in the early 1990s. Apart from a handful of political scientists, established Washington commentators, and some veteran members of Congress, few Americans were prepared to argue that the legislative branch of the American federal government was doing its job in anything like an adequate fashion.[1] Indeed, most members of the House and Senate appeared to be only too happy to participate in the public denigration of the institution in which they served. On television news, newspaper columns, op-ed pages, and talk radio, Congress had few if any defenders, and this distaste for the branch of government mentioned first in the U.S. Constitution was reflected in Congress's very poor public approval ratings (see Figure 1.1). Congress received significant public attention, it appeared, only when tawdry scandals involving money or sex dominated the political landscape. The institution where Madison, Monroe, Clay, Webster, Calhoun, Lodge, Russell, Johnson, and Rayburn had served was now associated with the sordid "money grabbing" of Jim Wright and Dan Rostenkowski or the "lechery" of Bob Packwood.

This chapter argues that Congress's problems stemmed from a variety of sources, but most of them were ultimately related to the decline in the power and authority of the legislative branch in the U.S. political system, a decline that became inevitable in an advanced mass society where the electronic news media serve as the primary vehicle of political communication and intermediation between citizen and government and where the norms of legislative government and representative democracy as set out in the 1787 Constitution no longer accord with the prevailing political ethos. Modern postindustrial society is ill suited to parliamentary government, a fact that became evi-

3

Figure 1.1 **Congressional Approval, 1980–94**

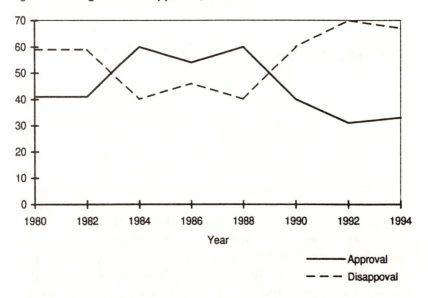

Source: Data kindly provided by Professor Kevin A. Hill from *American National Election Study Cumulative File, 1952–1994.* (Ann Arbor, MI: The Inter-University Consortium for Political and Social Research, 1995).

dent in several other mass democracies some time ago, but that has been obscured in the United States by a separation of powers that precluded the legislative branch from becoming a rubber stamp for the executive as in virtually all other advanced late twentieth-century democracies. While Congress retained significantly more of its prerogatives as a legislature than its counterparts elsewhere, this only seemed to contribute to governmental gridlock in the United States and popular disgust with the operations of an unwieldy body that had lost its political authority in a media-dominated mass democracy. The consequence has been that Congress seizes the public's attention only when its members accomplish nothing or get embroiled in scandal. Fundamental components of the legislative process, such as the brokerage of important political interests to produce compromises, not only fail to excite the American public but are also viewed as being at odds with the concept of "good government" in contemporary American political culture.

Thus it was long-term social and technological forces, rather than the foibles of its members, that brought Congress to its nadir in public approval and the concomitant crisis in its political authority in the early 1990s.

The Golden Age: Congressional Government
in the Nineteenth Century

For most of the nineteenth century, American government was more or less, as the title of Woodrow Wilson's classic work implies, *Congressional Government*.[2] This reflected the intentions of the Framers of the Constitution, who expected the legislative branch to be the predominant element in the federal government they were creating and thus delineated the structure and powers of Congress in the first article of the Constitution. Early American society lent itself easily to the concept of representative democracy or "Republican government" as Madison described it in *Federalist #10* and *#51*.[3] The country was still largely rural and highly decentralized governmentally, with the predominant political role being played by local elites and notables.[4]

Whig Republicanism—the belief that popular liberty required parliamentary as opposed to monarchical government—was the dominant ideology among the founding generation of Americans.[5] Nevertheless, the eighteenth-century English Parliament had one house composed of hereditary gentry and the second elected with a very limited franchise. In the early days of the American Republic the franchise was also limited, although the Framers still fretted about the potential for tyranny in the popularly elected House of Representatives. An explicitly "aristocratic" upper chamber on the lines of the House of Lords was precluded, however, by the absence of a native aristocracy and the egalitarian rhetoric of the Revolutionary War.

The legislative branch that the Framers created generally reflected the prevailing Whig view of what a parliament should be: a popularly elected House elected in single-member districts as the dominant element, with a Senate selected from the states by the state legislatures having several important prerogatives in approving treaties and federal executive and judicial appointments. The president was intended to be a quasi-monarchical restraint on popular power through his veto and was also given some important reserve powers in cases of national emergency.

What made parliamentary government possible in early America was the limited nature of government's activities, the absence of national emergencies most of the time, and, latterly, the strength of the national political parties. A federal government limited to adjusting the tariff and modifications in interstate commerce could fairly easily be directed from Congress. Moreover, the level of government that had the most impact on citizens during the nineteenth century was state or local government. For most of the first half of the nineteenth century the legislative branch predominated in a fairly limited federal government, as the Framers had intended that it would, and the greatest political figures of the age were leading members of Congress: Henry Clay, Daniel Webster, John C. Calhoun, and John Quincy Adams (who was far more influential as a member of the House than he ever was as president of the United States). Andrew Jackson was an exception to the rule of weak presidents, but the reaction to his crusade against the Bank of the United States was so strong that it probably weakened the office even further in the long term. It was in Congress that the great debates over slavery took place and where the numerous compromises on the issue were thrashed out.

National emergencies and a sudden rise in the significance of foreign and defense policy brought the presidency to life as the Framers had intended. Lincoln's "elective dictatorship" during the Civil War is the most obvious example. But the power that the White House accumulated in that conflict had receded within months of the war's end as Congress passed the Tenure of Office Act and almost removed President Andrew Johnson from office by impeachment. For the final quarter of the nineteenth century the presidency receded to its largely ceremonial position, to the extent that when Woodrow Wilson and James Bryce were writing their classic works on late nineteenth-century American national government, it was generally agreed that the most powerful office in the federal government was the Speakership of the House.[6]

The Speaker's power came not only from presidential weakness but also from the strength of the political party machines both within and outside Congress.[7] These organizations commanded unprecedented levels of loyalty from American voters but were primarily motivated by control of state and local governments, rather than national issues.[8] Congressional adherents were expected, however, to secure as much as they could from Washington for the local organization, and could do so only by currying favor with the party leadership, which controlled committee assignments, rules, and the legislative schedule on Capitol

Hill. Centralized leadership enabled Congress to overcome its inherent problems of fragmentation and coherence and to play the leading role in the federal government even as the scope of federal government activity was gradually expanding.[9]

Instead of being the prelude to the emergence of parliamentary government on the British model, however, the strong Speakerships of Thomas "Czar" Reed and Joseph "Uncle Joe" Cannon between 1890 and 1910 would prove to be an Indian Summer as far as Congress's influence in American government was concerned. Major international, social, and technological forces were already in train that, combined with opportunistic presidential leadership would change the balance of institutional power decisively in favor of the executive branch.

The Revolution of 1910 and the Committee Seniority System

The Progressive era marks the decisive turn in America's political development into an advanced industrial society. While Progressivism was composed of a variety of disparate movements, its underlying demand was for a more active role for the federal government, a role that the Progressives argued was necessitated by the changing national and international interests of the United States. The most influential strand of the Progressive movement in terms of leadership and ideas was the rapidly expanding urban professional class—teachers, lawyers, journalists—who, despite their considerable education and training, felt excluded from a political process dominated by corporate interests and party machines.[10] Progressives advocated a politics based on ideas, reason, and expertise: the regulation of the economy and society based on an objective "public interest" as opposed to the narrow interests of business or politicians. Congress was an unlikely environment for such a politics to thrive. Even under the strong Speakers of the turn of the century, Congress was an internally fragmented body geared to representing and brokering the multifarious particularistic interests of society instead of encouraging a broad national interest that transcended those particular interests to emerge. As such, it was an unlikely vehicle for the kind of extended government regulation in the public interest sought by the Progressives.

Instead, the latter regarded an activist presidency and a reformed and extended federal bureaucracy as crucial to the implementation of their vision of a more energetic and "rational" federal government, and the two Progressive presidents of the period were very much in sympathy with this view of government. Both Theodore Roosevelt and Woodrow Wilson aggressively promoted the notion of the presidency as a "bully pulpit" and the president as the unique representative of the "national will" or the "national interest" against the particularistic, "material" interests represented in the legislative branch.[11] In addition to the charismatic appeal of the Progressive presidents, by contrast with their dowdy, passive, late nineteenth-century predecessors, the Progressive approach to politics and government was buttressed intellectually by contemporary theories of professional management in the corporate world, which its adherents sought to replicate by establishing the rule of educated, expert "managers" in the political realm.[12]

Progressivism's faith in objective, technocratic solutions to political questions and a predominant role for an enlightened expert bureaucracy led by a charismatic president has never completely prevailed in the United States because it runs counter to the strong democratic strands in the national ideology, but it has retained and extended its influence among American social elites in the law, the media, and academia, to the point where its tenets are rarely, if ever, questioned in those arenas. Of course, those tenets are at odds with the politics of interest representation and brokerage characteristic of legislatures. As government has expanded and become more bureaucratic in advanced democracies, powerful legislatures have thus become expendable. In Great Britain, once regarded as the classic case of parliamentary democracy, the story of twentieth-century politics has been the loss of legislative power and independence to the cabinet and prime minister: a shift in the locus of governmental power, disguised only by the merging of the executive and legislative branches in a parliamentary system, through the medium of strong party government.[13]

The strict separation of legislative and executive powers, and the incompatibility of strong, centralized, European-style "mass parties" with American political culture, entailed that the rise of bureaucratic, executive-centered government would take a somewhat divergent course in the United States. Instead of submitting meekly to party dominance, the U.S. Congress, in fact, went in the opposite direction, weakening its centralized leadership and fragmenting its internal power structure. By so doing it enhanced the power of its individual members but precluded the possibility of something akin to a parliamentary system of government ever emerging in the United States.

Indeed it was the Progressives within Congress who were in the vanguard of the revolt against the power of Speaker Cannon in 1910. Progressive Republicans led by Congressman George Norris of Nebraska joined with the Democratic minority to strip Cannon of his control over committee assignments, the Rules Committee, and the scheduling of legislation. The Speakership had become so powerful under Reed and Cannon that it was interfering with the ambitions of individual members.[14] Reforms introduced by the Progressives to break the power of party bosses at the state and local levels—and particularly the introduction of the direct primary—had loosened the shackles of party loyalty on individual members of Congress.[15] Moreover, the primary made incumbent members in even the safest districts and states vulnerable to an electoral challenge. In such circumstances individual representatives and senators had a powerful incentive to try and obtain a share of congressional power to cater to the needs of their states and districts. The slow erosion of party machines also permitted ambitious young professionals to run for Congress outside the traditional party structure and win by securing a personal constituency of support.

These factors provoked the House Republican revolt that weakened Cannon and replaced the centralized leadership structure with the committee seniority system. In both House and Senate from 1910 to 1970, power devolved upon a system of permanent, specialized congressional committees, each monitoring a designated sphere of federal government activity. These committees were led by powerful chairmen, who essentially selected the membership and controlled the flow of legislation through their committee. To enhance the expertise of the committee and restrict the influence of party leaders or the executive, the positions of chairman and ranking minority member were awarded strictly on the basis of seniority. The committee seniority system enabled Congress to adapt to an expanded federal bureaucracy by encouraging members to develop policy expertise and thereby continue to monitor the various activities of the executive branch. Congress also retained its prerogatives on the federal budget through the power of its long-standing taxing and spending committees: Ways and Means and Appropriations in the House, and Finance and Appropriations in the Senate.

The price that was paid for this ability to scrutinize better the outputs of an expanded federal bureaucracy, however, was a loss to the presidency of the power of initiative and the ability to set the agenda of the federal government.[16] This began in the administrations of Theodore Roosevelt and Woodrow Wilson, but was not fully confirmed until the New Deal administrations of Franklin Roosevelt. While the president was now supposed to set the national political agenda, Congress was content to manage the details. According to Theodore Lowi, a "Second Republic" of the United States was erected on the basis of what Lowi described as "Interest Group Liberalism."[17] National emergencies or crises such as the New Deal brought forth new federal programs and agencies to administer them. Congressional authorizing committees sanctioned the creation of these agencies on the basis that the agencies would be answerable to that committee. In fact, powerful private interests concerned with the particular program came to dominate the committee and the agency in question to the extent that the program was administered for the benefit of those particular interests, rather than the interest of the taxpaying public. Moreover, personnel involved in particular programs tended to rotate from the agency to the committee and back to the major private interests concerned with the agency. Much of American domestic policy thus came to be controlled by "iron triangles" or "issue networks" of insiders and specialists— agency, relevant congressional committee(s), and relevant interest group(s)—largely impervious to influence by president, congressional leadership, or the wider public.[18]

None of this reflected well on Congress. Presidents, although they failed more often than not, were at least perceived as trying to perform their post–Progressive role in the political system of setting a national policy agenda in the public interest. The fragmented Congress under the committee seniority system was concerned with mundane and "narrow" constituent interests and the preservation of the policy status quo. While the legislative branch rarely took the initiative in establishing new government programs, once such programs were established and acquired a substantial constituency of support, Congress became their staunchest line of defense.[19] While the representation of powerful interests undoubtedly was a large part of the role that the Framers conceived for the legislative branch, it certainly did not accord with the Progressive concept of how politics should be conducted so prevalent among educational and professional elites in the United States.

Several other factors contributed to the erosion of Congress's public prestige and authority during the era of the committee seniority system.

The rise of foreign policy and national security issues to the top of the political agenda during World War II and the Cold War enhanced the influence of the presidency at Congress's expense, particularly as congressional "meddling" in foreign policy, as exemplified in the rejection of the League of Nations in 1920 and the passage of various neutrality acts during the 1930s, was widely held to have contributed to the eventual outbreak of World War II.[20] With presidents now acting as self-conscious "leaders of the free world" and possessing the further allure of having their fingers on the American nuclear button, Congress was ready to give the executive the benefit of the doubt on foreign and defense policy in the postwar years, even to the extent of turning a blind eye to violations of the constitutional prerogatives of the legislative branch in the area of war powers.[21] Presidents were now able to fight extended and bloody wars under the commander in chief power, as long as these engagements were largely militarily successful.

The committee seniority system had also accidentally led to the domination of Congress by conservative southern Democrats. The long period of largely Democratic control of both houses that began with the New Deal elevated to committee chairmanships those Democrats with the safest seats and longest tenure, namely white southerners. While many of these gentlemen were skillful and distinguished legislative leaders, and their fiscal conservatism acted as a constraint on pressures to expand the federal budget on the financial committees, even the great ones among them were unrelenting in their defense of southern racial segregation.[22] While this played well with their white southern constituents, nationally Congress as an institution of government became associated with resisting efforts to provide full civil and voting rights for black Americans. The association with "massive resistance" to civil rights became a further blot on Congress's public image during the civil rights revolution in the 1950s and 1960s.

Indeed, it took intervention by the U.S. Supreme Court in *Brown* v. *Board of Education* to finally break the congressional logjam on civil rights, and the post–New Deal period was conspicuous by the prevalence of federal judicial activism across a whole range of volatile political issues—civil rights, press freedom, criminal procedure, church/state relations, and sexual morality—at the expense of the legislative branch. The least accountable branch of the federal government was now effectively legislating on issues that were of major importance to Americans in their everyday lives, while the legislative branch either stood by or engaged in ineffectual protest at the scope and ambition of the judiciary. While much of the work of the Warren and Burger courts may have been merited, the extent of their activities did not reflect well on the status of a branch of government that is supposed to represent the people.

Congress reached its nadir in terms of the loss of institutional power in the first half of the 1960s. While the Warren Court was effectively legislating from the bench on a whole variety of issues, Congress still dragged its feet on the civil rights issue and completely abrogated its constitutional prerogatives as the Kennedy and Johnson administrations entangled the United States ever more deeply in the morass of Vietnam. Lyndon Johnson boasted that he did not need a congressional resolution giving him authority to escalate the Vietnam War, but he carried one in his pocket just in case the right opportunity arose to provide him with political cover. Johnson submitted his resolution after U.S. destroyers collided with some North Vietnamese fishing vessels in the Tonkin Gulf in July of 1964. The resolution, giving Johnson a free hand in Southeast Asia, sailed through the House and Senate in one afternoon with only two senators voting against it.[23]

With this careless abrogation of its constitutional duty Congress thus helped to entangle the United States in a brutal military conflict that divided and traumatized U.S. society, contributed to the downfall of two presidents, and undermined U.S. power in the world for two decades. The backlash against Vietnam, however, also provided Congress with an opportunity to exercise leadership and reassert its authority in the American system of government.

Congressional Resurgence: 1973–80

It took the cataclysmic impact of Vietnam and the excesses of Richard Nixon's administration, culminating in the Watergate scandal, to awaken Congress to the decline in its institutional authority. By the late 1960s a majority in Congress reflected popular exasperation with the conflict in Southeast Asia but nevertheless found it difficult to extract U.S. forces in the face of opposition from the commander in chief. The option of simply cutting off the military appropriations for the war existed, but it laid Congress open to accusations of exposing American forces to danger in the field or "stabbing our troops in the back." As if to rub salt in the wound, President Nixon extended the war into Laos and Cambodia without even consulting Congress.

Nixon moved against the legislative branch in other respects as well. Exasperated at the reluctance of the Democratic Congress to reduce spending, Nixon began to "impound"—that is, refuse to spend—funds appropriated by Congress.[24] It seems possible that without the intervention of the Watergate scandal, Nixon might well have reduced Congress's position in the political system to an even more lowly state, but with the presidency weakened by scandal, the legislative branch at last began to reassert itself in the face of the assault. In the summer of 1973 Congress finally cut off funding for the continued bombing of Cambodia. That same year, they passed the War Powers Act over Nixon's veto.[25] This piece of legislation was designed to prevent presidents from involving the United States in prolonged military conflicts abroad under their commander in chief power. The legislation obliged the president to consult Congress before making any such commitment of forces, gave Congress the power to end such commitments at any time by concurrent resolution of both houses, and stipulated that U.S. forces should be withdrawn after sixty days unless both houses of Congress had explicitly voted, by concurrent resolution, to approve a continuation of the military commitment. The following year, Congress also moved to reassert its power of the purse in the Budget Control and Impoundment Act of 1974. The budget act made all presidential impoundments subject to congressional approval and created a Congressional Budget Office (CBO) to provide Congress with data and information on the budget. The act also created a congressional budget process with budget resolutions and a reconciliation procedure, to reconcile taxing and spending decisions, for the first time in U.S. history. Alarmed by Nixon's assault on its fundamental constitutional prerogative, the power of the purse, Congress was determined to demonstrate that it could be fiscally responsible, and the new budget process was intended to recover legislative supremacy over the budget process from the presidential budget compiled by the Office of Management and Budget (OMB).[26]

The two legislative landmarks of the War Powers Act and the Budget Act were the most significant symbols of the congressional resurgence of the 1970s. But in addition to these measures the overall temper of both chambers had changed from a deferential to a much more aggressive posture vis-à-vis the presidency, an institution now viewed with suspicion by Congress and public alike in the aftermath of Vietnam and Watergate. A new generation of congressional Democrats elected in the aftermath of the antiwar movement and the Democratic congressional landslide of 1974 was eager to challenge the Republican-controlled executive branch at every turn. In 1974–75 Congress cut off military aid to U.S. allies in Turkey and Angola. Congress also began major investigations of the Central Intelligence Agency (CIA), an essential instrument of presidential foreign policymaking during the Cold War.[27] In the domestic sphere, Congress now habitually wrote "legislative veto" clauses into bills authorizing programs or agencies, giving itself a veto over executive branch actions of which it disapproved.[28]

Facing this new congressional assertiveness regarding the executive branch, even a Democratic president, Jimmy Carter, found it difficult to get Congress to go along with his objectives in foreign and domestic policy. Carter's ambitious energy program died in the Senate, his treaty returning the Panama Canal to Panama only barely obtained the requisite two-thirds Senate majority, and his SALT II Treaty died in that body in 1979.

Yet at the same time as the resurgent Congress was reasserting itself as a roadblock to the ambitions of the executive branch, it was also undertaking internal reforms that created an even more fragmented and diffuse internal power structure in both chambers and rendered Congress even less able to reconstitute itself as the active and dynamic element in the federal government. The same ambitious new generation of Democrats that sought to put the presidency in its place was not content to bide its time and defer to southern conservative elders, to whom they were fundamentally ideologically opposed. Instead, they sought to carve out a share of congressional power for themselves as soon as possible. For many of them, who had won election in formerly Republican districts, getting some power and visibility in policy areas relevant to their districts was also an electoral necessity. To this end they united with the liberals of the Democratic Study Group (DSG) to pass a series of reforms in the rules of the House Democratic majority that greatly weakened the power of the committee chairmen and devolved more power to subcommittees and individual members.[29] As a symbol of the change, three elderly southern conservative committee chairmen were deposed in a vote of the House Democratic Caucus in early 1975, just after the "Watergate" election.

Other changes in the wider political environment also made it harder for Congress to act as a cohesive unit. The televising of the House floor and the opening of all but a few congressional committee proceedings to the press and public made it harder for legislators to broker deals in private and encouraged members to be obstructive in asserting personal and constituent interests. And while the Democratic reforms by weakening the committee chairs had provided an opportunity for the party leadership to reassert itself, their overall thrust was initially in the opposite direction: fragmentation and diffusion, rather than the concentration of power.

The new generation of younger Democratic members, principally the seventy-four Democratic freshmen elected in the Watergate congressional election of 1974, helped to create a more assertive, energetic, and informed House, but a House that was fragmented internally and lacked the cohesion necessary to be the leading element in the U.S. political system. As far as producing coherent public policy was concerned, the House was also at a disadvantage. It was better equipped than ever for district service and oversight, criticism, and obstruction of the executive branch, but at the same time the House appeared decreasingly able to forge a national consensus on most areas of public policy.

To add to this situation, an increasing problem of congressional responsiveness, or the lack of it, began to develop in the 1970s. The revolution in the congressional power structure had made it easier for incumbent members to service their districts. Drastic changes in the financing of congressional campaigns following the Federal Elections Campaign Act (FECA) of 1974 precluded the financing of congressional campaigns by large individual donors and forced candidates to rely more on small-donor fund raising and political action committees (PACs). Business PACs in particular tended to give money to incumbent members on relevant committees, thus enabling incumbents to compile huge warchests that deterred an effective challenge in most instances.[30] Reelection levels for incumbent members exceeded 90 percent during the 1980s, with the liberal Democratic majority becoming ever more entrenched in a time of increasing conservatism and Republican presidential landslides. Conceived as the most responsive branch of the federal government by the Framers because it was the branch closest to the people, by the 1980s the House had become arguably the least responsive element in the federal political system owing to the distorting effects of incumbency; it was an institution geared toward reelecting its members, instead of leading the country in producing effective public policy or even articulating public demands.

Ironically, during the 1980s it appeared that the supposedly more "aristocratic" Senate had become more responsive to changes in national public opinion than the "people's House." Control of the Senate changed hands between the parties in 1980 and again in 1986. The reelection rate for Senate incumbents was also somewhat lower than the House during the same period, perhaps because the more visible senators found it more difficult to control their public perception than their House brethren. Of course, the Senate had not been immune to many of the same fragmentary and individualistic tendencies that characterized the House. As late as the 1950s, it was expected that junior senators would defer initially to their elders and serve an "apprenticeship." This tradition began to erode with the election of a large contingent of activist and assertive liberal Democratic senators in the late 1950s and early 1960s. They succeeded in breaking the power of elderly white southerners over the institution and persuaded the Senate leadership to devolve power to more junior members. During the 1970s the Senate also voted to reduce the number of votes needed to end debate to sixty (rather than sixty-seven) senators, but despite this significant change, the dispersal of power actually made the Senate even more difficult and cumbersome to manage. The situation became more serious still when the conservative Republican counterparts of the liberal Democratic activist senators began to get elected during the 1970s and 1980s. Both sides began to resort to guerrilla tactics, being ready to tie up the Senate to get their way, regardless of seniority or status.[31]

By the mid-1980s, while Congress had undoubtedly reasserted itself in terms of its ability to restrain the president and exercise executive oversight from the nadir of the early 1960s, the legislative branch was still hampered by its fragmentation and lack of cohesive leadership—problems that had actually been exacerbated by the internal reforms of the 1970s. The War Powers Act made presidents more wary of defying Congress, but in practice Congress found it hard to make presidents adhere to the letter of the act's provisions in an era of high technology and the need for rapid global military response. Only once, when President Reagan sent U.S. Marines to Lebanon in 1983, were the terms of the act ever officially invoked, and Presidents Ford, Carter, and Reagan all undertook various military missions overseas of brief duration without paying much attention to its provisions. The Budget Act and the CBO made Congress a much more effective participant in the budget process, but in the absence of any consensus between a Democratic House and a Republican Senate and president on taxes and spending issues, it could not prevent the escalation of the federal budget deficit in the 1980s. Indeed, during that decade, as appropriations bills often failed to be passed on schedule, the federal budget process degenerated into threats of government shutdowns and the passage of stopgap "continuing resolutions" to keep the federal government going. The final admission of failure was the passage of the Gramm-Rudman-Hollings legislation of 1986, in which Congress delegated the power to the president to order an automatic schedule of draconian reductions in discretionary domestic spending if mandatory annual deficit-reduction targets to reach a balanced budget by FY 1992 were not met.

By the early 1980s Congress had, in fact, dissipated much of the institutional goodwill that had fallen upon it after the disgrace of the executive branch under LBJ and Nixon. What might have been an opportunity for the legislative branch to reassert its authority was squandered by the inability of Congress to organize itself to be the preeminent governing institution in the federal government. On the contrary, in response to a changing electoral and communications environment, Congress decentralized itself even further, moving from committee government to subcommittee government. As the incumbents and the Democratic House majority entrenched themselves through reliance on staff, perks, and PACs, the House actually began to become impervious to popular electoral pressures. The same features also characterized the always more fragmented Senate, as the "inner club" of the 1950s broke down.

While the Republicans maintained a tight grip on the presidency, due to astute leadership by House Speaker Thomas P. "Tip" O'Neill, public opinion did not accept the Republican charge that the fiscal profligacy of the Democratic House was largely to blame for the record budget deficits during the 1980s. Indeed, the Democrats were returned to power in the Senate elections in 1986, when it seemed that the country had had enough of "Reaganomics." To some members of the Democratic leadership this also looked like an opportunity to demonstrate that, with a lame-duck president in the White House, they might be able to lead the nation from Congress.

Disgrace, Scandal, and the Rise of Newt Gingrich: 1987–94

The procedural reforms of the 1970s had contributed initially to an even greater diffusion and fragmentation of power within Congress by weakening the committee chairs. But those reforms also revived the party caucus and created the potential for a more assertive party leadership. The conservatism of the Reagan administration and the Republican Senate, combined with more aggressive partisan leadership from Speaker O'Neill, led to a marked rise in Democratic (and Republican) Party unity in the early 1980s (see Figure 1.2).[32] The return of a Democratic Senate in 1986 inspired Tip O'Neill's successor as House Speaker, Jim Wright, to make a daring attempt to overcome the endemic fragmentation of "subcommittee" government and reestablish the authority of strong, centralized party leadership in the House. Taking advantage of the weakened state of the Reagan administration following the 1986 elections and the outbreak of the Iran-*contra* scandal, Wright sought to impose a more disciplined leadership over the House Democrats and bring the committee and subcommittee chairmen into line behind a specific agenda of legislative measures, including farm credit, catastrophic health insurance, Clean Water Act amendments, and trade. To an extraordinary extent Wright was successful in getting his agenda through the House and adopted by the Senate. The Speaker also played an unusually large diplomatic role by negotiating directly with the Sandinista regime in Nicaragua in an effort to broker a cease-fire in the civil war there.[33]

It was not only Wright's attempts at diplomacy in defiance of their president that outraged the normally placid Republican minority in the House but also the more partisan and high-handed approach that the Speaker adopted toward them on the House floor.[34] Some of the younger and more ambitious GOP members, such as Georgia Congressman Newt Gingrich, were also concerned that if Wright's experiment of a stronger Speakership and the return of central control over the House was successful, it might become all but impossible for the Republicans to succeed in their long-term goal of taking over the chamber. It was Gingrich who was at the forefront of the systematic attacks on Wright's personal business ethics, a strategy specifically directed not only at undermining the public image of the Speaker but highlighting the broader point that Gingrich wanted to make about the

Figure 1.2 **Party Unity in Congress, 1980–94**

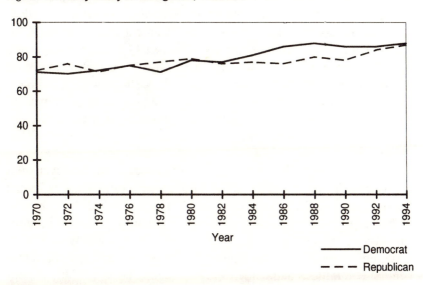

Source: Norman J. Ornstein, Thomas E. Mann, and Michael J. Malbin, *Vital Statistics on Congress: 1995–1996* (Washington, D.C.: American Enterprise Institute, 1996), pp. 209–10.

Note: The figure shows the percentage of members voting with a majority of their party on party unity votes (i.e., when a majority of one party and a majority of the other party are on opposite sides of the issue).

systematic "corruption" within the House after almost forty years of Democratic rule.[35]

As Gingrich's allegations began to find an echo in the press, Wright found that he had few strong allies even among his own troops. His legislative successes in the 100th Congress had been achieved at the price of treading on the toes of powerful Democratic committee chairmen and junior members who had gotten used to getting their own way in the fragmented House power structure. Thus, when the leader came under strong attack, Democrats who had chafed under the strictures of strong leadership did not hurry to his defense, particularly once the national news media had joined the Gingrich-led Republican assault on Wright's character and ethics.[36]

After Wright was forced from office in the spring of 1989, Democratic rule in the House reverted to the more fragmented, decentralized mode characteristic of the modern Congress. Bold, centralized partisan leadership along the lines intended by Wright was possible for a short time, but could not be maintained in the face of the centrifugal tendencies that the contemporary political environment forced on the Congress. Democratic members beholden electorally to their districts and financially to political action committees had little incentive to submit to the authority of their leadership. Wright's successor, Tom Foley, reverted to what Ron Peters has described as the more "therapeutic" approach of Speaker O'Neill, a style of leadership that House Democrats found much more congenial than the strong-arm style of Jim Wright.[37]

One aspect of Wright's Speakership that persisted, however, was the focus on scandal and the ethics of the Democratic majority by the Republicans and the news media. Much of this resulted from the rise of Newt Gingrich to a position of power among the House Republicans. By the mid-1970s it appeared that the GOP had almost entirely given up on controlling the House, and its leaders and ranking members on committees had come to rely on cooperation with the Democratic majority to achieve any influence at all. The conciliation strategy was epitomized by the amicable relationship that existed between Minority Leader Bob Michel and Democrat Speaker Tip O'Neill, who were golfing partners during the early 1980s.

Frustrated at this conciliatory attitude, several more junior House Republicans, led by Gingrich, formed the Conservative Opportunity Society (COS) in 1982, to pursue a more aggressive, partisan strategy.[38] The decision to pursue the ethics allegations against Speaker Wright was part of this strategy, and the success of that venture contributed to Gingrich's election over the more traditional and conciliatory Republican endorsed by Michel, Edward Madigan of Illinois, as minority whip, the number-two leadership position in the House GOP in the spring of 1989.[39] From that platform Gingrich continued his assault on the Democrats, not just by promoting orchestrated attacks by Republicans on the House floor but also by building a national network of Republican challengers, through GOPAC, a political action committee under his personal control.[40] Gingrich believed that the lesson of the Reagan presidency was that only through controlling both houses of Congress could the Republicans really undertake the radical scaling-back of the federal government that Reagan had envisioned but had been unable to implement after his first year in the White House. Moreover, destroying the old order in the House would require the systematic undermining of the underpinnings of Democratic rule: incumbency, the committee system, seniority, and PACs. If the public could be convinced that this system was the explanation for inefficient and ineffective government, the Republicans might be able to break through.[41]

Gingrich's strategy was thus not only predicated on questioning the ethics of individual Democrats but on denigrating Congress as an institution. Of course, the Republican leadership was not alone in playing this game. Democratic incumbents had also worked out some time before that they could, ironically, enhance their own electoral security by publicly disparaging the institution in which they served.[42] The systematic exposure and utilization of scandal by Gingrich, however, raised this to a level that became dangerous for the Democratic majority. Bob Michel might criticize the Democrats but not bring opprobrium on his own members. Gingrich pursued the issue of members keeping large overdrafts at the House bank, even though Republican members were affected as well as Democrats.[43] His point was that in order to break the Democratic mold voters had to be convinced that the whole institutional structure of Congress under the Democrats had become totally corrupt. Only when that became the dominant perception of voters would the Republicans be able to "nationalize" a House election and win control.[44]

Gingrich had help from several external factors in pursuing his strategy. After the Jim Wright affair, the national news media had seen the newsmaking potential in congressional scandal. The constituent politics, brokerage, and "special interest" representation that characterized Congress under Democratic rule did not sit well with the progressive, reformist, "good government" orientation that characterized the news media's view of the political world.[45] Indeed, the whole business of legislative politics did not accord with a political universe where the news media served as the main conduit between citizens and government. Thus, when scandals involving the House bank, the House post office, and the chair of the powerful House Ways and Means Committee, Daniel J. Rostenkowski, emerged, the news media pursued them as avidly as the GOP.

Developments in the programming of AM-radio were, moreover, creating a new media outlet that also served the interests of conservative and Republican critics of Congress. AM-radio talk shows were a prime arena for the generally conservative hosts and callers to vent their frustrations at Congress and the Democratic majority therein. The impact of talk radio was first demonstrated by the orchestrated (and successful) campaign by several hosts against a proposed congressional pay raise in the spring of 1989. Talk radio would serve as a continuing source of bitter public criticism of Congress until the GOP finally took control of the House in 1994.[46]

While relative comity prevailed in the more genteel Senate in the early 1990s, as opposed to the fervid partisanship of the House floor, the media's appetite for scandal and sensation also helped create an adverse public perception of the Senate. The catalyst for this was President Bush's nomination of Clarence Thomas to the Supreme Court in 1991 and the subsequent allegations of sexual harassment against Thomas by his former aide, Anita F. Hill. Public hearings and interrogations of both Thomas and Hill involving alleged actions and language with which the senators were clearly uncomfortable only served to make the Senate Judiciary Committee and the body as a whole appear ridiculous before a rapt national television audience.[47] When another scandal developed in 1993 concerning sexual harassment allegations by more than twenty women against a senior and respected senator, Republican Robert Packwood of Oregon, this perception of tawdriness on the Hill was merely reinforced. Senators' almost habitual resort to dilatory devices such as the filibuster also contributed to the image of "gridlock" and "stasis" in Washington increasingly held by the American public beyond the Capitol beltway and exploited by both Bill Clinton and Ross Perot in their 1992 presidential campaigns.[48]

From the mid-1980s, a grassroots movement for congressional term limitations had gotten under way in several western states. Initiative proposals began to appear on state ballots limiting the terms not only of state legislators but also those states' members of Congress.[49] Despite the dubious constitutionality of such measures, over twenty states—including the largest state, California—had adopted congressional term limitations by the time the 104th Congress opened in January 1995. In national surveys at least 70 percent of the public expressed support for a constitutional amendment establishing congressional term limits, despite the almost united opposition of the majority of members of Congress and political commentators in the news media. Many Republicans, frustrated by the Democratic manipulation of incumbency at both the congressional and state levels, eagerly jumped on the term limits bandwagon.[50]

The widespread success of the movement in the face of such concerted opposition was testimony to the increasing public exasperation
with the federal government and, most specifically, Congress. A further indication of this unrest was the rise of Texas billionaire Ross
Perot as a national political figure, based largely on Perot's assertions
that "gridlock" in Washington, created largely by the undue influence
of powerful lobbyists and PACs over the legislative process, was at the
root of the seeming inability to deal with major domestic problems,
such as the budget deficit. Despite his evident eccentricities, Perot's
attacks on Congress and the culture of Washington were instrumental
in his winning 19 percent of the popular vote for president in 1992.

By the early 1990s then, public support for Congress (never very
high in recent decades) had collapsed to abysmal levels. As a result of
media scrutiny, Republican attacks, and the apparent inability of the
Democratic majority to address the major problems facing the nation,
Congress had become a despised body associated in the public mind
with scandal, corruption, and ridicule. Speaker Wright's effort to address these problems by recentralizing party leadership and attempting
to implement a national political agenda from Congress collapsed in
the face of the attacks on Wright's ethics by the Republicans and the
news media. More important, however, Wright's downfall illustrated
the distinct lack of enthusiasm for Wright's project, from a House
Democratic majority that had gotten used to independence, decentralization, and "therapeutic" leadership. Newt Gingrich, who had been
the key figure in removing Wright, expanded his target to embrace the
entire institution in which he served, even at the cost of implicating his
fellow Republicans in the mess. Gingrich perceived the public dissatisfaction with Congress earlier than most, and he sought to get the Republicans to capitalize on such symptoms of that discontent as the
Perot campaign and the term limits movement. By thoroughly discrediting the institution and riding the popular wave of discontent with
Congress, Gingrich reckoned that a Republican House majority might
finally be achieved.

Congress at Nadir: Legislatures and Modern Politics

It is tempting to attribute the American public's disgust with Congress
in the early 1990s to short-term factors like the fall of Speaker Jim
Wright, the Thomas-Hill affair, or the House bank and post office

scandals. If this were the case, then simply throwing the Democratic "rascals" out, as Newt Gingrich advocated, might suffice to rectify the problem. Replacing the particularistic and incremental interest-group liberalism characteristic of the long decades of Democratic rule with a partisan majority committed to an ideological agenda addressing the broad problems facing the nation, and taking back the initiative as the "popular" branch of the American federal government, might then succeed in transforming Congress into the kind of vehicle that would better satisfy the public's conception of what a legislature should be.

In the 104th Congress Gingrich would get the opportunity to put his concept of government from the Congress into action, and the remainder of this book focuses on the part his most ardent disciples and "shock troops," the 1994 Republican freshmen, would play in the endeavor to restore the authority and legitimacy of Congress.

From this summary of Congress's evolution during this century, however, it should be apparent that Gingrich might well have underestimated the extent of the forces militating against congressional government in the contemporary United States. Congress had lost authority in the federal political system because legislative politics with a fragmented internal power structure and a fairly loose party system could not meet the social, economic, and military demands made upon the American federal government in the twentieth century. Since the Progressive era, there has been a consensus among American political elites on the need for federal government regulation of the economy, society, the environment, and the international situation in the "interest" of the nation as a whole. Congress, for most of the twentieth century, has been a body so constituted as to represent the parts. An unwieldy, querulous legislature might be good at articulating the ephemeral demands of the public (although even that became highly dubious as congressional incumbents entrenched themselves in the post–World War II period), but by definition it cannot govern.

Partly by design and partly by default, power passed to the other branches of the federal government. The president, embellished by modern electronic communications and the imperatives of rapid and concealed decision making after the United States became the predominant global power, is now the agenda setter and dynamic element in the federal system, playing something like the role of a Weberian "charismatic leader" in a system otherwise characterized by bureaucratic and legislative "gridlock."[51] On issues that have been so politically or socially sensitive that they do not lend themselves to the bargaining characteristic of the legislative process, the role of the legislature has effectively fallen to the Supreme Court since the *Brown v. Board* decision in 1954. Where Congress fears to act, or cannot act because of determined resistance by a legislative minority (or majority!), the Court has asserted its authority to step in and set society to rights. Wrapped in a glow of constitutional/legal authority that today's Congress can only dream of possessing, the Court may indeed be more efficacious in assuming a leadership role as far as pursuing social change in American society is concerned. But whatever else we might call legislation by judiciary, it is not "democratic." It is a mark of Congress's loss of authority that the Court has been able to effect this change with so little resistance from the American public. Americans will apparently accept a great deal as long as it is done by judges, but very little that their own elected representatives accomplish appears to meet with their approval.

The electronic media now serve as the primary means of communication between citizens and government, and their view of politics is based on the progressive credo of rationalism and expertise. The "right" answers (scientifically and morally) are there, but the "special interests" represented in the legislative process get in the way. Correct action gets compromised in the brokerage politics endemic to legislatures and therefore gets lost. When the media treat politics in this fashion, and enterprising politicians like Perot and Gingrich pick up the same theme, it is small wonder that the legislature appears to be not only inefficient but ignoble in the living rooms of American citizens.[52]

The loss of power by legislatures has been a common feature of advanced industrial democracies for the reasons mentioned above. Yet in other advanced democracies there has not been any significant public outrage over the loss of legislative authority because in those systems it is accepted that governments should be formed by strong, disciplined political parties. In the United States, with a strict separation of powers and a weak party system, Congress has survived as a much more powerful legislative body than in other democracies, with more independent control over the bureaucracy and a greater ability to thwart the will of the executive. Congress is probably better informed, better staffed, and gives more power to the individual member than any other legislature in the Western world. The price it pays for that power is that it had become probably the most popularly despised legislative body in the Western world.

Newt Gingrich believed that restoring strong, centralized, ideological leadership to Congress would restore its public esteem and allow the House of Representatives to act as the dynamo for a conservative revolution in American government. The remainder of this book demonstrates that strong, centralized, ideological party leadership could temporarily transform Congress, but not sufficiently to reverse the long-term forces that had contributed most to its decline.

2
The 1994 Election, the Contract, and the Freshmen

Despite the widespread disgust with Congress, the Republican victory in the 1994 congressional elections still came as a tremendous surprise. While it was anticipated that the normal midterm swing against the party controlling the White House might well enable the Republicans to gain the seven seats necessary to control the Senate and to make a considerable dent in the apparently impregnable Democratic majority in the House, the net shift of fifty-two House seats from Democrat to Republican, enabling the GOP to take control of the House by a majority of 230–204 (with one Independent), was completely unexpected. In a time of peace abroad and relative prosperity at home, such a decisive repudiation of the party controlling both Congress and the White House appears even more unusual.

The Republican landslide in 1994 occurred because of a combination of factors that favored the Republicans, the most important being public disgust with Congress (addressed in the previous chapter), the perceived failure of the Clinton presidency, astute strategic leadership by Newt Gingrich, the effects of the 1990 reapportionment and the unusually large number of Democratic retirements in 1992–94, the recruitment of an excellent crop of Republican challengers, and perhaps least important despite all the subsequent attention, the Republicans' Contract with America.

This chapter discusses each of these factors in turn, together with an analysis of the 1994 results. Adhering to the main subject of this book, the story is told as far as possible from the perspective of the successful challengers of 1994: the House Republican freshmen. In their accounts of why they ran for Congress and won, the common theme is the public repudiation of congressional "politics as usual," which, with more than a little help from the foibles of President Clinton, the Republicans were finally able to turn to their advantage in 1994. The election results contained two possible pitfalls for the newly elected Republican freshmen, however. First, they might have aroused unrealistic expectations among voters about the extent to which the direction of the country could actually be changed from Congress. And second, the freshmen (and the Republicans in general) might be tempted by the scale of their triumph to interpret the 1994 election result as a public endorsement of the GOP policy agenda, as expressed in the Contract with America, rather than an electoral repudiation of Bill Clinton and the Democrats. Both factors would create serious problems for the Republican freshmen later in the 104th Congress.

Democratic Meltdown Under President Clinton

Little noticed in Bill Clinton's victory in the 1992 presidential election was the fact that his party actually lost ten seats in the House and made no gains in the Senate. Clinton himself won office as a "minority president" with only 43 percent of the popular vote against divided opposition and no electoral mandate except that he was the most convincing alternative to the unpopular Republican incumbent, George Bush. While campaigning as a "New Democrat" who would "end welfare as we know it" and repudiate the traditional Democratic reliance on federal government programs to address economic and social problems, Clinton in the 1992 campaign had also promised to boost the economy through an "economic stimulus" package, address the burgeoning budget deficit, reform the health-care system, and deliver a "middle-class" tax cut.[1]

Even before he could address these issues in his initial "honeymoon" period in office, Clinton spent the first week of his presidency defending his campaign pledge to end the U.S. military's policy of automatically discharging gays and lesbians on the basis of their sexual orientation, thereby highlighting the very social-issue liberalism that had been the party's greatest electoral vulnerability over the previous two decades. While this alienated socially conservative middle-class voters from Clinton, the passage of his 1993 deficit-reduction package, which included significant tax increases, by a single vote in each House of Congress over united Republican opposition, also alienated several middle-income voters, who never received their anticipated "middle-class" tax cut. Meanwhile, his mild "economic stimulus package" was successfully blocked by a Republican filibuster in the Senate. Aside from the budget package, Clinton's other signal achievement of his first year was congressional approval, thanks to strong Republican support, of the North American Free Trade Agreement (NAFTA) largely negotiated by the preceding administration.[2]

After a mixed beginning, the Clinton administration's main legislation before Congress in 1994 was the "managed care" health-care proposal devised by First Lady Hilary Rodham Clinton and White House adviser Ira Magaziner. Clinton had campaigned hard on the issue of health-care coverage for all Americans in 1992, but the fate of his proposal highlighted the increasing Democratic difficulty in managing Congress, despite their comfortable majorities in both houses. The Clinton plan never got out of committee in the House, where it became mired in jurisdictional disputes between the Ways and Means Committee and the Energy and Commerce committees. Without the strong backing of the Ways and Means chair, Dan Rostenkowski, who was under criminal indictment as a result of the House post office scandal, the Clinton plan collapsed and never even made it to the House floor. The perception of the plan as another example of "Great Society style" social engineering also made Clinton's "New Democratic" credentials appear hollow.[3]

Things got even worse for the Democrats during the summer of 1994, when a major crime package endorsed by the president and the Democrats was defeated on a procedural vote on the House floor. Although the bill eventually passed, the temporary loss again reflected on the competence and division among congressional Democrats, and the Republicans successfully highlighted several provisions, including "midnight basketball" for inner-city youth, as typical examples of Democratic liberalism and the "pork barrel."[4]

By the fall of 1994, the relative legislative successes of the Clinton administration, such as the budget package, the Brady gun-control bill, and the Family Leave Act, had been eclipsed by the failure of the health-care package and the perception that the president and the congressional Democrats lacked the will or the competence to deal with the country's domestic problems. While many of the Democratic freshmen in the 103rd Congress had been elected on a reform agenda in 1992, no significant internal reform of Congress had taken place, and

Republicans continued to make hay with their charges of corruption and incompetence against the Democratic majority.[5] Combined with the apparent failure of the Clinton presidency, these charges were now beginning to resonate beyond the Capitol beltway, as voters started to connect their discontent regarding Congress with the party that had prevailed there for forty years.[6] Bill Clinton had proven to be the catalyst.

Most of the Republican freshmen members interviewed mentioned Clinton's unpopularity as a major factor in their victory in 1994. This was particularly apparent among members from socially and economically conservative districts in the South:

> The reason I won was that the district was more conservative and Bill Clinton was very unpopular, and still is. Instead of being a new kind of Democrat, voters thought he was saying "I know how to fool you." I came out with a conservative agenda: something you could feel good about voting for. They could support someone close to where they were and vote against something that was bad for the country. But the most decisive reason was the Bill Clinton factor.[7]
>
> *Congressman Lindsey O. Graham (S.C.)*

> The Third Congressional District is a conservative district. Bush carried it in 1992, and [U.S. Senator] Jesse Helms is extremely strong there. Bill Clinton's approval rating in the district was 36 percent the first time we polled in 1994, and Senator Helms had a 58–62 percent approval rating. In southern and eastern North Carolina the conservative trend is continuing to grow and becoming stronger. Folks feel impatient with half of their money going in taxes, and they see welfare needing to be reformed, and they want a balanced budget. I also have three military bases, which also tend to encourage conservative views.[8]
>
> *Congressman Walter B. Jones, Jr. (N.C.)*

> The Democrats had controlled the House for forty years, and people were dissatisfied with high tax rates, bureaucracy, the size of government, and regulations. They were also concerned that welfare was contributing to the destruction of the work ethic. Bill Clinton was very unpopular for passing the largest tax increase in history. In his first two years the liberal agenda was directly contrary to his posture as a New Democrat. I think personal dislike of Bill Clinton and forty years of Democratic rule were the two main factors that contributed to the turnaround in 1994.[9]
>
> *Congressman Ed Whitfield (Ky.)*

Even in more socially liberal New Jersey, moderate freshman Bill Martini believed that disgust with Clinton's failure to live up to his promise as a New Democrat had been the most significant factor in Martini's 1994 victory:

> In 1994 people still wanted the changes that they wanted in 1992 when Bill Clinton articulated their needs and sentiments on issues like a balanced budget, a middle-class tax cut, changing welfare, and smaller government. By 1994 people realized that he had contradicted every one of his commitments, but the desire for those things was still there. Middle America wanted tax relief and saw deficit spending as a positive peril to the country. In 1994 they rejected Bill Clinton, who broke his promises, and voted for the Republicans because they stood for the same principles they thought Clinton stood for in 1992.[10]

In several cases, disgust with Clinton had served as a *personal* motivation for members to run in 1994:

> Bill Clinton did everything he could to repudiate social conservatives early in his presidency. In the first days we had "Gays in the Military" and he repealed every pro-life government ruling. Then he passed the biggest tax increase in U.S. history and pledged to turn OSHA into an enforcement agency again, which alienated business and small business—the economic conservatives. On the Wetlands issue he drove farmers nuts. Then came the National Health Plan and the crime bill, smoking laws, and Joycelyn Elders. He managed to unite doctors, insurers, gun owners, religious conservatives, motorcyclists, smokers, country-club Republicans, and blue-collar workers. Clinton brought many conservatives out of the woodwork, including people who had never thought they would run for office, like me.[11]
>
> *Congressman Mark Edward Souder (Ind.)*

The decisive thing was [Democratic incumbent] Earl Hutto voting for the 1993 Clinton budget. You hear so much about the social issues—abortion, prayer, and gays—as the hot button issues, but it was the May 1993 Clinton tax increase that got most of my classmates off the couch and into the political arena. That was the defining issue, because the Democrats stood for the largest tax increase in the history of Congress, and it passed without a single Republican vote in either the House or the Senate. That got an awful lot of members running, especially after Bill Clinton had campaigned on a middle-class tax cut and broke his

promise after bashing Bush on the issue in 1992. That made me decide
to go ahead and run.[12]

Congressman Joe Scarborough (Fla.)

I thought that Bill Clinton was the worst president the country had ever
had, and without a Republican Congress to balance his views we
wouldn't recognize the country anymore.[13]

Congressman Van Hilleary (Tenn.)

In a couple of other cases, successful freshmen attributed their defeats
of incumbent Democrats to those Democrats' votes for the tax increases in the 1993 Clinton budget plan. According to Congressman
Bob Barr of Georgia, who defeated Democratic incumbent Buddy
Darden:

There were two main issues: the gun issue because Buddy Darden
supported the Clinton gun ban, and he also supported the Clinton tax
increase. Both of these were fundamentally important, but if I were
forced to choose one decisive issue, I would say the tax increase.[14]

Freshman Democrat Marjorie Margolies-Mezvinsky had switched her
vote at the last minute in 1993 to save the Clinton budget package,
which passed the House by only one vote. Jon Fox, the Republican
who lost to Mezvinsky in 1992 but defeated her in 1994, believed that
Mezvinsky's budget vote accounted for the different outcomes of the
two elections:

She had a record. She said she wouldn't raise taxes, and she then voted
for the largest tax increase in congressional history.[15]

Freshman Republicans in the 104th Congress and their leadership
were well aware that the failures of the early years of Clinton's presidency had played a particularly important role in putting them in office. As we later see, however, this freshman class did not wish to be
perceived merely as fortunate beneficiaries of the temporary unpopularity of Clinton and the Democrats. Instead, the House Republican
freshmen not only wanted to take advantage of this opportunity to
reform Congress as an institution but also to employ the House of
Representatives as the launching pad for a "revolution" in American
politics and public policy. In these objectives they were encouraged by

their leader, Newt Gingrich, who had had just such a purpose in mind since he launched the Conservative Opportunity Society back in the dark days of 1983.

The Gingrich Factor

> It would be difficult to overestimate his role, and hard to come up with the words to describe it. He provided the vision that allowed us to win. The man is absolutely brilliant.[16]
>
> *Congressman Bob Barr (Ga.)*

In addition to leading the Republican assault on the Democrats inside the House, Republican Whip Newt Gingrich and his allies in the Conservative Opportunity Society had also been playing an increasingly significant role in congressional election campaigns in the early 1990s. When it became evident that Gingrich would challenge (and likely defeat) veteran incumbent Robert Michel for the Republican leadership in the 104th Congress, Michel announced his retirement, and Gingrich became de facto leader of the House Republicans and chief director of Republican electoral strategy for the 1994 congressional elections.

As mentioned in the preceding chapter, Gingrich had been preparing for this moment for some time. He and several other relatively junior House Republicans had formed the Conservative Opportunity Society (COS) after the Republican setback in the 1982 midterm elections in order to mount not just a more militant opposition to the Democratic majority on the House floor but to challenge the entire basis of the domestic "welfare state," which Gingrich perceived as both the cornerstone of the Democratic grip on the House and the source of most of the economic and social problems of contemporary America. Gingrich and his COS compatriots, Bob Walker and Vin Weber, wanted to move beyond the tax cutting of "Reaganomics" and replace that welfare state with an "opportunity society":

> The greatest moral imperative we face is replacing the welfare state with an opportunity society. For every day that we allow the current conditions to continue, we are condemning the poor—and particularly poor children—to being deprived of their basic rights as Americans. The welfare state reduces the poor from citizens to clients. It breaks up families, minimizes work incentives, blocks people from saving and

acquiring property, and overshadows dreams of a promised future with a present despair born of poverty, violence, and hopelessness.[17]

In terms of strategy, the COS originally concentrated on relentless partisan attacks on the Democratic leadership, using the "one minute" speeches at the beginning of the day's business in the House and the "Special Orders" provisions after the legislative business for the day had been completed on the House floor. This tactic gained attention among viewers of the House proceedings on the cable television network C-SPAN and eventually provoked Speaker O'Neill into an intemperate response on the House floor, for which he was later admonished.[18] Later, Gingrich's sustained attacks on the ethics of the majority would also lead to the downfall of Speaker Wright and Minority Whip Tony Coelho and to the publicizing of the House bank and post office scandals. The Georgian's focus on the "corruption" of the Democratic majority, the failure of "big government," and the need to create an "opportunity society" propelled him into the House Republican leadership and served as the unifying focus and inspiration of what had been a rather dispirited House Republican minority. David Dreier, the second-ranking Republican in the House Rules Committee in the 104th Congress, and a member since 1981, testified to Gingrich's importance in leading the long march to a House majority:

> Newt Gingrich has been the progenitor of the whole thing. He is the single person who brought us to majority status.[19]

Another senior House Republican, Steve Gunderson of Wisconsin, concurred:

> Newt Gingrich has been of the utmost importance. He has been the vision, the intellect, the emotion, and the motivation of the party.[20]

As the Democratic majority remained entrenched, however, Gingrich and his allies soon realized that to meet their long-term goal of creating a Republican House majority they would have to work outside Congress in mobilizing public opinion. They also began to absorb a message from the consensus among scholars of congressional elections that the quality (in terms of experience and ability) of challengers and open-seat candidates was of the utmost importance in House contests.[21] Gingrich's long-time friend and COS lieutenant, Congressman Bob Walker of Pennsylvania, described how the COS operation expanded beyond the beltway into an effort to recruit and train candidates supportive of the confrontational COS approach to run in competitive House races:

> We had a lot to learn about building national movements, before you get the critical mass that allows you to win elections. I thought it [winning control of the House] would take two to four years, when, in fact, it took us more than a decade. We learned a lot about national leadership and what it really takes to foment and lead a national movement. We created a farm system for the horses we needed to win. Tom Delay and Dick Armey both came out of the farm system. They watched us on the floor, our message appealed to them, and they came to Washington to join us. They were soldiers who became leaders in the revolution. Bill Paxon learned at the knee of Jack Kemp. Most of them regularly listened to Newt Gingrich's GOPAC tapes and regularly watched us on the floor.[22]

GOPAC was to be one of the major vehicles in the Gingrichite campaign to take over the House. Delaware's then Republican governor, Pierre S. "Pete" DuPont, had founded GOPAC in 1979 to help recruit GOP candidates at the state legislative level. When DuPont decided to run for president in 1988, Gingrich took over GOPAC and transformed a relatively small and obscure operation into what his biographer has described as "the academy of modern Republicanism": an apparatus specifically designed to recruit, train, and sustain a cadre of Republican challengers with the eventual objective of taking control of the House.[23] In 1991–94, Gingrich raised and spent more than $8 million in recruitment and candidate training efforts through GOPAC.[24] Its primary vehicle was a series of audiotapes that were available to aspiring Republican candidates, offering advice and encouragement on the campaign trail and relentlessly inculcating Gingrich's Opportunity Society message. Journalists Dan Balz and Ronald Brownstein described the content of the GOPAC tapes as follows:

> Instead of cash, Gingrich sent audiotapes and videotapes. They would arrive unsolicited nearly every month in the mailboxes of candidates around the country, tapes on tactics and strategy and ideas and issues, lectures from Gingrich or his political advisers, interviews with other

successful Republicans. It was like subscribing to a motivational course, with Gingrich a cross between Norman Vincent Peale and a marine drill sergeant.[25]

The positive impact of the GOPAC tapes on aspiring Republican candidates is evident in the comments of Arizona Republican freshman J.D. Hayworth:

> Matt Salmon [another Arizona Republican freshman] was plugged in as a state legislator to GOPAC and had all the GOPAC training. Once people expressed interest, those GOPAC tapes would appear on your doorstep. GOPAC was a resource that was free and open to all of us. It was a good strategy of empowerment with practical tips and philosophical argument.[26]

Although Gingrich had reoriented GOPAC toward his long-term goal of securing control of the House, it still made most of its direct campaign contributions to state and local races, rather than federal offices. This enabled GOPAC to circumvent the $1,000 limit on individual donations and the reporting and disclosure requirements of the federal campaign finance laws. Gingrich was thus able to raise large sums of money from individual donors, which he used to establish a network of tangential organizations and activities, including a think tank—The Progress and Freedom Foundation—and a college course, which he taught at various small Georgia colleges and marketed to Republicans nationwide.[27]

More directly related to the 1994 campaign, Gingrich also revitalized the almost moribund and bankrupt National Republican Congressional Committee (NRCC). Having installed one of his allies Congressman Bill Paxon of New York, as chairman, Gingrich strongly encouraged incumbent Republicans with safe districts to contribute money to the NRCC to help out more vulnerable GOP incumbents and challengers in 1994 and to urge their political action committee (PAC) allies to contribute to the Republican effort. These efforts paid off spectacularly for the GOP in 1994, assuring that their challengers were dramatically better financed than in 1992. According to James Gimpel, 130 of the 178 House Republican incumbents made a contribution to the NRCC's campaign effort and raised over $5 million to help GOP challengers (compared to a meager $50,000 in 1992).[28] The

Speaker himself campaigned in more than 127 congressional districts and helped raise over $3 million for the 1994 campaign.[29] Better-financed challengers of course, considerably enhanced the Republicans' prospects of winning the House in November.

There can be little question that Newt Gingrich's leadership helped lay the groundwork for the Republican triumph in 1994, strategically, materially, and psychologically. Gingrich had been campaigning for a Republican House majority since he founded COS in 1994. His confrontational approach of unmitigated confrontation with the Democratic majority had come to predominate among the House Republicans and had influenced a whole generation of Republican House candidates. The Gingrich approach of slowly building a cadre of "Opportunity Society" Republicans from the bottom-up through GOPAC and his other related enterprises paid off in 1994 when a large number of experienced Republican challengers was available to capitalize on the unpopularity of the Clinton administration. Gingrich's overhaul of the Republicans' fund-raising and campaign machinery, together with NRCC chairman Paxon and Republican National Chairman Haley Barbour, also ensured that those challengers had the necessary funds to mount a credible challenge to the Democrats.

The centerpiece of Gingrich's 1994 election strategy, however, was the Contract with America, a specific program of measures that a large majority of Republican House candidates pledged to enact if elected to office. It is to the genesis and the impact of the Contract on the 1994 campaign that we now turn.

The Contract with America

> In Congress you had traditionally been able to win by saying: "Here's what I've done for the district." With the Contract one party was able to say: "Here's what we want to do for the country."[30]
>
> *Congressman Jon Fox (Pa.)*

The Contract with America was the centerpiece of Newt Gingrich's strategy for the 1994 campaign, and would also subsequently set the Republican agenda for the 104th Congress. At the time the Contract was signed in September 1994, however, it appeared as a bold, but probably unsuccessful, attempt to nationalize the congressional elections around a set of measures that the Republicans had pledged to implement once in office. The conventional wisdom regarding modern congressional elections, adhered to by both politicians and political observers, is aptly summarized in former Democratic Speaker Tip O'Neill's dictum that "all politics is local." The decline of party identification, the expansion of the domestic state, and the advantages available to incumbents in terms of perks, privileges, and technology had only reinforced this conviction and enabled the Democrats to consolidate their grip on the House though the brilliant exploitation of those advantages.[31] Running a party-based campaign on a national agenda was regarded as likely to be ineffectual, and probably ultimately harmful to challengers who needed to prove to local voters that they would put their district's interests ahead of the demands of their national party.

The origins of the Contract lay in the successful Republican national campaign of 1980, where Ronald Reagan won the presidency by a landslide and the Republicans gained thirteen seats to take over the Senate and also gained thirty-three seats in the House. The main event of that party effort had been a rally held on the Capitol steps in Washington in which presidential candidate Reagan and the Republican House and Senate candidates all made a commitment to a common platform. As a House GOP freshman, Newt Gingrich had been involved in the planning of the 1980 rally, and he believed that it had made a strong contribution to the Republican electoral success in that year:

> In early October, the entire Republican ticket assembled, calling for the Kemp-Roth tax cuts, a strengthened national defense, and significant cuts in federal spending. David Broder, one of the century's leading political journalists, wrote a favorable column about it. A number of our senate and congressional candidates profited. We picked-up thirty-three seats in the House and won a majority in the Senate after several very close races. Without the event at the Capitol we might not have won the Senate.[32]

Gingrich was somewhat disappointed that this kind of occasion had not been repeated in subsequent elections:

> While the 1980 event seemed worth repeating, circumstances did not lend themselves for the next six elections. Either the political environment was wrong or the platform was not universally popular or the leading candidates did not want to risk tying themselves to the party. There was always some reason.[33]

In 1994, with no incumbent Republican president to preclude the congressional Republicans from setting the party agenda, Gingrich got his chance to replicate the 1980 Capitol steps event on an even more ambitious scale.

Gingrich first proposed the idea of a national statement of policy and principle for House Republicans at a retreat for GOP congressmen at Salisbury, Maryland, in early 1994, which produced the "Salisbury Statement" setting out broad themes such as economic opportunity, limited government, and personal responsibility that would form the basis of the Republican campaign in the fall.[34] Gingrich envisaged the launching of a more detailed, but still concise, version of the Republican "vision statement" at a Capitol steps rally for House GOP candidates, and set 27 September as the date. Believing in the significance of the number "10," Gingrich argued that the document should include ten specific items that the Republicans would pledge to bring to a vote on the floor within a hundred days, should they take over the House. The Contract thus had a threefold purpose: to unify the Republican Party; to nationalize the 1994 election campaign around a set of issues favorable to Republican challengers; and to provide a clear legislative agenda should the Republicans take control of the House, which appeared as a still remote, but by no means inconceivable, possibility in the summer of 1994.

The drawing up of the Contract involved a two-stage process: deciding which items to include, and how to sell it to the voters. The first task was given to Gingrich's deputy, House GOP Conference Chair Dick Armey of Texas, and his staff. Issues that were extremely popular with voters, such as the balanced budget amendment to the Constitution and congressional term limits, were obvious items for inclusion. The Contract would also have to include only items that could realistically pass through the House within the hundred-day time limit. Issues on which the Republicans were divided, therefore, had to be avoided. For this reason, much of the emphasis of the Contract was on economic issues such as the balanced budget, reducing the size of government, and welfare reform, rather than social issues such as abortion, affirmative action, and school prayer. According to Gingrich ally Steve Gunderson:

> The Contract with America focused on what united the party—economic issues—and not on what divided us.[35]

To appease Christian conservatives, however, a $500 per child "family" tax credit was included in the Contract, and the gun lobby was promised a repeal of Clinton's ban on the sale of assault weapons. Apart from these, there was little else in the Contract to excite the social conservatives, who constituted such an important component of the GOP electoral base.[36]

During the summer of 1994 working groups of House GOP members from the relevant committees drafted the necessary legislation so that the Republicans would be up and ready to begin implementing the Contract from the moment they took power. Once the items were agreed on, pollster Frank Luntz was commissioned to work with focus groups of voters to find out how the Contract's proposals should be worded to maximize their electoral appeal, particularly to the 1992 Ross Perot voters Republican congressional candidates needed to win over in 1994.[37] Thus, instead of the usual mundane policy-oriented titles, the Contract items were designated as the American Dream Restoration Act (tax reform); the Personal Responsibility Act (welfare reform); and so on (see Table 2.1). In order to capitalize further on the voters' disgust with "politics as usual" in Washington, the Republicans also explicitly invited voters to "throw them out" if they did not fulfill all the items of the Contract.

On 27 September 1995, 367 Republican House candidates arrived in Washington to sign the Contract in a ceremony held, as in 1980, on the steps of the Capitol. All but five of the seventy-three Republican freshmen elected in 1994 would ultimately sign the Contract.[38] Three successful Republican candidates mentioned how the rally and signing ceremony for the Contract raised their morale and contributed to the strong initial sense of solidarity among the members of the House Republican freshmen class:

> The Contract has been overhyped. There was hardly a Republican member who didn't have every point in the Contract in their election brochures six months before it was signed. The Contract was not anything new. What was new was bringing us all to Washington for the signing. We found it very exciting to meet so many kindred spirits.[39]
>
> *Congressman Mark Souder (Ind.)*

> When I signed the Contract with America in September 1994, and stood on the west steps of the Capitol, I said: "This is a very significant and historic day." I went back and ran on the Contract with America.[40]
>
> *Congressman Dick Chrysler (Mich.)*

Table 2.1

The Contract with America

Item	Policy proposal(s)
Fiscal Responsibility Act	Balanced budget constitutional amendment Line-item veto on appropriations bills
Taking Back Our Streets Act	Anticrime package
Personal Responsibility Act	Welfare reform
Family Reinforcement Act	Tax incentives for adoption Parents' rights in education Child support enforcement Tax credit for elderly dependents
American Dream Restoration Act	$500–per-child tax credit Repeal marriage tax penalty
National Security Restoration Act	More defense spending No U.S. troops under UN command
Senior Citizens Fairness Act	Raise social security earnings limits Repeal 1993 tax hikes on social security benefits Incentives for private long-term health insurance
Job Creation and Wage Enhancement Act	Capital gains tax cut Deregulation Unfunded mandate reform
Common Sense Legal Reforms Act	Limits on punitive damages Tort reform
Citizen Legislature Act	Congressional term limits

Note: The Contract also included a package of institutional and procedural reforms of the House to be passed on the first day of the 104th Congress, including applying federal legislation to Congress, an audit, cuts in committees and committee staffs, term limits on committee chairs, a ban on proxy voting, open committee meetings, and a three-fifths majority for tax increases.

> The Contract was a great high. . . . We were coming in with a unity of purpose, and I can't begin to explain how gratifying and emotionally satisfying that is. It's the antithesis of the truism that misery loves company: success loves replication.[41]
>
> *Congressman J.D. Hayworth (Ariz.)*

Initially the Democrats and many political commentators believed that the Contract was at best a waste of resources and at worst would actually damage Republican prospects by giving Democratic candidates a specific agenda to attack and thereby turn the election away from being a referendum on the unpopular Clinton administration. By ignoring the Tip O'Neill rule and emphasizing national over local concerns, the Republicans were violating all the norms of House elections over the previous quarter century. Gingrich believed, however, that the Republicans could actually win control of the House, and he wanted to be sure they would be ready if that occurred. Despite an advertisement in the mass-circulation *TV Guide*, Democratic attacks, and considerable attention from the Washington press corps, most voters still had not heard of the Contract by November, and few students of the election believed that it had played an important role in determining the outcome of the 1994 vote.[42]

Most successful freshmen also did not believe that the Contract had been a decisive factor in the success of their campaigns. Joe Scarborough of Florida summarized this view:

> I didn't mention it [the Contract] once. I signed it on the very last day because the campaign committee kept faxing it to us. The Contract was an aggregate of the popular issues that we ran on. These were things that we were campaigning on anyway. Most voters agree with what was in there. These issues were no-brainers that 80 percent of Americans support. Who's not for the Shays Act [making Congress subject to its own laws], unfunded mandate reform, a balanced budget, or the line-item veto?[43]

David Funderburk of North Carolina agreed:

> Nobody in my district had heard of it, and it was not a major factor.[44]

Another successful freshman, Steve LaTourette of Ohio, mentioned that his Democratic opponent made more of the Contract with America than he himself did:

I didn't go to the signing ceremony in Washington, but faxed my signature later. While the items in the Contract—the balanced budget, the line-item veto, welfare reform, and legal reform—were all ideas I support, the Contract itself was not a high campaign issue. My opponent talked about the Contract adding a trillion dollars to the national debt, but as the legislation hadn't even been written, I thought that was a silly argument.[45]

There were exceptions, however. Bob Barr of Georgia, Richard "Doc" Hastings of Washington, and Dick Chrysler of Michigan all emphasized the significance of the Contract in their successful races;

The Contract was very important. It presented something that everybody understood and meant that I didn't have to explain my philosophy because everybody could quickly identify what I stood for. It was a good contrast with [Barr's Democratic opponent] Buddy Darden, who was associated with Clinton. The Contract was a clear, concise, easily identifiable, easily understood, alternative message to Bill Clinton.[46]

I ran on the Contract with America. I came back and endorsed it and talked about it. The Contract was designed so we could say, "This is a blueprint, and we promise to address this blueprint if you elect us." The issues in the Contract hit home in my district. My opponent had campaigned on some of those issues in 1992, but didn't support them as a congressman.[47]

In Michigan five races were fully funded by the NRCC, and the other four Republican candidates pulled away from the Contract and toward the center. I think that when you move to the center, people see you as being the same as the other guy, and as they know what they have, they decide to keep him. I said, "Here's an agenda that I stand for and believe in," and I was the only one of the five that won.[48]

The general consensus among the freshman members, however, was that while the Contract may not have been the decisive factor in their races, the document did play the role that Newt Gingrich had intended by providing both a positive common platform for Republican candidates, in addition to just attacking Clinton and the Democrats, and a governing agenda for which the Republicans could claim an electoral mandate if they did take control of the House. The following comments from freshman members were typical in summarizing the impact of the Contract:

At the state level I was an elected official, and if I could show you tapes of some of my presentations from ten years ago, you would see that long before I got into office, I was talking about the things we dealt with in the Contract with America: the balanced budget, term limits, welfare reform, and tax breaks for families. I was talking about all of these long before the Contract with America came down the pike. Families need tax breaks, and 80 percent of the public supports a balanced budget. The Contract with America was nothing new, but it was a savvy idea by the leadership, who were willing to put their fate on the line, rather than just criticize the Democrats.[49]

Congressman J.C. Watts (Okla.)

We wrote our own contract with the people of Wisconsin. The Contract with America was good because it gave us something to go back to, and it highlighted two or three issues like the balanced budget, term limits, and the line-item veto. Beyond that, most of the voters in my district didn't have a clue about it. But I did like the idea of writing down what I stood for and the voters later holding me accountable.[50]

Congressman Mark Neumann (Wisc.)

The Contract was not all that important. People did not vote for Gil Gutknecht because of the Contract, but the Contract moved the Republicans off the image of Nyet, Nyet, Nyet. The Contract was positive, and we ran a positive campaign. The most important word in the English vocabulary is "attitude." The Contract gave the Republicans a positive attitude and a positive agenda.[51]

Congressman Gil Gutknecht (Minn.)

So while the impact of the Contract on the 1994 election result was considerably overstated, the document ironically would become much more important after the election, when it set the legislative agenda for the new Republican Congress.

The Unappreciated Factors: Redistricting and Retirement

While President Clinton's unpopularity, the Contract with America, and inspirational leadership from Newt Gingrich assisted the Republican effort in 1994, Republican House candidates also benefited from the less obvious impact of the 1990 reapportionment and redistricting of the House. During the 1970s and 1980s, when the Democrats' grip on the House appeared close to impregnable, it became evident that some of this impregnability was related to the redistricting process. Democrats used their control of most state legislatures and state governorships to draw U.S. House district lines advantageous to themselves or, at least, to protect incumbents of all parties, which, of course, "locked-in" the Democrats' overall advantage, since they had more incumbents. Redistricting as a factor in maintaining the Democratic majority in the House became particularly egregious after 1980, when Democratic legislatures in many states used "state-of-the-art" computer technology to pack Republican voters in a few overwhelmingly Republican districts, while allowing the Democrats to win the remainder and also reducing the number of truly competitive districts to zero.[52] Skillful redistricting thus enabled Democrats to mitigate the possible long-term advantage to the Republicans from the movement of population and House seats toward the more conservative South and West, which Republican presidential candidates generally carried by comfortable margins after 1968.

California was the most notable example of a redistricting tailored to maintain the Democratic advantage in House seats. Jolted by the Republicans' gaining twenty-six House seats in 1980, with Ronald Reagan at the head of the GOP national ticket, California Congressman Phil Burton drew a map with the aid of computers that maintained minimal variation in population between districts but that blatantly discriminated against the Republicans by packing their voters into seventeen overwhelmingly Republican districts and thereby leaving Republican candidates with hopeless prospects in almost all of the remaining twenty-eight. In 1984 Republican House candidates won 49 percent of all votes cast for the U.S. House in California to the Democratic candidates' 48 percent, but thanks to creative redistricting, the Democrats' won twenty-seven of the forty-five California U.S. House seats to the Republicans' eighteen.[53] On a national basis a similar effect was evident (although not on quite such a dramatic scale), as can be seen from Table 2.2.

For the 1990 redistricting, the Republicans were very much on guard to prevent a repetition of such blatantly partisan gerrymandering of U.S. House district lines by Democratic legislatures and governors. This time they also had a weapon at their disposal that had not been available to them during the preceding redistricting cycle. In 1982,

Table 2.2

**Democratic Popular Vote and Seats Won in U.S. House
Elections, 1980–94**

	Democratic % of national House vote[a]	Democratic % of House seats won	Difference
1980	50	56	6
1982	55	62	7
1984	52	58	6
1986	54	59	5
1988	53	60	7
1990	53	61	8
1992	51	59	8
1994	45	47	2

Source: Norman J. Ornstein, Thomas E. Mann, and Michael J. Malbin, *Vital Statistics on Congress: 1995–1996* (Washington, D.C.: American Enterprise Institute, 1996).
[a]Excludes districts where candidates ran unopposed.

despite the opposition of the Reagan administration, Congress had passed an extension and revision of the 1965 Voting Rights Act that effectively mandated the creation of minority electoral districts at all levels of government, in cases where blacks and Hispanics did not hold a number of seats roughly equivalent to their numbers in the overall population of a city, county, or state. Thus in redistricting the U.S. House after the 1990 census, state legislatures were virtually compelled to create "minority-majority" districts wherever possible or else invite challenges in federal court. In a hypothetical state with ten U.S. House districts and a black population of 20–25 percent, the legislature would thus be more or less legally required to create at least two majority-black electoral districts.

The problem for Democrats was that in most parts of the country, and particularly in the expanding southern states, minority voters were the most reliable Democratic electoral constituency. Packing these voters into a number of overwhelmingly minority districts would thus greatly weaken Democratic prospects in the remaining "lily white" districts. The Republican National Committee and the Bush administration's Justice Department were well aware of this possibility, and both allied themselves with black and Hispanic leaders in mounting federal court challenges to Democratic redistricting plans that did not meet the strict requirements of the Voting Rights Act. Thus, even

Table 2.3

Republican Gains From Redistricting in Three Southern States, 1990–94

	North Carolina			Georgia			Florida		
	WDª	BDᵇ	R	WD	BD	R	WD	BD	R
1990	7	0	4	8	1	1	9	0	10
1992ᶜ	6	2	4	4	3	4	7	3	13
1994	2	2	8	1ᵈ	3	7	5	3	15
Net gain/loss	–5	+2	+4	–7	+2	+6	–4	+3	+5

ªWD = White Democrat.
ᵇBD= Black Democrat.
ᶜNorth Carolina and Georgia each gained one U.S. House seat after the 1990 census. Florida gained four seats.
ᵈGeorgia's last remaining White Democrat, Congressman Nathan Deal, switched to the Republicans in April 1995.

states such as Florida and Georgia, where the Democrats controlled both the governorship and the legislature, witnessed the imposition of court-ordered redistricting plans that were much more favorable to minorities, and the GOP.

Although the Democrats were still able to draw redistricting plans advantageous to their incumbents while adhering to the strictures of the Voting Rights Act in states such as North Carolina and, most notably, Texas (where Democratic candidates won only 42 percent of the House vote in 1994, but still won nineteen (63 percent) of the Lone Star state's thirty U.S. House districts), their triumphs were likely to be short-lived as the bizarre district lines, required simultaneously to protect incumbents and satisfy minority demands for representation, attracted further federal court challenges. In states with Republican governors, the latter strove to prevent Democratic legislatures from promoting blatantly partisan gerrymanders. This was particularly evident in California, where Republican Governor Pete Wilson fought successfully to prevent a repeat of 1980.

The overall effect of the 1990 redistricting was to enhance Republican prospects in House elections. In the conservative southern states that generally gained U.S. House districts in 1990, the effects of the Voting Rights Act Amendments definitely assisted the GOP, as can be seen from the examples in Table 2.3.[54] Moreover, unfavorable redis-

Table 2.4

Retirements From the U.S. House, 1980–94

	Democrats	Republicans	Total
1980	21	13	24
1982	19	21	40
1984	9	13	22
1986	20	20	40
1988	10	13	23
1990	10	17	27
1992	41	24	65
1994	28	20	48

Source: Norman J. Ornstein, Thomas E. Mann, and Michael J. Malbin, *Vital Statistics on Congress: 1995–1996* (Washington, D.C.: American Enterprise Institute, 1996).

tricting also contributed to the large number of retirements by white Democratic incumbents, many of whom now faced either a very diffi-cult primary against a minority candidate or a general election against a Republican in 1992–94. As can be seen from Table 2.4, forty-one Democrats retired in 1992, and another twenty-eight in 1994, consider-ably in excess of the mean number of Democratic retirements since World War II.

The case of North Carolina freshman Walter B. Jones Jr. demon-strates the impact of the 1990 redistricting on both parties. As a white conservative Democrat, Jones failed to gain the Democratic nomina-tion in 1992 in North Carolina's First Congressional District, where his father, Walter B. Jones Sr., had been the Democratic incumbent for almost thirty years, but where the district boundaries had been drasti-cally altered to accommodate the requirements of the Voting Rights Act after 1990. In 1994 he won election as a Republican in the adjoin-ing Third District:

> In the 1992 redistricting, my county was split between the First District and the Third District. The First District was a minority-majority dis-trict, and the legislature had taken my hometown and put it into that district. In 1992 I won the Democratic primary in the First District with 39 percent of the vote, but in North Carolina you need 40 percent to avoid a runoff, and Eva Clayton [a black candidate], who finished sec-ond, called for one, and she won.

After that, in August 1992, my father and I met. He was seventy-nine years old and in the sunset of his life, and he was real disappointed that I didn't seem bitter about it. I said it was God's will, but that I did feel that I didn't fit in with the direction of the Democratic Party, and that I didn't feel there was a place in the party for people like myself. My father said, "I don't blame you and I support your decision. The Democratic Party has become too liberal for me and certainly for you."

I stayed Democrat in 1992 to head "Democrats for Jim Gardner," the Republican candidate for governor, but on the fifteenth of April 1993, I changed my party affiliation with no intention of being a candidate. I saw the Republicans as the best party to advance my Judeo-Christian principles, family issues, and my belief that people are overtaxed. The party asked me to travel in eastern North Carolina to energize the Republican leadership and reach out to frustrated conservative Democrats, and the local Republican leaders said "we think you would be a good candidate for Congress yourself." I agreed that I had a duty to advance my principles.[55]

The effects of retirements and redistricting were not immediately apparent in 1992, although the Republicans were able to make a net gain of ten House seats, despite Democrat Bill Clinton's victory in the presidential contest. Interestingly, however, the overwhelming majority of the 1992 Republican gains were in the South and could be attributed to redistricting and retirements.[56] After the 1994 returns were in, the long-term fallout of the 1990 redistricting for the GOP in the South was clearly in evidence (see Table 2.3). Finally, it should be noted that of the thirty-four Democratic incumbents who were defeated, sixteen, or almost half, were freshman Democrats elected in new marginal districts in 1992 who had not been able to entrench themselves and were therefore highly vulnerable to the anti-Clinton electoral backlash in 1994.

The 1990 redistricting thus served to "loosen up" the House in the early 1990s in such a way that the Republicans' prospects of making substantial gains were considerably enhanced. New seats in the South and the packing of Democrat-voting minorities into minority-majority districts contributed to Democratic retirements, more open seats in "lily white" districts, and Republican gains in 1992–94. Elsewhere, the generally fairer partisan lines after 1990 made it easier for the national swing toward the GOP to be reflected in significant House gains in 1994. The unusually high number of Democratic incumbent retirements in 1992 and again in 1994, which were certainly encouraged by the 1990 redistricting, created a large number of open seats and electorally fragile Democratic incumbents for the Republicans to defeat in 1994.

The 1990 redistricting, and the Democratic retirements it inspired, was thus an understated but very significant factor in the Republican takeover of the U.S. House in 1994.

Why Did They Run? The Successful 1994 Republican Challengers

The role of President Bill Clinton in motivating Republicans to run for Congress and in driving voters toward Republican congressional candidates in 1994 was discussed earlier in this chapter. Of course, dislike of the White House incumbent was not the sole reason that motivated Republican challengers to run for Congress in 1994, and many of the successful Republican freshmen, particularly those who had little or no previous political experience, believed that district-level factors were as important as national issues in explaining their success.

For those Republican candidates who had already been serving in state legislatures, more traditional motivations for running predominated. These ambitious Republican legislators had noted that 1994 was likely to be a good Republican year, and the opportunity of winning a U.S. House seat would have to be grasped while that prospect was open. Congressman Mark Foley of Florida was typical of the more politically experienced Republican challengers who noticed the possibility to advance their political careers:

> When Tom Lewis [the previous GOP incumbent] retired, it was assumed that I would seek the seat. I already represented a good portion of the district in the Florida Senate, and since I was five years old I had wanted to serve in Congress. I saw a rare opening that might come along once in ten years. It was too good to pass up.[57]

Similar considerations motivated South Carolina freshman Lindsey Graham and Maryland's Bob Ehrlich:

> In 1992 I was the first Republican elected to the state House from the Second District. Around March 1994, Butler Derrick [the Democratic

House incumbent] announced he was going to retire. The district had clearly changed, and 53 percent of the vote was from the counties that I come from. I was single, I had a little money, and I thought this was the best chance I'd ever have. The dynamics were there for a Republican victory.[58]

I got interested in politics because I like competition. I was a jock, and politics seemed like the closest thing to athletics I could find. I also thought that what legislatures do was important. It was at the back of my mind in college, where the strong academic environment at Princeton helped develop my views. At twenty-seven I ran for the legislature and won my primary by ninety-three votes. I enjoyed the legislature, and when this seat opened up, it was a natural progression.[59]

Minnesota Republican state legislator Gil Gutknecht found that his belief in legislative term limitations coincided with the opportunity to seek higher office:

I think that luck happens when preparation meets opportunity. I served in the Minnesota legislature for twelve years and I enjoyed it very much. But I also believe in term limits, and rather than press my luck, I decided that I should press on. I seriously considered running for the U.S. Senate seat being vacated by David Durenberger. I was the front-runner and had formed an exploratory committee and had raised $100,000. Then when I was campaigning in western Minnesota, I heard that [Democratic Congressman] Tim Penny had announced he was not going to seek reelection. A lot of people called and urged me to switch and run for the House seat because I was very well known in the district. So it was partly term limits and partly serendipity.[60]

Ray LaHood of Illinois also had an inside-track in the district represented by retiring Republican House Leader Bob Michel, because LaHood was already serving as Michel's chief of staff:

People knew me from my involvement in the community, so it was a natural succession for me. I had the best of all worlds. I came up under Tom Railsback [another former congressman from Illinois] and established a record of strong constituent service. I did the same for Bob Michel. I commuted every week, and I never moved my home from Peoria. I also had an advantage in learning the process here in Washington.[61]

Several freshmen came to Congress directly from local government. Virginia freshman Tom Davis, who had served for many years in local government in Fairfax County, Virginia, ran for Congress after getting encouragement from more senior Republican officeholders in his state:

> I was recruited by Senator [John] Warner and Representative [Frank] Wolf. I had won five elections in Fairfax County, representing 80 percent of the congressional district, so they thought I would have a good shot.[62]

Two California freshmen—George Radanovich of Mariposa and Brian Bilbray of San Diego—also both served in county government and frustrated by federal mandates, decided that the issues that most concerned them could be resolved only in Washington:

> I wanted to develop my ideas about the proper place of government in society, and it seemed to me that they didn't fit anywhere but at the national level. After redistricting, I thought about running for the assembly, but the heart of that district was in Modesto, and I was always more oriented toward Fresno. I also couldn't see how my vision of society could be put to use at the state level.[63]

> When I served as a San Diego county supervisor, I administered a lot of federal programs and experienced the federal government's detachment from reality on welfare and environmental issues. I was infuriated by the problem of illegal immigration.[64]

For those members who came to Congress with little or no legislative experience, issues appeared to have played a more significant role in their decision to run for Congress. The federal budget deficit and their personal experiences in business were a particularly significant factor for "outsider" candidates Mark Neumann of Wisconsin and Mark Sanford of South Carolina:

> The business I was in charted the debt. Homebuilding is very sensitive to changes in the interest rate, and I had watched the growth of the debt since 1980 and had seen it leading to the fiscal collapse of our nation if we didn't get to a balanced budget. I had no financial motive to do this, and I would have a better lifestyle outside Congress, but I thought that we had to start to get things under control, so we can have hope for the

future of our children. Frankly, as soon as I get the job done, I'll go home.[65]

I went to a Renaissance Weekend and heard Jim Davidson of the National Taxpayer's Union, make an apocalyptic presentation on the future of the country, with some scary economic projections. Not long after I was complaining about this at a business luncheon, and someone said: "Don't complain! Go and run for Congress." My first thought was that that was very narcissistic, but the idea wouldn't go away. I talked to my wife and to my friends, and they agreed that I should get it out of my system.

So I ran. Although I didn't think I could win, I thought I could shape the debate on the economic impact of the debt and the deficit, and if I happened to win, do something about it.[66]

Other "outsider" candidates, such as J.C. Watts of Oklahoma, mentioned a broader set of moral and cultural issues that were not being addressed by the Democratic Congress as a primary motivation for seeking election to the House in 1994:

I had no interest in running for Congress. I thought someday that I might run for the U.S. Senate, but I was not really interested in fighting a two-year reelection battle. I was involved in a Youth Ministry in my local church that was doing well, and my small business was doing OK. Why come to Congress?

The reason that I needed to be in D.C. was that my values as a father, youth minister, husband, and businessman are under attack in the United States today as never before. So I finally gave in to running, after much encouragement and prayer.[67]

Television sportscaster J.D. Hayworth of Arizona also set aside family and career considerations to take advantage of an opportunity to run for Congress, although he was more motivated by a general notion of public service than any specific issue or set of issues:

I was always interested in politics. In college I was a speech and political science major, and, as a broadcaster, I was always interested in the political process. I was active in debate, and there's a synergy between broadcasting and politics—especially in Arizona.

My predecessor was going down the line for the Clinton tax increase, and she was out of touch with the district, so I decided to take a serious look. It was just before my thirty-fifth birthday, and developmentally I had reached the point in my life where I had done so much in my profession and I wanted to give something back. I had been a precinct chairman and an active Republican, so it seemed the next logical step. I had to make a decision about leaving my profession and feeding my family while running for Congress all at once, but after a lot of blood, tears, and prayer, I decided to do it. As my old political science professor said: "Timing is everything."[68]

In addition to some differences in their motives for running, there was some distinctiveness in the nature of the campaigns conducted by "insider" and "outsider" candidates. Experienced state or local office-holders, with deep roots in the Republican Party, such as Tom Davis and Gil Gutknecht, tended to conduct more traditionally party-oriented campaigns while emphasizing their local roots and name recognition:

> I have been a Republican all my life. I was the chairman of the Republican committee in Fairfax County, and I was president of the Young Republicans at Amherst. I also served as a page on Capitol Hill, and I got my picture taken with Everett Dirksen and President Eisenhower.
>
> I had the *Washington Post* endorsement and a good strong local base. Both my wife and I grew up inside the beltway. I took her home precinct by 200 votes, the same margin that Clinton carried it by in 1992.[69]

> In my own district I had been in the state legislature for twelve years and I was well known in the district. I had an advantage in that the seat had been held by a Republican for almost a century, and Tim Penny [the retiring Democratic incumbent] was the first Democrat to be re-elected.[70]

For those successful freshmen who came from outside politics and won "against the odds" in 1994, ties to the Republican Party were much less significant. Mark Neumann, Joe Scarborough, and Mark Sanford were typical of this breed of Republican freshman:

> I've voted both ways, but I was never involved in politics prior to 1989–90. I usually voted a split ticket. I decided to run as a Republican because they stood for values and principles I believe in, and they're more inclined to tell the truth. They're also the party less willing to spend the taxpayers' money.[71]

> I was a Democrat through November 1992. After Bill Clinton was elected, I switched to the Republicans. If you look at the freshmen in

the House, you'll see that there's not as much identification with the Republican Party, or with the traditional party stances, as is the case with those elected before 1994.[72]

I don't define myself as a Republican or Democrat. If I had to define myself, I would define myself, first, as an American; second, as a South Carolinian; and third, as conservative or liberal. Most Americans would define themselves as conservative or liberal rather than Republican or Democrat. I don't view myself as hung up on party labels.[73]

Although initially disadvantaged in terms of money and name recognition—the two major prerequisites of success in congressional elections—because of their nonpartisan backgrounds, the outsider candidates were ideally situated to exploit the general public disgust with Congress and to emphasize a populist, Perot-style "reform agenda," including congressional term limits. In Republican primaries against established state and local officeholders, the outsiders had little option but to emphasize these issues. Indeed the reform agenda became the major theme of many outsider campaigns, such as Mark Sanford's:

I was an outsider and that was the only card I had, so I ran my campaign tied to two issues: first, the government is spending too much money; and second, maybe the type of person who goes to Congress had a lot to do with this. I ran on the idea of a "citizen legislator." I wasn't going to stay around, and in the primary debates while everybody supported term limits, I could say I really supported them, because I was only going to be there for three terms. Voters are sick of the disconnect between politicians' words and their actions, so I wanted to reconnect them. I also didn't want to get caught on the money train. I said that I wouldn't take PAC money, and I wouldn't take a congressional pay raise until we had balanced the budget.[74]

The outsiders, being short of money and resources, also had to resort to unconventional media outlets, or stunts and gimmicks to attract "free" media coverage in order to raise their visibility. Joe Scarborough of Florida's First District, running in a multicandidate field with a limited budget against a well-known state legislator, Lois Benson, discovered the potential of cable-access television:

I had decided that instead of paying $10,000 to get on the ballot, I would do it by collecting door-to-door petitions. I was also aggressively

using alternative media outlets. The other candidates were blowing
money on thirty-second commercials at prime time on local news. We
used the fax aggressively and talk radio. We also used cable-access—
the slum of TV land! Lois Benson or [Retiring Democratic incumbent]
Earl Hutto would never dare appear on that. But I appeared on something called BLAB TV, where people just go on and talk and hawk
products. I raised $18,000 to $20,000 in the first six months and spent it
all on yard signs. In six to eight months the district was covered with
yard signs because I asked everyone who would sign my petitions if
they would take a sign.

In June and July I needed to get my face associated with the name,
so I went on a cable-access show and bought time at low prices. I just
had a desk, a face, a sign background, and a phone, and I would take
thirty minutes answering phone calls. I bought in such large volume that
it made a big difference. We could go up to 200 shows a week to get the
message out. While Lois Benson was in there, we had a mainly hostile
press, so in the final five days I bought up all the time on two channels
for "Joe TV," and you could not turn on the TV without seeing me on
the cable-access shows.

It worked because of channel surfing. Nobody watched the shows
for the whole thirty minutes, but if they switched channels three or four
times every thirty minutes, they would see me. In the off hours you
could buy thirty minutes on cable-access for $150. I got twelve hours
of time for every thirty-second commercial Lois ran on the networks.[75]

Mark Souder of Indiana had worked for years as a congressional
aide to Congressmen and later Senators Dan Quayle and Dan Coats,
but when he decided to challenge Democrat incumbent Jill Long in the
district held by both Quayle and Coats, he also adopted an "outsider"
strategy:

My district was not on the NRCC target list, and I was outspent in the
primary by two opponents. [Democratic incumbent] Jill Long had high
reelection numbers. I built a grassroots organization, and nobody saw it
coming. In a six-way primary race that everyone thought would be
close, I won with 40 percent to 18 percent for the next guy.

It was the same story in the general election. I was on the radio on
seven stations a month before Jill Long even realized it. I did over
2,000 cable spots on small local channels. The national party was cau-
tioning me to save all my money for the last two weeks, when it would
get close. I disagreed with them and argued that my job was to get into

the race. We had a "loaves and fishes" strategy. We never had enough, sometimes only about $75 in the bank, and only 8 percent of my money came from PACs. In the end I outspent Jill Long, but my money came late. Early on, I relied on a lot on free media, like [presidential candidate Pat] Buchanan.[76]

Mark Sanford's approach was to use a smart gimmick to attract free media attention and highlight his central issue, the budget deficit:

The media wouldn't cover us in the beginning, but they began to cover me when I walked all over the district handing out fake billion dollar bills to voters.[77]

Successful Republican outsider campaigns also frequently sought support among Democratic voters or Independent supporters of Ross Perot, with some measure of success, even at the expense of alienating some traditional Republican voters. Joe Scarborough and Mark Souder typified this approach:

We were very influenced by the Independents who found Ross Perot as a vehicle to channel their anger in 1992. A lot of his positions in 1992 were our positions in 1994.[78]

The national tide was something of a myth. It maybe explained 2–3 percent but not a 13 percent win. There was no uniformity in my returns, but if you looked at the individual precincts you could work out my strategy. In Noble County, for example, I lost all the majority Republican precincts, but I won a blue-collar town in the Northwest, and was even in another. I won with the same themes that Pat Buchanan is sounding: concern that we were losing our national sovereignty and that we were not negotiating good trade deals.

When I would go to meetings, I would find guys rising with long hair, tattoos, and a cigarette who were agreeing with me! People who were upset by motorcycle helmet laws and smoking restrictions. These people were fed up with the intrusion of the federal government.

The Perot voters also moved in our direction. If you take two-thirds of the Perot vote and add it to the Bush vote in 1992, that just about matches my vote in 1994.[79]

While the national Republican Party was campaigning on the basis of the Contract with America and against Bill Clinton and the "corrupt" Democratic Congress, at the district level the 1994 campaign revealed some important distinctions between Republican challengers. Even while the election outcome was apparently determined by national trends, local Republican campaigns were tailored to districts and circumstances. Politically experienced Republican challengers ran on the basis of their experience and familiarity to the voters. Many of them were effectively recruited by the national party or powerful Republicans in their states. They also entered their campaigns with much more potential to raise money rapidly. Their motivations for running were often based on ambition and timing.

Outsiders who succeeded naturally did not have such deep roots or ties with the Republican Party. Many of them, such as Mark Neumann and Mark Sanford, were successful businessmen, who had been inspired to run by concern over the economic course of the country. Others were motivated by deeper concerns over values and the country's moral direction. What they generally had in common was a campaign strategy that made a virtue of their outsider status, and in the climate of 1994 successful outsiders were able to capitalize on public discontent with Congress by emphasizing issues such as congressional term limits and campaign finance reform, and running as "citizen legislators." They put together their own organizations from scratch, and they often got the better of more established Republicans by using alternative forms of campaign media such as talk radio and cable-access television.

The differences between insider and outsider candidates was somewhat obscured by the national trend toward the GOP in 1994. In the 104th Congress, however, it would be the outsiders, with their militant commitment to reform and a balanced budget, who would define the freshman Republican class.

Analysis of the Republican Victory

On a turnout of 36 percent of eligible voters (up 3 percent from the previous midterm congressional election in 1990), the Republicans made a net gain of fifty-two seats to take control of the House by a margin of 230–204 over the Democrats, with the remaining seat being held by Independent Socialist Bernard Sanders of Vermont. In the Senate the Republicans made a net gain of eight seats for a 52–48 margin, which increased to 53–47 when Senator Richard Shelby of Alabama switched parties on the day following the election.

In the share of total votes cast for the House in contested races the Republicans got about 52 percent to the Democrats' 45 percent, a gain

Table 2.5

Republican House Gains by Region (1994)

	Net GOP gain	%
Northeast	4	8
Midwest	15	28
South	19	36
West	14	27
Total	52	100

of more than 6 percent for the GOP over 1992.[80] Thirty-four Democratic incumbents lost their seats, the highest figure since 1966, while no Republican incumbent lost. Interestingly, over 90 percent of House incumbents seeking reelection were returned, and of those who lost, sixteen were freshmen. When this is added to the Republicans' net gain of eighteen in the open-seat contests, the effects of the Democratic retirements in 1992 and 1994 in "loosening up" the House are apparent. In terms of seats, the Republican gains were largest in the South, but also substantial in the West and Midwest, while much less significant in the Northeast—the traditional bastion of liberal Republicanism (see Table 2.5). The impact of the 1990 redistricting and electoral realignment in the South was evident as the Republicans for the first time controlled more of the regions' House seats than the Democrats. The conservative southern states also now accounted for almost a third of the House Republican conference. The growing southern impact on the GOP would become a significant factor in the 104th Congress.

As mentioned previously, there was also evidence that the Republicans benefited from having stronger candidates than usual—particularly in the open seats. According to Gary Jacobson, 1994 was one of the few times since 1945 when Republican House challengers were more experienced in terms of having held elective office than their Democratic counterparts, and this was particularly important in the open-seat contests.[81]

Evidence from exit polls indicated that the key to the Republican victory lay in significant shifts toward the Republicans among certain key categories of voters, particularly Independents and supporters of Ross Perot in 1992 (see Table 2.6). The Republicans also had phenomenal advantages among categories such as evangelical Christians (76

Table 2.6

Voters Shifting Toward the Republicans in 1994

% of total	Category	% Rep. 1992	% Rep. 1994	% shift to Rep. 1992–94
24	Southern whites	53	65	+12
40	White men	51	62	+11
20	White "Born Again" Christian	66	76	+10
28	Whites 30–44 years old	51	61	+10
24	Independents	46	56	+10
41	White Protestants	57	66	+9
26	Whites 60 and over	46	55	+9
79	Whites	50	58	+8
17	Men 30–44 years old	49	57	+8
35	Republicans	85	93	+8
11	Income under $15,000	31	38	+7
34	Conservatives	72	79	+7
12	Men 60 and over	44	51	+7
23	Whites 45–49	52	59	+7
49	Men	48	54	+6
22	High school education	42	48	+6
32	Some college	47	53	+6
40	White women	49	55	+6
14	Unmarried men	42	48	+6
59	Country on "wrong track"	—	67	
49	Disapprove of Clinton	—	82	
12	1992 Perot voters	—	67	

Source: Data from exit-poll surveys by Voter Research and Surveys and Mitofsky International published in the *New York Times*, 10 November 1995, and 13 November 1995.

Note: Table shows categories of voters who moved more than 5 percentage points to the Republicans from 1992 to 1994.

percent Republican) and white men (62 percent Republican). Of the almost 50 percent of the voters who stated they "disapproved" of Bill Clinton, the Republicans won 82 percent.

Despite the great attention given to Speaker-elect Newt Gingrich and the Contract with America by the news media in the weeks following the election, voter surveys appeared to confirm the experiences of most successful Republican candidates that the election was a repudiation of Bill Clinton and "big government," rather than an endorsement of the Contract, with which most voters were still unfamiliar on polling day. Electoral mandates are created after the event rather than at the polls, however, and with the election over, the Contract was vastly magnified in importance as it became a policy agenda for the new Republican Congress. In the hoopla over the election result, both pundits and the Republicans themselves forgot the basic reasons for their victory and how tenuous their mandate for a "revolutionary" change in the direction of American politics really was. They also appeared to have forgotten that the arcane rules of the U.S. Senate and the constitutional prerogatives of even an apparently badly wounded chief executive would present serious obstacles to the implementation of that agenda.

3

The Republican Revolution: Institutional Reform and Passing the Contract

Given Newt Gingrich's belief in the power of symbolism over the popular imagination, it was hardly surprising that the Speaker-elect would resort to the notion of a "first hundred days," reminiscent of Franklin Roosevelt's New Deal and the glamour of John F. Kennedy, in his legislative strategy for the 104th Congress. The Contract with America committed the Republicans to the passage of its ten items through the House in the first three months of the 104th Congress, a frenetic schedule given the momentousness of many of those items.[1] Of course, in acting while their electoral mandate was fresh in the minds of both press and public, the House Republican leaders were following the conventional Washington wisdom—more usually applied to newly elected presidents—of getting the main points of their agenda enacted before the endemic "inertia" and "gridlock" of the American governmental system set in.

In the heady aftermath of the Republicans' electoral triumph and the early weeks of the new Congress, as the new Republican House majority, voting in lockstep, succeeded in bringing all the items of the Contract to the House floor as legislation, the Republican leadership and the news media began to talk about a "Republican revolution" in Washington. As we have seen from the previous chapter's analysis of the 1992 results, however, there was slight evidence of revolutionary fervor among the less than 40 percent of the American electorate that voted in the 1994 congressional elections. But carried away by their own rhetoric and press sensationalism, the Republican leaders and their freshman Republican troops in the House did begin to regard themselves as "revolutionaries," all the while forgetting that the public perception of "radicalism" or "extremism," intrinsic to the concept of revolution, has rarely been a recipe for political success in U.S. history.

The "Republican revolution" was more than a change in the direction of public policy, however. The Contract, and the pervasive public dissatisfaction with Congress as a governing institution on which the Republicans had capitalized in the 1994 elections, demanded that the new Republican majority also address the issue of institutional reform within Congress. In the weeks before taking office Speaker-elect Gingrich and his colleagues undertook a number of significant changes in the structure and procedures of the House, to emphasize the contrast with the old Democratic regime and make that body run more efficiently. Congressional accountability had been a major part of the Contract, and other items that had not been specifically included, such as lobbying reform and campaign finance reform, were taken very seriously by many of the freshman Republican members.

This chapter discusses the Republican record on procedural reform during the 104th Congress, including the procedural changes in the House initiated by Speaker-elect Gingrich prior to the opening of the new Congress (the congressional gift ban, lobby reform legislation, and the failure of campaign finance reform are discussed in chapter 6). It also includes a discussion of the passage of the various Contract items through the House and an explanation of the Republicans' tactics in the exhilarating early days of the "revolution." In accordance with the central theme of this book, these aspects of the 104th Congress are discussed from the perspective of the seventy-three House Republican freshmen, the vanguard of the Republican revolution.

Before addressing these issues, however, we begin with a brief social profile of the freshman Republican class of 1994, to assess just how exceptional they actually were in terms of their social and economic background, by comparison with their fellow Republicans and the House as a whole.

The House GOP Freshmen: *Plus Ça Change?*

By virtue of their sheer numbers and their status as front-line troops in the Republican triumph in 1994, the freshman class of Republicans in the 104th Congress was bound to have an extraordinary impact. No other House freshman class, including the equally large (seventy-four) Democratic freshman class of 1974 (the so-called Watergate Babies), had attracted so much publicity and notoriety or had such an elevated conception of its own significance. As is evident from the previous chapter, many of the newly elected freshmen of 1994 preferred to think of themselves as political "outsiders," a new breed of congressmen who would sweep-clean the "mess" in the nation's capital. This self-characterization was also reflected in epithets such as "inexperienced," "revolutionary," and "zealous" applied to the freshman Republicans by the news media and, particularly when these attributes appeared to be politically damaging by their Democratic opponents.

A glance at Table 3.1, which compares the social profile of the freshmen to the House Republicans and the House as a whole, reveals that, in its social makeup at least, the freshman class of House Republicans was not as different from the modern congressional norm as both they themselves, the press, and their detractors suggested.

In terms of gender, the freshmen were only marginally less overwhelmingly male than their GOP colleagues, and at about the same percentage level as the House as a whole. As far as racial and ethnic background was concerned, the freshman class, like the House GOP as a whole, was highly unrepresentative, with only one black member— the former college football star J.C. Watts of Oklahoma—and no Hispanics. The regional background of the freshmen reflected the regional electoral strengths and weaknesses of their national party. The Northeast (New England and Middle Atlantic) region was somewhat underrepresented by comparison with the House GOP and markedly underrepresented by comparison with the House as whole. The western region (the Mountain and Pacific states) was somewhat overrepresented, while the proportion of freshman members from the Midwest and South was almost exactly the same as the House Republican Conference and the House as whole.

With regard to religious adherence, no significant differences were evident. The freshmen were marginally more Roman Catholic than the House Republican Conference, but marginally less so than the entire House, and there were no significant differences evident with regard to the major Protestant denominations. Freshman Republican ranks included only one Jewish member—Jon Fox of Pennsylvania—but this was not far out of line with the whole Republican Conference, which included only four of the House's twenty-five Jewish members.

Table 3.1

Demographic, Social, and Professional Backgrounds of the 1994 House Republican Freshmen

	% 1994 GOP freshmen (n = 73)	% All House Republicans (n = 230)	% Whole House (n = 435)
Race/Ethnicity			
White	98	98	87
Black	1	1	9
Hispanic	0	1	4
Gender			
Men	90	93	89
Women	10	7	11
Region			
Northeast	15	19	23
Midwest	25	26	24
West	27	23	21
South	33	32	31
Religion			
Roman Catholic	25	23	29
Baptist	15	12	13
Episcopalian	11	9	8
Methodist	8	13	11
Presbyterian	8	13	11
Other Christian	26	28	22
Jewish	1	2	6
Prior occupation(s)[a]			
Agriculture	5	6	5
Business/banking	49	50	37
Education	5	15	17
Law	32	34	39
Medicine	5	3	2
Public official/ politician	15	21	23
Other	4	2	9

Sources: Norman J. Ornstein, Thomas E. Mann, Michael J. Malbin, *Vital Statistics on Congress 1995–1996* (Washington, D.C.: Congressional Quarterly Press, 1996); and Michael Barone and Grant Ujifusa, *The Almanac of American Politics 1996* (Washington, D.C.: National Journal Inc., 1995).

[a]Because of members' overlapping occupations and professions, the percentages in each column in this category do not total 100.

As far as occupation and professional background are concerned, the freshmen did not differ much from their more senior Republican colleagues, and the more significant differences were between the latter and the entire House. The freshman class did contain a much lower proportion of members with a professional background in education,

Table 3.2

Political Experience of the 1994 Republican House Freshmen

	% of freshman class[a]
Government experience[b]	
Federal	15
State	36
Local	15
Legislative[c]	34
None	37
Campaign experience	
Ran previously for Congress	27
Ran for the House in 1992	21
Ran for state or local office	36
Never previously ran for public office	37

Source: Michael Barone and Grant Ujifusa, *Almanac of American Politics 1996* (Washington, D.C.: National Journal, 1996).

[a]Column does not add to 100 percent due to overlapping categories (e.g., members who had served in both state and local governments).

[b]Includes elected office, service in administrative capacity, or as executive or legislative aide.

[c]Includes state and federal levels and service as legislative aide.

and doctors were slightly overrepresented. The really interesting disparity, however, was in the number of freshman Republican members who were serving as *full-time* politicians or public officials at the time of their election. Their proportion in the freshman ranks was only 15 percent, in comparison with 21 percent among all House Republicans and 23 percent of the total House membership.

Thus far, the claims of the freshman Republicans to be political "outsiders" appear to be corroborated from the data. Yet, a glance at Table 3.2 reveals that the freshman Republicans, while obviously less politically experienced than their House GOP brethren, were hardly the political naifs occasionally described by the press and themselves. More than 60 percent of the class had served in the government in some capacity at the state, local, and federal levels, and more than a third of the class had some previous legislative experience at the state or federal level. Moreover, over three-fifths of the freshman Republicans had previously run for Congress or some state or local office, and more than one in five had run unsuccessfully for Congress only two years previously.

Analysis of the social and professional backgrounds of the Republican "class of '94" consequently reveals the freshmen to be surprisingly socially and demographically similar to the House Republicans in general. Differences between Republicans per se and the whole House were much more significant on most indicators. Interesting differences were apparent in two areas. First, the freshman Republicans were somewhat less likely to be from the Northeast than their GOP colleagues, and more likely to come from the West. In terms of setting the tone for the freshman class and the House GOP on environmental issues, this factor would become important. Second, the freshman Republicans were less likely to be politicians or public officials by profession, thus confirming their image as "outsiders" and "citizen-politicians." Nevertheless, the outsider status of the freshman class was qualified by the fact that an overwhelming majority of its members had served as civil servants, legislators, or elected officials at some level, and most had previous experience of political campaigning.

In sum, the House GOP freshmen of 1994 were not "political outsiders" to quite the degree reflected in their own rhetoric or that of their critics.

A New Regime and New Rules for the House

If the Democratic regime in the House had been generally characterized by weak leadership and a decentralized power structure oriented around powerful committee, and later subcommittee chairmen, the first Republican House in forty years would be defined by exactly the opposite power structure. From the time he became Speaker-elect after the November election victory, Newt Gingrich was clearly the dominating figure in the 104th Congress. Not since the time of the legendary Joseph Cannon at the turn of the century had America witnessed such a powerful Speakership.[2] The actions taken by Gingrich and his chief lieutenants in the weeks before the 104th Congress had even met set the pattern; the Speaker-elect exploited his dominant position as the architect of the Republican revolution to consolidate his power in the forthcoming Congress. And since the seventy-three House Republican freshmen had provided the Republicans with their first House majority in forty years and accordingly embodied the spirit of the revolution of 1994 to a greater extent than the more senior Republicans, their endorsement of the newly empowered Speakership was crucial.

The changes in House procedures introduced in the interregnum before the new House convened in January 1995 were monumental in their significance. The committee/subcommittee system, the basis of the House's internal power structure under Democratic rule, was the first object of the Republican leadership's attention. Reducing the number of House committees and subcommittees and the overlapping jurisdictions between them, a long-time Republican goal, was the first issue they tackled.[3] David Dreier of California, a leading Republican on the House Rules Committee, was given the task of devising proposals to streamline the House committee system with an eye toward eliminating superfluous committees and subcommittees:

> My goal was to enhance the deliberative nature of the institution. We had 266 committees and subcommittees, and the congressional bureaucracy was way too great. People were not accountable because of the joint referrals of legislation, and legislation was getting bottled up.[4]

On the face of it, Dreier had only limited success in his objective. Republican members, committee staffers, and lobbies closely associated with House committees fought mightily to preserve the existence of threatened committees such as Veterans Affairs. Another committee threatened by abolition, Small Business, survived because of the Republicans' strong political links to small-business lobbies, and because the new Republican committee chair, Congresswoman Jan Meyers of Kansas, had been the only woman in line for a full committee chairmanship. In the end just three full committees—District of Columbia, Merchant Marine and Fisheries, and Post Office and Civil Service—were eliminated. An additional 31 (27 percent) of the 115 House subcommittees were abolished, however, and the jurisdiction of the extremely powerful Energy and Commerce committee (which had dealt with much of the ill-fated Clinton health-care plan) was substantially reduced. House committee staffs were also reduced by over one-third.[5]

A final interesting aspect of the reforms of the committee process was the decision to rename ten of the twenty-eight remaining committees. The reason for this was more substantial than a mere indication of a new regime. According to David Dreier,

> Renaming was about shifting the agenda away from big government. For example: Government Operations became Government Reform and

Oversight, Education and Labor became Economic and Educational Opportunity, and Public Works and Transportation became Transportation and Infrastructure. The old names implied a desire to perpetuate and expand the size and scope of government. The new names were needed to put our *imprimatur* on Congress and indicate the direction in which we're taking the institution.[6]

Perhaps of more direct significance with regard to the role of the freshmen were changes in the status and power of committee chairs. Gingrich exploited the authority he had earned by leading the Republicans to their first House majority in forty years to handpick the chairs of congressional committees. No Democratic Speaker in the modern era would have presumed to attempt this, and although the 1970s reforms in the Democratic Caucus rules had led to the occasional removal of a committee chair by a vote of the entire caucus, seniority had remained the norm. Speaker-elect Gingrich did not believe that the longest-serving Republicans on the major committees should automatically be elevated to the chairmanships, however. Many of these members had formed close relationships with committee Democrats and interest-group representatives who dealt regularly with specific committees. As committee chairs, they might lack the necessary commitment to passing the Contract and implementing the Republican revolution. So while Gingrich by and large adhered to seniority, several senior Republicans were bypassed for important committee chairmanships, which were given instead to younger and more energetic "true believers." A clear instance of this was the selection of Robert Livingston of Louisiana, only the fifth-ranking Republican in terms of seniority, to chair the critical Appropriations Committee. California Republican veteran Carlos Moorhead also became the unluckiest member of the new majority when he was passed over for the chairmanship of *both* the Judiciary and Commerce committees, which were to be chaired instead by Henry Hyde of Illinois and Thomas Bliley of Virginia.[7]

In addition to making committee chairs beholden to the new Speaker, as part of the Contract's promised package of "opening-day" procedural reforms the new House Republican majority ended the practice of "proxy voting," by which committee chairs had controlled the votes of absent members, thus guaranteeing a party majority even in the physical absence of many majority party members. This was held to be characteristic of the "corrupt" and "despotic" manner in which the Democrats had conducted the House, and naturally was especially well received by the freshman members. Indiana Republican Mark Souder, who had experienced the Democratic House as a congressional aide, believed that this was a particularly significant change:

> The biggest change I've noticed is the end of proxy voting, which has freed us up to be free agents. Before, on a critical vote, a committee chair could demand your proxy, and if you didn't behave, he could cut off your funding, because he controlled the flow of PAC dollars. Now the breach in proxy voting has turned the internal pre-meetings of committees before hearings into chaos. Everybody is a free agent, and no one takes orders.[8]

Another Gingrich innovation that appealed to the freshmen was imposing a six-year term limit on committee chairs (and an eight-year limit on the Speakership), which accorded with the "citizen legislature" concept that was widely held among members of the freshmen class (see chapter 2).[9]

As mentioned in the previous chapter, the operations of GOPAC and Gingrich's high media profile had already allowed him to forge close ties to many members of the freshman class, and at the beginning of the 104th Congress it was clear that the large freshman class had not only fulfilled the Speaker's long-term vision of providing the House Republicans with a majority but was also proving to be his strongest bastion of support in enhancing his power as Speaker vis-à-vis the committee chairs. According to Mark Souder,

> There couldn't have been a better time to be a freshman: (1) because of the size of the class; and (2) because of the nature of Newt Gingrich's commitments. Before we arrived, Gingrich's hold on the conference was tenuous, but because of the size of the freshman class, Gingrich had no opponent for Speaker, neither did Armey. Most of the freshmen voted for Delay, Boehner, and Cox as well. We elected a leadership that agreed with the freshman class.[10]

Florida freshman Mark Foley concurred:

> Newt really enjoys seeing some of us work because he sees the same rabble-rouser that he was a few years ago. Without Newt, the class wouldn't be such a dynamic class. Newt Gingrich asks: "What do the

freshmen think?" And he's giving us more than anyone else would have.[11]

In return, the Speaker, much to the irritation of several senior Republicans, gave out slots on the most important "exclusive" committees—Rules, Ways and Means, and Appropriations—to freshmen. Three freshmen were appointed to Ways and Means, seven to Appropriations, and one to the Rules Committee. Another move that had been virtually unheard of under the old House regime was the appointment of two freshman members—David McIntosh of Indiana and Tom Davis of Virginia—as subcommittee chairs.

Several major factors were involved in explaining the unusual degree of freshman influence over the committee selection process. First, as the House Appropriations Committee chair, Bob Livingston, pointed out, was the sheer size of the class:

> It was only because there were so many freshmen and they represented 20 to 25 percent of our members that the leadership made the decision that it was important to accommodate them.[12]

Congressman Bob Walker, an intimate of the Speaker and a member of the GOP leadership, agreed, but he also emphasized the point earlier mentioned by Mark Souder concerning the special rapport between Speaker Gingrich and the freshmen, who were more "in tune" with the revolutionary aspirations of the leadership than many of the more senior members:

> Given the size of the class, I think it made very good sense to allow them to interact with powerful committees. It was also important that those committees have representatives from the freshman class who understood the dynamic that the entire House had to deal with, and in most instances the chairmen of those committees have been quite pleased with the freshman members, who've made a positive contribution to the legislative agenda.[13]

The unusual circumstances of the Republicans taking control of the House for the first time in forty years also enhanced the freshman Republicans' influence, a point noted by both Appropriations chair Livingston and Tennessee freshman Zach Wamp:

> It was also due to the fact that we were a new majority for the first time in forty years and the transition from minority to majority status. On

taking over the leadership we had to learn how to chair and staff committees from scratch with no experience, and that inexperience worked
in favor of the freshmen.[14]

I hit the ground running and I did not have a slow learning curve. This
freshman class was conceded more influence than its predecessors because the transition to Republican rule gave us more influence and
allowed us to come up to speed on legislation far quicker. In fact, I
don't feel like a freshman anymore, because I feel that I can move
legislation, move the conference, and effect change as much as a senior
legislator.[15]

One final factor, of course, was the need to protect the most vulnerable
freshman members electorally. Of the seven freshman members on
Appropriations, six had won previously Democratic districts in the
1994 election, as had the three freshmen on Ways and Means, and the
freshman member on the Rules Committee.[16] Another senior member
close to Speaker Gingrich, Wisconsin Representative Steve Gunderson, conceded this point:

Freshmen have gotten more attention because so many of them are from
vulnerable districts, and the leadership has to care and feed them to
ensure they are reelected.[17]

This point was reiterated by a freshman member who had hoped to get
an exclusive committee assignment:

I had a big win in the general election, but there are three guys on the
Ways and Means Committee who won by 300 to 1,500 votes. The
Committee-on-Committees wanted to shore-up our areas of weakness
and put the marginal guys on good committees, as opposed to those
who won by big margins. I naively thought that I would be a candidate
for Ways and Means because of my background in finance, but I didn't
understand the politics.[18]

Among the more senior Republicans, the aggressive assertion of
power by the Speaker and the attention given to the freshmen did not
go unnoticed. Ray LaHood, an Illinois freshman who knew the senior
members well due to his previous position as Bob Michel's chief of
staff, was in a better position than most freshman members to note the
reaction of the seniors:

In the beginning, when the Speaker and the leadership decided to put freshman members on the Rules, Appropriations, and Ways and Means committees, the senior members resented it a little bit. They believed that if you kept quiet, and did your work, you would eventually get slots on those committees. The leadership also gave subcommittee chairmanships to freshmen, and there was also a little resentment about that. There was a great deal of resentment when the leadership decided to overlook members' seniority on some committees, and picked their own people to chair those committees, ahead of people like Carlos Moorhead and John Myers. But the Speaker decided that he wanted to be a strong Speaker.[19]

Several other freshmen, such as the militant budget-cutter Mark Neumann of Wisconsin, were more wary of the senior Republicans, many of whom, they believed, had been coopted by the Washington "system":

Those [senior members] that have not been corrupted by the system and are willing to do something for the future of our country, I get along with. The ones that aren't, I don't get along too well with. The ones that want to spend my kids' money.[20]

While most members interviewed for this study confessed to inevitable tensions between the old and the new guard among the House Republicans, those on both sides were nevertheless generally keen to emphasize what united the 1994 freshmen and their more senior Republican colleagues, rather than what divided them. Three fairly senior and influential House Republicans, Bob Walker, Bob Livingston, and Florida's E. Clay Shaw, all stressed the gratitude felt by most of the senior Republicans toward the freshman class that had made the GOP a majority in the House for the first time in forty years:

Every senior member recognizes that, without the freshmen, they would not be in positions of leadership in this Congress. It happened that these guys made us a majority.[21]

Among some members I've heard some resentment about the undue influence of the freshmen, but we then recall that we would not be a majority without them, and we appreciate them more.[22]

I don't think there's any resentment. Perhaps there's a little impatience among the older, more seasoned, members. For example, chairs of committees having to do so much work to convince freshmen of their positions. It's also important to realize that the Speaker gave the freshmen great importance from the start. He made it clear he would support them and what they stand for.[23]

These sentiments were also noted by the freshman members, including Maryland's Robert Ehrlich:

I think that most of the senior members have a gleeful appreciation of why we're here. Gerry Solomon [chairman of the Rules Committee] was hugging all of us freshmen for six months.[24]

Most of the infrastructure of what would later be termed the "Gingrich revolution" was thus already in place before the 104th Congress had even met: the seniority system had been seriously assaulted, the power of the committee chairs had been circumscribed, the large class of freshman Republicans was already making an unprecedented impact, and Newt Gingrich had become the most powerful House Speaker in living memory. The new Republican majority was apparently rewriting the textbook view of the House as characterized by decentralized power; weak, conditional, party leadership; and seniority.[25] As the new House met in January 1995, the Republican majority would have to sustain its discipline and demonstrate its effectiveness by passing the provisions of the Contract with America within the hundred-day deadline the members had set for themselves. In doing so, the Republican Party leadership and their allies in the freshman class would find the new power structure they had put into place to be indispensable.

Passing the Contract: The First Hundred Days

Once the 104th Congress met on 4 January 1997, the Republican majority wasted no time in getting down to the business of passing the Contract with America. On the very first day of the Congress, as promised in the Contract, the new Republican House passed a ban on proxy voting in House committees, term limits for the Speaker (eight years) and committee chairs (six years), a reduction by one-third in committee staffs, the opening of committee and subcommittee meetings to the public as a matter of right, the inclusion of committee voting records in committee reports, the first independent audit of the House's books in living memory, the abolition of publicly funded congressional caucuses or Legislative Service Organizations (LSOs), a ban on members' altering their remarks in the *Congressional Record*, and a rule making the latter and other House documents available for free on the Internet. On that hectic opening day they also found time to pass a new House rule requiring a three-fifths majority to raise income rates, and the Congressional Accountability Act, which made Congress for the first time subject to federal laws on workers' rights and conditions, such as civil rights acts and labor legislation.[26]

The agenda for opening day reflected the Republican leadership's awareness of the need to address immediately the issue of congressional reform that had contributed so heavily to their electoral triumph, and what they had long regarded as the worst excesses of Democratic rule. Of the measures passed above, by far the most symbolic was the Congressional Accountability Act, which directly addressed the widespread public perception that Congress was out of touch with the American public. The perception of Congress as having become corrupt and unresponsive to public opinion was, of course, most deeply ingrained in the freshman class. Congressman Zach Wamp's reaction was typical:

> Whether it's term limits or campaign finance reform, or the gift ban, or cutting pensions, it's extremely difficult to cut through the mindset of members who put this institution above the American people. We want an institution that deserves the trust of the American people, but doesn't put itself above the people. It's an institutional corruption, not a legal or ethical corruption, but senior members want to make excuses for a situation that benefits them, and they are unwilling to be objective. If you look at it objectively, you have to say that we have to clean up the campaign system and introduce term limits. This institution needs to be reconnected to the American people.[27]

In order to adhere to the hundred-day deadline for getting the Contract through the House, the Republicans had committed themselves to an intensive and hectic schedule in the first three months of the 104th Congress. Acting on their electoral pledges assumed tremendous importance to the party leadership and the freshman class because they had to demonstrate that they were politicians who would keep faith with the voters and thereby restore integrity to the institution of Congress. Although Maryland freshman Republican Bob Ehrlich believed that the distinctiveness of the freshmen was exaggerated, he acknowledged their more idealistic approach to politics:

We've been overly demonized by our enemies and overly praised by our friends. By and large, our ideas are in conformity with the vast majority of Republican members. We're maybe a bit more hard-edged, and have more philosophical grounding. We think that politics should be about ideas and principles. That why we have such utter disdain for the president, and nothing that has happened has disabused us of that notion![28]

The schedule became even more problematic because of the Republican commitment to reform House floor procedures to make them more "open" and "fair," in contrast to what the Republicans perceived as the increasingly unfair rules for floor debate under which they had had to operate as a minority under Democratic rule.[29] To this end the opening-day package of rules changes also included provisions guaranteeing the minority party the right to offer "a motion to recommit with instructions" (i.e., a vote on an alternative measure just prior to final passage of legislation on the House floor), and a ban on time-consuming commemorative legislation (designating days, weeks, or months after certain trades or products). In addition to these changes, the Rules Committee under its new chair, Congressman Gerald Solomon of New York, promised to allow far more "open rules" (providing greater opportunities for amendments) in floor debate on legislation.[30] While these changes did lead to somewhat fairer and more open procedures on the House floor, there is no question that giving the minority more opportunity for amendments in combination with the strict schedule for passage of the Contract put tremendous time pressure on the Republican membership and made strong leadership and strict party discipline even more important.

Aside from institutional reform, the issue that defined the freshman class and constituted the priority item in the Contract was the balanced budget. The Republican strategy for the budget issue involved, first, the passage of a balanced budget amendment to the Constitution, and, second, the construction and passage of a budget package that would achieve that objective in the near future. The Contract version of the balanced budget amendment included a provision that a three-fifths majority in both Houses of Congress be required for revenue increases, but it soon became apparent that most Democrats, and a sizable number of Republican moderates, could not support this provision. As a result, the eventual vote on the balanced budget amendment on 26

January 1995 was on a version of the amendment drafted by veteran conservative Democrat Charles Stenholm of Texas, which did not include the provision on revenue raises. The Stenholm amendment passed the House by the requisite two-thirds majority, 300–132.[31] When the balanced budget amendment failed to pass the Senate by one vote in March, the onus was still on the Republicans to produce a balanced budget package, with consequences that are discussed at greater length in the next chapter.

Meanwhile, the passage of the Contract items through the House continued apace. On 6 February 1995, the House approved legislation, by a 294–134 margin, that would give the president a line-item veto on individual items in appropriations bills. The House also passed an "unfunded mandates" measure preventing the federal government from imposing new federal mandates on state governments without providing the funds to pay for them. On 3 March, the House passed the package of measures known as the Job Creation and Wage Enhancement Act, which included the easing of federal environmental and safety regulations on businesses, subjecting such regulations to "risk assessment" and "cost-benefit" analysis, and providing more generous compensation to property owners whose property was affected by federal environmental and wildlife protection laws.

On 8 February, the House approved a package of six separate bills dealing with crime, collectively entitled The Taking Back Our Streets Act in the Contract, that included a limit on death penalty appeals in federal courts, mandatory minimum sentences for drug-related offenses, a repeal of much of the increased spending on crime prevention included in President Clinton's 1994 crime bill by converting these individual programs into a single block grant, increased funds to the states for building prisons, and a relaxation of the rules on the admissibility of evidence obtained without search warrants. All passed the House without much difficulty. The Republicans also passed a package of measurers on 7–10 March entitled the Common Sense Legal Reform Act, the essence of which was reform of tort laws to limit "frivolous" lawsuits and "excessive" damages awarded by juries in product liability and medical malpractice suits.

One of the Contract's most significant measures was a welfare reform proposal designed to deal with the alleged connection between welfare benefits and widespread illegitimacy among the inner-city poor. The Personal Responsibility Act transformed the main federal welfare program, Aid to Families with Dependent Children (AFDC), from an entitlement into a block grant to the states, and barred teenage mothers under the age of eighteen from receiving AFDC, food stamps, or public housing. It also introduced strict time limits for welfare benefits and cut off benefits to resident aliens. This legislation finally passed the House on 24 March 1995, in a fairly close (234–199) party-line vote. Another close (234–188) party-line vote occurred on the Contract's tax cut proposals, including a 50 percent reduction in capital gains taxes, and a $500 per child tax credit for families with incomes under $200,000 a year. Described by Newt Gingrich as the "crown jewel" of the Contract, the tax reduction was the final item to pass the House on 5 April 1995, the ninety-second day of the 104th Congress.[32]

While the Republicans adhered to their pledge to allow all the Contract items to come to a vote on the House floor within the first hundred days of the 104th Congress, two Contract items failed to achieve passage. The first occurred in the Contract's foreign policy and defense measure—The National Security Revitalization Act. The act's provisions prohibiting the use of Pentagon funds for UN peacekeeping operations and advocating the expansion of NATO membership to the former Warsaw Pact nations of eastern Europe passed easily on 16 February 1995, but another provision, which would have established a space-based antiballistic missile system, was weakened by a successful Democratic amendment that changed the emphasis from space-based to ground-based, short-range or "theater," antimissile systems, as advocated by the Clinton administration.[33]

The second defeat, on a constitutional amendment to limit congressional terms, was more significant in that it once again highlighted the reformist, populist orientation of the freshmen and exposed tensions with more senior Republicans, such as Judiciary Committee chair Henry Hyde, who vociferously opposed term limitations. Even the party leadership that had drawn up the Contract was deeply ambivalent about term limits, perhaps because, unlike the other Contract items, there was no overwhelming consensus within the House Republican conference on the issue. In his comprehensive study of the Contract and its implementation in the House, James Gimpel noted:

> While Newt Gingrich (Ga.) publicly supported the entire Contract, he had never been enthusiastic about term limits and the new majority leader, Richard Armey (Tex.), had suggested in interviews that he had

little ardor for them. . . . Given the popularity of term limits, it was just too difficult to ignore the issue. GOP leaders could assure opponents within the party that the Contract's promise was to bring term limits to a vote, not to pass them.

Still, term limits was a divisive issue within the Republican Conference. . . . Several members, including the influential Henry Hyde (Il.), had such strong reservations that they nearly refused to sign the Contract.[34]

As we have seen, however, there was considerable enthusiasm for term limits among the Republican freshmen, many of whom had made term limits a major theme of their successful election campaigns. Oklahoma's J.C. Watts was one of these:

One reason I'm in favor of term limits is that in any elected body, the longer you stay, the more mechanical the process becomes, and when the process becomes mechanical, it's bad for America and bad for one's integrity and values. It's a tough system to operate in if you've got a conscience and convictions. So many members see this as a mechanical process.[35]

Congressman Walter B. Jones Jr. of North Carolina further argued that term limits were essential to the freshmen's maintaining their profile as "outsiders":

We want to ensure that we maintain our outside view as we serve in Congress. That's why I am for term limits. I am also fortunate to be so close to the district, which means that I have been home almost every weekend, despite the fact that it's a ten-hour drive there and back. I simply didn't want people to think that I didn't want to meet them. That attitude is what makes the freshmen different. We've always understood that we've been given a special opportunity by God and the people to change America, and the only way to keep it is to keep in touch with the people back home.[36]

Tennessee freshman Van Hilleary, a leading proponent of term limits whose draft amendment was debated on the House floor, again remarked on generational differences among House Republicans as far as this issue was concerned:

Young folks want term limits and older folks don't. It doesn't cut across party lines, but more on generational lines. We have to hold the line on the balanced budget and term limits, because they would have the longest-lasting, widespread, and positive effect on Congress of anything we can do. . . . The freshman class is more reform-oriented and slightly more conservative. The liberal/conservative spectrum is defined by whether you're a Republican or a Democrat. The status quo versus reform spectrum is defined by how long you have been here.[37]

While this observation generally held in the debates over term limits, support for the latter was not unanimous among the freshmen members. Bob Ehrlich of Maryland was an outspoken opponent of term limitations:

I'm against term limits because I want positive ideas for a party that prides itself on limiting government, and true democracy. People knew my position when I ran for the legislature, where I voted against term limits, and my opponent in the last election attacked me on it. I want to vote for whoever I'm going to vote for, and I don't agree that longevity in office makes you more corrupt. In fact, it's probably the reverse. If you are going to be corrupt, you'll be corrupt early in your career.[38]

Gingrich appointed a task force on term limits heavily stacked with junior members, but could not reach a consensus on a proposal with six-year, eight-year, and twelve-year limits all having support among advocates of term limits. Things got worse in the Judiciary Committee, where senior Republicans led by Chairman Hyde vehemently opposed the whole concept, and the only proposal that got voted out was a twelve-year limit, with a provision that term-limited members could sit out one term and then run again: a clear abandonment of the Contract's promise of a "clean" vote on a term-limits amendment. While the freshman Republicans enthusiastically supported Congressman Hilleary's proposal for a twelve-year absolute limit with states being permitted to set stricter limits, the leadership eventually rallied behind a proposal sponsored by Congressman Bill McCollum of Florida that set a twelve-year limit for both houses with states being preempted from establishing stricter limitations. In the end, House floor votes took place on four term-limits constitutional amendments, including a Democratic substitute that would have applied the twelve-year limits retroactively (thereby ending the political careers of most of the House Republican leadership) on 29 March 1995. None of them came close to the necessary two-thirds majority of 290 votes, although the leadership-backed McCollum version came closest with 227.[39]

The confusion and lack of Republican consensus over term limits was the exception rather than the norm during the "hundred days," however. In those hectic first three months of the 104th Congress, the new Republican majority fulfilled their commitment to bring all the items in the Contract with America to the floor of the House within the promised time, and with the exceptions of term limits (a constitutional amendment that required a two-thirds majority) and the highly technical issue of space-based missile defense, each item was approved by the House. While the Republicans had only promised to bring each item to a vote, it was nevertheless somewhat disappointing that only the two least politically controversial measures—the prohibition on unfunded mandates and the Congressional Accountability Act—were quickly approved by the Senate and signed into law by President Clinton. The reasons why the Contract inevitably got bogged down in the Senate are discussed in a separate chapter on that chamber. The opposition of the Clinton administration to most of the Contract was only to be expected, and the Republican House majority was too slim to override the president. But all the hyperbole over the Contract and the "Republican revolution" almost led the GOP to believe that it could change the direction of American politics from the House of Representatives alone. Events in the following months would provide a rude awakening.

First Impressions: The Freshmen Encounter Washington

For the self-styled "revolutionaries" of the freshman class of Republicans, life on Capitol Hill in the early months of the new Congress provided quite a few surprises, both pleasant and unpleasant. After all, this was the very same institution that many had been describing in their campaign rhetoric as "unresponsive" and "corrupt," so it was interesting to discover whether these views of Congress were confirmed by actual experience with Washington. Before the grim realities of the budget struggle with President Clinton hit at the end of 1995, the GOP freshmen were giddy with the attention they had been receiving from their leaders, the news media, and the wider public. Hitting the ground running, and in a far more privileged position than other freshman classes in recent times, the seventy-three House Republican freshmen found the "hundred days" an exhilarating, but also physically demanding, experience. Joe Scarborough, from Pensacola, Florida, who had never held any kind of political office prior to his election, found the time demands of the job of congressman to be the most surprising feature of life in the U.S. House:

Most of us campaigned against an "Imperial Congress" and talked about the "affluent lifestyle" of Congress. We were told that we would begin work on Tuesday, Wednesday would be our long day from 10 A.M. to 7 or 8 P.M., and on Thursday we would vote in the morning and fly out in the afternoon.

That was the old way. We started working early on Monday morning and left Friday afternoon. The last plane to Pensacola is at 4 P.M., and I run from the last vote to the plane. We usually have events on Friday night, three of four town meetings on Saturday, and some more events on Sunday. I have no time to sit behind the desk and get any work done or read the papers and magazines. I have no time to plan the next day, let alone the next month.

In the first year there was the added pressure that we came in as freshmen on 4 January, and instead of the traditional three weeks off, we went straight to work. We still had boxes sitting unpacked in the office while we were getting up and running. By April, we felt like grizzled veterans. The schedule was insane during the hundred days and stayed insane through the budget debacle.[40]

Mark Sanford of South Carolina, another political neophyte among the freshmen, expressed similar sentiments:

It was a trial by fire last year. I had never pulled an all-nighter when I was in college, but I pulled a few during the first hundred days. It was a wrenching adjustment. I wore myself out in the first year. I had no political base, and I didn't know that many people. So both here and at home we had little priority setting. Because I was just trying to survive that first year, I would meet every single group of people that I'd never met before. It was an awkward year. Unless you have been in the state legislature for ten years, you try and do too much. By year two, you are so exhausted that when they come for the second visit, you just stick your head out and say "hello." And you get into a system and structure that was not here during the first year, but is necessary for survival.[41]

In fact, four freshman members who had served in state legislatures— Gil Gutknecht of Minnesota, Jon Fox of Pennsylvania, Walter B. Jones, Jr. of North Carolina, and Florida's Mark Foley—also emphasized the workload and pressure by comparison with that level of government, and the impossibility of effective scheduling:

I think moving from the state legislature to Congress was like moving from triple-A ball to the major leagues. It's the same game, and the issues are the same, but of course everything is more nationalized and internationalized. To pursue the baseball analogy: there's more spin on the curve balls, and the fast ball gets to the plate faster. It's a faster game, but I enjoy this more. Congress is like being in the first grade every day.[42]

Here you try to do everything at once. You have committee meetings, votes on the floor, you meet constituents, and respond to letters all at the same time. Everything happens at once, so the challenge is to use time efficiently, but it's a challenge that I love. Of course, in the Pennsylvania House, where I served for seven years, I had only 60,000 constituents, whereas in Congress I'm representing 600,000.[43]

Another thing I have noticed is the lack of time that I have in my office. My day is about fourteen hours, and it's a rarity if I have one solid hour to myself during the day. I am also surprised that I am so dependent on my staff. I have no time to read or research issues myself, so I'm very dependent on their research. In the General Assembly I did a lot more of my own reading and research. We had a staff of experts in particular areas, but no one individual was attached to you unless you chaired an appropriations committee. Much of my day here is spent outside the office, and when I am here, I am usually meeting staff or constituents.[44]

In Tallahassee the committee process always came to an end. Here it never seems to end. You always have more mark-ups and hearings. Committees are much larger here, too. The whole complex was much smaller in Tallahassee. Here you can have two committees on the same day and a bunch of votes. It's a very stressful environment.[45]

Several other freshman members also commented that they were genuinely surprised by the degree of power and influence that the leadership conceded them. California freshman Brian Bilbray's cousin, James Bilbray, had served as a Democratic member from Nevada (he lost to a Republican, John Ensign, in 1994), and the Republican Bilbray had expected his experiences as a junior member of the majority to be similar:

I have been shocked that the new majority has been so open to allowing the freshmen—the outsiders with new ideas—into the system. After I asked my cousin from Las Vegas and [the Democratic incumbent from the adjacent San Diego congressional district] Bob Filner about the old

majority, they said I would be told to shut up and be quiet until the
leadership had indoctrinated me to the ways of the House. But, in fact,
the new majority appreciates being in the majority and even the president is saying that the freshmen get everything. That has really surprised me. Seniority is not the only determining factor in the House of
Representatives, as it has been for the past forty years.[46]

Mark Souder of Indiana, who had extensive experience of the *ancien
regime* in the House as a minority staffer, also noted how the unique
circumstances of the 104th Congress and procedural reform in committees and on the floor had enhanced the influence of the junior
Republicans and contributed to their extraordinary public visibility:

It has been the changing of the House rules that has led to the rise of the
freshman class. Of course, the fact that we have not controlled the
House for forty years has meant that the whole structure is fluid. Every
chair is brand new, and we now run the hearings and get the witnesses.
You have tremendous fluidity when over half of the conference has
been in the House for two years or less. The opening up of amendments
on the floor has also been important. In the old days, there would be one
Democratic, and one Republican amendment, and that was it. Now you
see ten or twenty amendments on the floor. With a more flexible policy
on the floor, freshmen are offering amendments and speaking on the
floor, and with the one-minute and special orders on top, we are getting
far more attention than freshmen usually do. At three different town
meetings in my district this month, I have been asked about bills introduced by freshmen.
    I have been overwhelmed by the media. At one point I was asked to
do something for CBS, NBC, and CNN in one night. I'm not quoted as
much as some, though. I prefer to do background interviews. On any
week I'll get interview requests from the *New York Times*, the *Washington Post*, or the *Los Angeles Times*. I get requests from *Time* and *News-
week* every other week; NPR about once a quarter, and even the BBC![47]

Many of the freshman Republican members were also initially surprised at the degree of partisanship in the House. Ed Whitfield of
Kentucky's reaction was common:

I have been most surprised at the intensity of the rancor of the Democratic leadership in the House and the degree of partisanship on the
floor. After I thought about it, I realized that I shouldn't have been so

surprised because this was the first time in forty years that we were trying to reevaluate every program of the Great Society. We were threatening the groups that had grown up around those programs, and we should have expected the intense opposition.[48]

Other freshman Republican members, who had come from state legislatures where there was less partisanship and more influence on the floor for individual members, did not appreciate the degree of opening to freshman influence noted by freshmen more familiar with the ways of Washington like Mark Souder and Brian Bilbray. Instead, they bemoaned the partisanship of Congress and their relative lack of influence over floor proceedings:

> In Congress there's much more partisanship. In the legislature we were all on the floor together. Here we're off the floor and in our offices most of the time. When there's a debate going on, I have to ask for time to speak, and usually you just get a minute. You don't really get the opportunity to debate legislation. Here it's much more partisan, too partisan.[49]
>
> *Mark Foley (Fla.)*

> Parliamentary procedure was different in the state legislature. I came from a system where you could write an amendment at your desk and submit it on the floor—a "catfish" amendment. Here you have to pre-file your amendment. It's more formal. Debate on the floor is a very interesting process. We have heated debate, but it's all very organized and orchestrated.[50]
>
> *Walter Jones (N.C.)*

Tom Campbell of California, who joined the 104th Congress late, after winning a special election at the end of 1995, had also served previously in the House Republican minority during the 1980s. He put the increased partisanship and apparent "incivility" in the House down to the frustrations of the Democrats, who had unexpectedly found themselves in the role of the minority after forty years:

> When I was here in the minority, we could never chair a committee or subcommittee. You could not even hold the gavel while the chairman left the room. In four years only one of my bills was permitted to go to mark-up, and that was defeated in subcommittee without ever going to

full committee. But I was elected in 1988 knowing that those were the rules. Every Democrat in the House today was elected expecting to be in the majority, and that is a very important factor that has not been written about. I knew I would be subjected to those rules, but a Democratic friend recently told me: "I had no idea that's how we treated you!"

The incivility will pass. It's an artifact of the disappointment of 193 Democrats who were expecting to be in the majority. If we maintain a majority, that will lead to a kind of stasis and that will lead toward an increased level of civility, when each party has become accustomed to the role it has.[51]

The intense partisanship of the 104th Congress and the expectation that Republican members were expected to adhere to the leadership line created problems for some of the more "moderate" freshman members from the northeastern United States. Representing districts where some of the items included in the Contract (particularly with regard to environmental and property rights) were viewed rather less favorably than elsewhere, these members had to balance the requirements of representing their constituents with those of passing the Contract. The conventional wisdom regarding Congress under Democratic rule can be summarized in the dictum "Vote Your District First." While this still obtained to a large extent in the 104th Congress, and Speaker Gingrich was attentive to the concerns of northeastern moderates, the fervid partisan rhetoric on the House floor created some discomfort for moderate freshman members from marginal districts who might have benefited electorally from a less polarized atmosphere. Steve LaTourette of Ohio and Californian Brian Bilbray were particularly surprised by the degree of partisan conflict they discovered in the House:

I never realized the House was so leadership driven. Although when we deviate from the leadership on certain votes, we're not taken out and flogged, a quiet ostracism does develop, and that has surprised me more than anything else. I had always thought that you came here to do the best you could for the country and the district, and not always what's necessary to get 218 votes on an issue. Some things we've been asked to get 218 votes on are not good for the Nineteenth District of Ohio.[52]

It's the partisanship! "I don't care if it's a great idea, you're in the wrong party so I'm against it." Somebody attacked me because I supported a bill of Barney Frank's, but even Bernie Sanders and Barney

Frank have a good idea once in a while. I came here to vote as an individual: as Brian Bilbray who happens to be a registered Republican, not as a Republican who happens to be Brian Bilbray. I didn't check my mind and independence at the door.[53]

Another moderate, Bill Martini of New Jersey, also believed that the virulent partisan rhetoric so prevalent on the House floor in the first year of the 104th Congress was getting in the way of congressional effectiveness in lawmaking:

One thing there wasn't much of was to stop, pause, and reflect a little bit, and take a little time to stop and think about what we're doing. Freshman members like Steve LaTourette, Tom Davis, and myself have beliefs even though we're not out on the floor leading the charge against the Democrats. If anything doesn't help the process, it's beating up on each other more that we have to. Some of my colleagues could benefit from keeping the rhetoric down, and still get the job done.[54]

Freshman members varied considerably in their reactions to committee work. For more low-key, moderate, or pragmatic members such as Bill Martini, this was the most stimulating aspect of congressional service. These freshman members might be regarded as untypical, since they did not fit the stereotype of the voluble, ideologically committed, "revolutionary" freshmen, but instead were more oriented toward the traditional congressional role of district/constituent service. Steve LaTourette was a freshman member who fitted this pattern:

Before I came here, I had been a prosecutor so I wanted the Judiciary Committee. Then Ralph Regula said that we didn't have anybody from Ohio on Transportation, and they could use an Ohio member on three subcommittees. I have to tell you that the committee work has been one of the most enjoyable aspects of being in Congress for me. I'm not big on going to the floor and talking. I'm most active in committee where I've written legislation that boosts the environmental health of Lake Erie. I have also enjoyed working on ISTEA reauthorization. I'm glad that Ralph Regula pointed me in that direction. I enjoy it. I think it's rewarding and the work is important. It's important for me to be here and move legislation in a certain direction.[55]

This division between committee-oriented members, who put serving their district first, did not fall along "moderate" versus "conservative" lines. Richard "Doc" Hastings, a more conservative freshman Republican from Washington State, also found his committee and district service work more fulfilling than the partisan donnybrook on the House floor:

> I got the committees I wanted: Resources, because it deals with water issues and without irrigation my district would be a desert, and National Security, because that is the authorizing committee for the biggest federal installation in my district—the Hanford Nuclear Reservation. What I set out to do was to address the issues that were important to my district. The balanced budget and other things are important, but I let others carry the lead on that. In the defense authorization this year I was able to get rebates to Hanford, and on another committee, on which I don't serve, I got another piece of legislation important to my constituents. I focused on those activities.
>
> I find the committee work more rewarding than the floor—particularly as we're in the majority. . . . The experience I have had here as a majority member has allowed me to do things that I thought were important vis-à-vis legislation that dealt with my district. So I made a conscious effort in working on this legislation.[56]

Even a very conservative Georgia freshman, Bob Barr, emphasized the importance of constituency connections in committee service:

> The one I enjoy most is Judiciary, because it comports with my background. I spend most of my time on judiciary-related matters, and so does my legislative staff. The Banking Committee gives me the opportunity to deal with the banks back in my district, and that helps me to keep in touch with what's going on in local communities. Dealing with community branches keeps me in close contact with the needs of different communities.[57]

District connections and background also were important in the unprecedented awarding of subcommittee chairmanships to freshman members: David McIntosh of Indiana was awarded the chairmanship of the new National Economic Growth, Natural Resources and Regulatory Affairs Subcommittee of the Government Reform and Oversight Committee because of his experience as an aide to former Vice-President Dan Quayle, and the leadership's desire to push for a strong deregulation agenda:

> The Washington experience helped me get started. I was very involved in regulatory reform as the staff head of Dan Quayle's Competitiveness Council, so I carved out that area of expertise. I also had a sense of how

Congress worked that helped me get my bearings. . . . [Senior Republican] John Mica was a bit upset because he was due to chair a subcommittee, but he later got another one as compensation. Some senior members have been a bit put out by some of the freshman rhetoric. I think a little humility carries a congressman a long way, and we needed to learn that as a class.[58]

By contrast, the other freshman member to receive a subcommittee chairmanship, Tom Davis of Virginia, benefited from a more district-oriented concern for expertise in being awarded the chairmanship of the Governmental Reform and Oversight's Committee's District of Columbia subcommittee:

Of all the subcommittee chairmanships, I suppose mine made the most sense. I had been president of the Washington area Metropolitan Authority, and Fairfax County government is the second largest county government in the country. It was a good decision on the merits. Even [Washington pundit] Charlie Cook, who disapproves of freshmen being given subcommittee chairmanships, stated that Davis is an exception, and that in many ways I had had more government experience than some of the more senior members.[59]

While most freshman members expressed satisfaction and interest with their committees, relatively few placed their committee work at the center of their activities, perhaps because the Republican agenda in the 104th Congress was so leadership driven, and so much freshman energy was devoured by floor activity. The freshmen interviewed generally found their committees to be interesting, but something of a distraction from their broader mission of congressional reform and a balanced budget. They also found the time demands of committee and subcommittee service to be a particular strain. The comments of Bob Barr, Joe Scarborough, and Van Hilleary were fairly typical:

It's very tiring serving on three committees and trying to keep the hearings and mark-ups straight.[60]

[My committees] have been interesting. I am on National Security because I have always been interested in the military, and it's a good ideological fit for me. It's the same at Government Reform, where we have held interesting hearings on downsizing. The problem is that I'm on too many subcommittees: three on Government Reform and two on National Security, and I don't have the time to attend all these meetings. The number-one challenge has been time management. I've got to vote on the floor, attend subcommittee hearings, full committee markups, and meet people in the office.[61]

My committee work has been less satisfying because I'm so far down the food chain that I usually don't get the chance to say anything. I guess it's part of the learning process.[62]

On the International Relations Committee, conservative North Carolina freshman David Funderburk found the freshman Republicans were largely marginalized by a bipartisan foreign policy coalition:

There is a foreign policy division on International Relations between the upperclassmen who tend to support the conception of a bipartisan foreign policy and the freshman members who are less anxious about that and more anxious to stand for the issue of the moment. We don't worry so much about the niceties of some tradition, but about what's going on currently in Cuba or China, for example. We're populists who represent the masses in our districts. In our voters' view, foreign aid is a waste of money, and our European allies are not carrying their fair share of the burden. Like them, we don't want to squander money on NATO and foreign aid. Domestic concerns are tied more to foreign policy for us. . . . The bipartisan consensus has been the engine that drives foreign policy in the house, because out of 435 members, only thirty or forty focus on foreign policy. Those have the greatest impact. For the freshmen being on the International Relations Committee is not necessarily an asset, because most of our districts are concerned about what you are doing for the district.[63]

More senior Republicans, though initially wary, were generally impressed with the performance of the freshman members on committees. On the Ways and Means Committee the skeptical E. Clay Shaw found that the freshman members had been an asset to the committee:

The freshman members—John Ensign, Phil English, and Jon Christensen—are doing a good job. . . . I was very skeptical about putting freshmen on Ways and Means, and I didn't think it made sense. But as it's turned out, they've been a great asset.[64]

Moderate senior Republican Steve Gunderson concurred, and he emphasized the susceptibility of the freshmen to constituency considerations:

On the Agriculture Committee, with the exception of John Hostettler [Indiana], who's a free market purist, most of the other freshman members are people with a deep sensitivity and commitment to representing their district. Even Helen Chenoweth [Idaho] and Wes Cooley [Oregon] are very pragmatic legislators on behalf of their constituents from Agriculture. On the Education Committee there's a large group who are more ideological purists, like Funderburk, Souder, and McIntosh.[65]

From the other side of the aisle, a veteran Democrat and former chair of the Foreign Affairs Committee, Lee Hamilton, noted that most committees had become less relevant in the 104th Congress with a strong Speaker committed to the implementation of a legislative agenda. In Hamilton's view committees had simply ceased to be independent power centers within the House:

We don't have a committee system anymore. The Republican style of operation is to concentrate power in the Speaker's office to an extraordinary degree, and it has almost made the committees irrelevant. They operate on an ad hoc basis, and I don't really know how laws are made. It's a secretive, ad hoc, informal process. Important things are being done with Omnibus bills by the leadership. The committee system as we've known it is on the verge of breakdown and disappearance.[66]

Perhaps the last word on this matter should go to a voluble and highly visible freshman Republican who was unapologetic about the decline of committee work and the enhanced influence of the floor (and the freshmen):

On the floor I don't do it to be a show-horse. I do it because that's why I was elected: as a communicator and a broadcaster. If I had my druthers there'd be no constituent or committee work, and I'd just go and sit on the floor. After all, the citizens believe Congress is the floor. The floor is where it happens, and it's a big thrill being part of the majority.[67]

Solidarity in Numbers: The Unity of the Freshman Class

Despite the differences alluded to in earlier sections, the single most conspicuous feature of the freshman Republicans in the first months of the 104th Congress was their degree of unity and cohesion as a class. Although our earlier analysis has revealed that the freshmen were not such political neophytes as they themselves and their critics believed, the conviction of their being outsiders ready to change the system was deeply held among most freshman members. Minnesota freshman Gil Gutknecht accurately summarized the class's perception of its mission in the 104th Congress:

> The freshmen see themselves as different. They see themselves as har-
> bingers of change. I call them the "bumblebee" brigade. Look at Lindsay
> Graham, Zach Wamp, or Mike Flanagan, who are representing districts
> that have never been held by a Republican. Scientifically the bumblebee
> can't fly. Aerodynamically its wings cannot support the bee's body
> weight. A lot of the freshmen didn't know that they weren't supposed to
> win. They have a can-do attitude and they didn't know that they were
> supposed to sit down quietly and let the old bulls call the shots. Many of
> us have had success in other fields, and we believe in the reform of
> government and a balanced budget. It's not just rhetoric. We didn't know
> that "you can't do this." The old guard believes in the politics of the
> possible, but that just doesn't compute with the freshmen.[68]

Another freshman member used similar themes in discussing his GOP classmates:

> Traditionally, freshmen were supposed to sit at the end of the bench,
> and once in a while they might get to ask a question. However, most of
> us were used to horizontal, not vertical organizations. We were sent to
> Washington because Washington has gotten too big, and takes too
> much. . . . Instead of being woven into the fabric of Washington, we
> formed our own caucuses: the New Federalist Caucus, the Family Cau-
> cus, etc., consisting of freshman and sophomore members. The fresh-
> men constitute about one-third of the House Republican Conference.
> Most of us are the political offspring of Ronald Reagan. Strong populist
> themes came along with our election. There has also been a religious
> revolution: a fourth Great Awakening.[69]

In interviews with freshman Republican members, the belief in the freshmen as more responsive to, and more representative of, the American people, kept recurring. Former footballer J.C. Watts of Oklahoma was typical:

> The freshmen take as much pleasure in being called "Mom" or "Dad"
> as "Congressman" or "Congresswoman." If we don't get reelected, that

isn't the end of the world. We came here with a mission, and we really do want to make a difference. The freshman class, because of its dynamics and makeup—mothers, grandmothers, doctors, small-business people, footballers—is a group that needs to do whatever it has to do to get the country on the right track.[70]

The sense that the freshman members were not generally interested in a career in the House also contributed to their sense of urgency on the reform agenda, according to late-joiner Tom Campbell of California:

Another factor is the shortness of time many of this class will be here. Many of them have pledged to serve only two or three terms, and many are concerned that we may not be a majority, so there is more of a sense of urgency. The cohesive element in this class is not the social issues. It is the idea of spending less that unites everybody.[71]

This last point was a particularly accurate observation. While many members of the freshman class were committed to the political agenda of the Christian Right, there were two issues that defined the class above everything else: the balanced budget and the need for institutional reform, with the former clearly paramount. Almost every member interviewed emphasized the budget issue, and most made reference to institutional reform in Washington, but despite the determined resistance of the most committed institutional reformers in the freshman class, such as Washington State's Linda Smith, political reform issues—most notably campaign finance reform—were clearly relegated to a secondary position on the Republican legislative agenda by the leadership after the opening-day reforms. Instead, the importance of the balanced budget became emphasized and reemphasized to the point that it graduated from being a strategic move to unite the GOP in the 1994 campaign to an almost sacred mission. For the majority of the freshmen in their symbolic role as "keepers of the flame" of the 1994 revolution, the budget issue overshadowed everything else. According to the Wisconsin firebrand Mark Neumann:

The central theme is the balanced budget, and preserving the nation for our children. We also want to restore the values and principles of our nation: the moral and ethical sense that has been lost in the last thirty years.[72]

Even the moderates, Bill Martini and Steve LaTourette, who might have departed from Congressman Neumann on the "moral" part of his remarks, shared his commitment to a balanced budget and emphasized how it was the key to the solidarity of the class as a whole:

> At the first meeting of the freshman class, we shared war stories about how we got here, but it seemed that one commitment that was shared by everybody was to address the fiscal irresponsibility of the federal government. That was shared throughout, even though we had different opinions about how to get there. There was a commonality of purpose that was driving the process and was shared by other, more senior Republicans who had been around here a while and didn't have such zeal. The freshman class was an incendiary device, and when there was conflict we also took most of the blame.[73]

> The freshman class is important because we are identified most within the Republican conference with getting the senior members to make difficult economic choices, and to bring those issues to the table for discussion. I always chafe when I read about the "seventy-three Republican freshmen," which implies that we are in lockstep all the time or that there is 100 percent agreement. As Republicans in general come in different flavors, so do the freshmen. If you looked beyond the issue of a balanced budget in seven years, depending on the region of the country, you will find ten or twelve different paths to get there. The core of the freshman class is very conservative, but a number of us from the Northeast don't share those views on every issue.[74]

The balanced budget had become the central issue for the Republicans as a strategic move to build a united front against Bill Clinton in 1994, but the passion and rhetoric of the freshmen on the issue, together with the failure of the balanced budget constitutional amendment to pass the Senate in March 1995, greatly elevated the importance of the budget issue for the new Republican congressional majority. Failure to demonstrate that America was finally on the path to fiscal rectitude would demonstrate to the voters of 1996 that the Republicans had been unable to address what they themselves had declared to be the most urgent political issue facing the country; that they were just another bunch of politicians who promised and failed to deliver. As the balanced budget emerged at the forefront of the Republican agenda after April 1995, the freshmen would thus remain the most militant Republican members on the issue, regardless of geography or ideology. As Speaker Gingrich's confidant, Bob Walker defined their role:

> The freshman class is one of the marks of the success of the revolution. They are the guardians of the flame, and they have an energetic and dynamic role in defining the fundamentals of the revolution and dealing with the legislative agenda.[75]

Despite the pace and the intense work schedule, the first hundred days and the passage of the Contract through the House were indeed a honeymoon period for the freshman Republican members. In the forthcoming battles over the balanced budget, where they were pitted against the president of the United States, and over institutional reform, in which they were pitted often against their fellow Republicans, the freshmen would need every ounce of their solidarity and zeal to keep their issues at the forefront of the congressional agenda. As we see in the following chapter, they were largely successful in this objective, although it came at the cost of straining their hitherto close alliance with the party leadership and consequently engendered a massive loss of public support for the Republican Congress as a whole. After the spring of 1995, nothing would ever be so easy again in Washington for the Republican House freshmen.

4

A Lesson in Political Reality: The 1995–96 Budget Battle

There are three essential reasons to balance the federal budget. First, it is morally the right thing to do. Second, it is financially the right thing to do. Third, each of us has a personal stake in it. In fact, your personal stake is probably a lot bigger than you realize.[1]

Newt Gingrich

As mentioned at the conclusion of the previous chapter, a balanced federal budget was the keystone of the Republican legislative agenda in the 104th Congress. This renewed emphasis on fiscal rectitude was in conformity with the Republican Party's heritage. In the first quarter of the twentieth century, the balanced budget had been regarded not only as one of the essential tenets of classical economics but also as a moral imperative for a party grounded in North American Calvinist Protestantism. Even the shock of the New Deal and the prevalence of less strict fiscal policies had not shaken the fundamental Republican faith in a balanced budget. Republican Presidents Dwight Eisenhower, Richard Nixon, and Gerald Ford all placed the balanced budget at the center of their domestic policy agendas, and conservative Republican leaders on Capitol Hill, such as Robert Taft, Everett Dirksen, and, latterly, Robert Dole, railed against the fiscal profligacy of congressional Democrats and Democratic presidents, even as they accepted the substance of the New Deal interventionist state.

It should be added, however, that since the New Deal era this emphasis on fiscal conservatism had hardly served the Republicans well electorally. Republican strictures against government spending and their willingness to inflict tax raises and government spending cuts on voters reinforced the GOP's image as the party of hard-faced businessmen and the wealthy, an association that continued to damage Republican presidential candidates from the electoral routs of 1932 and 1936 right up until Gerald Ford's defeat in 1976. In congressional elections, where the Republicans' inability to play the game of distributive politics effectively was a reflection of the unrelenting fiscal stringency of their candidates, they paid an even heavier electoral price in losing control of the U.S. House for forty years. Traditional, fiscally conservative Republicanism might have been economically sound, but it generally made for a poor electoral strategy for Republicans in the post–New Deal era. Republican administrations that "deflated" the economy in order to deal with inflation and budget deficits induced economic recessions that reinforced the party's "hard-faced" image and contributed to the narrow presidential defeats of 1960 and 1976.

The situation changed dramatically with the advent of Ronald Reagan and "supply-side" economics in the late 1970s.[2] Supply-side doctrine enabled Republicans to continue to advocate a balanced budget and simultaneously support massive tax reductions, by arguing that the latter would eventually "pay for themselves" through enhanced economic growth. "Reaganomics" did not supplant traditional Republican fiscal stringency, however, but instead made it secondary to the political imperative of reducing personal tax rates for the middle class and sharply raising defense spending to deal with the renewed Soviet threat in the wake of the invasion of Afghanistan. While the Reagan administration did effect some significant reductions in discretionary domestic spending in 1981, these were nothing approaching the scale of the reductions that would have been necessary to compensate for the tax cuts and defense spending increases.[3] Moreover, after the Democrats increased their majority in the House in the 1982 midterm elections, any further domestic spending reductions were effectively placed off the political agenda.

The price that was paid for "Reaganomics" was, of course, a federal budget deficit of unprecedented proportions. Reagan's main rival for the 1980 Republican presidential nomination, George Bush, had described the Reagan program as "voodoo economics," but he swallowed his reservations in accepting the vice-presidential nomination from Reagan at the 1980 Republican National Convention. Reagan's first budget director, David Stockman, also realized the likely fiscal consequences of Reaganomics and openly revealed his skepticism in a series of interviews with journalist William Greider.[4] It was also around this time that Senate Finance Committee chair and later Senate majority leader, Bob Dole, (who was instrumental in negotiating a 1982 compromise budget package that included significant tax *increases*) made his famous quip about the busload of supply-siders going over the cliff, with the bad news being that there were two empty seats!

Yet, however much Republican traditionalists might have been uneasy about Reagan's economics, they found it hard to quarrel with the political impact of his program. While deficits might have reached heinous proportions, the economy began to boom after the 1979–82 recession bottomed out, and Reagan was overwhelmingly reelected in 1984. Unemployment and inflation also continued to fall in Reagan's second term, and George Bush was able to ride the 1980s boom to a third consecutive Republican presidential triumph in 1988. Republican presidents were able to evade responsibility for the deficit by pointing to the booming economy and blaming Democratic Congresses for not addressing the problem of high domestic spending. George Bush demonstrated that he had learned the political lesson of the Reagan years by making a pledge not to raise taxes the centerpiece of his 1988 presidential campaign. Essentially, American economic policy was in a state of stalemate after the Democrats regained a comfortable congressional majority in 1982. Democratic Congresses refused any further large reductions in domestic discretionary spending that affected their major constituencies, while Republican presidents refused to raise taxes. Neither side wanted to address the spending on "uncontrollable" entitlement programs, which constituted the most rapidly expanding portion of the budget. The Republicans had hinted at some changes in Social Security in the early Reagan years, but backed off sharply after the Democrats made political capital out of the issue in the 1982 midterm elections. The result was a ten-year period of stalemate, or "gridlock," on budgetary issues between 1982 and 1990, with neither side—Republican presidents nor Democratic Congresses—being willing to give ground. Budgets that were not passed on schedule, short temporary "shutdowns" of the federal government for lack of funds, and temporary expedients such as stopgap "continuing resolutions" or phony "quick-fixes" such as the mid-1980s Gramm-Rudman-Hollings legislation became pro-forma.[5]

George Bush's decision to return to his fiscal conservative roots, violate his tax pledge, and conclude a 1990 budget agreement with the congressional Democrats that included tax increases changed the equation for congressional Republicans. They had been loyal cheerleaders for Reaganomics—particularly on the House side—but the prospect of tax raises led to a revolt by a majority of House Republicans, including Minority Leader Michel and Whip Newt Gingrich, that embarrassed the Bush administration.[6] Unfortunately for the hapless President Bush, the onset of the early 1990s recession undermined the public's faith in Republican economic policy, and Bill Clinton, and particularly Ross Perot, were able to make inroads among Republican voters in the 1992 election by establishing a connection in voters' minds between the escalating deficits and the parlous economic state of the country, and blaming the situation on "gridlock" in Washington.

But by the time that the new Republican Congress took office in January 1995, the balanced budget was back at the forefront of the agenda of the new Republican leadership in Congress and had become a particularly important issue for the House Republican freshmen. Part of the reason was strategic. The budget deficit had been an especially critical issue for the 1992 Perot voters that the Republicans had won over to their side in 1994. Moreover, the deficit was also symbolic of a wider malaise in the American body politic that the Republicans were claiming to address in the Contract with America. More than anything else, it was the apparent inability of the political system to deal with the deficit that indicated the need for significant political reform in Washington. For Republicans, the predominance of the federal budget deficit as a major issue had the additional welcome effect of precluding a further expansion of the domestic state and providing, moreover, an excellent justification for the drastic reductions in the role of the federal government that the "Republican revolution" envisaged.

Most important, however, the deficit and the need to further reduce federal government spending to address it united all sectors of the Republican Party. As long as tax raises were off the table—and having witnessed the fate of President Bush, no Republican of any significance, including Bob Dole, was willing to advocate them—all Republicans could unite on demands to reduce government. Not a single Republican in either chamber supported Clinton's 1993 budget package, which included some major tax raises. Indeed, the Republicans of 1994 were committed to a balanced budget and simultaneously to carrying out some further major tax reductions directed at business and the middle class.

The Republicans had hoped to effect this strategy by the passage of a balanced budget amendment early in the 104th Congress, but when the amendment failed in the Senate, the Republican congressional leadership was still committed to enact a serious plan to reach a balanced budget. While there appeared to be a broad national consensus that the budget should be balanced, reaching that goal in the absence of tax increases and without further reductions in defense spending would necessarily involve draconian reductions in discretionary domestic spending or finally addressing the escalating costs of entitlement programs that benefited politically active, middle-class, and elderly citizens. To achieve this with a small House majority and a Democrat in the White House would inevitably prove difficult. Republicans also appeared to be unaware of the potential risks entailed in advocating such a program for a party, which even sixty years after the defeat of Herbert Hoover still retained powerful popular associations with wealth and privilege. All of this would become brutally apparent to the Republicans in the budget battle of 1995–96.

The Freshmen and the Budget

> In the first year the House Republican freshmen were tied together by the balanced budget. That was our Holy Grail if you like. Northeastern moderates who are worried about social issues and western conservatives who support property rights were all talking about a balanced budget, and everything else was sacrificed to that end. The balanced budget melded us together and led to an extraordinary amount of unity.[7]
>
> Congressman Joe Scarborough

In their almost universal enthusiasm for a balanced budget, the freshmen of the 104th Congress resembled their Republican forebears of the pre-Ronald Reagan era more closely than the enthusiastic supply-siders of the early 1980s. But there were differences between those members for whom balancing the budget was an end in itself and those who viewed the balanced budget as a convenient vehicle for reducing the size of the federal government. For the former group, the primary imperative to balance the budget was the fear that prolonged national insolvency would leave an enormous volume of debt to be borne by future generations of Americans. Moderate Republican Sue Kelly of New York definitely fell into this category:

> We represent a new attitude that government shouldn't spend more than it takes in. We want to hold the line on spending, and make sure that the budget is balanced for the sake of our kids and grandkids.[8]

Dick Chrysler of Michigan expressed a similar view:

> The balanced budget is the only thing that matters for America. If we continue with what we have been doing, by the year 2000, eighty-two cents out of every federal dollar will be spent on paying interest on the debt and entitlements. Balancing the budget is doing the right thing for our kids.[9]

By contrast, Richard "Doc" Hastings of Washington and John Fox of Pennsylvania tended to emphasize the balanced budget as a vehicle to reduce the size of government, rather than the moral/generational aspect:

> The freshman class all ran on getting our fiscal house in order and a balanced budget. We also want to take power away from Washington and give it back to states and localities. We agree on different areas to differing degrees, but we're all part of the freshman class, and we take our general philosophy to the senior members and put together a majority, and all of a sudden we're setting the political agenda along the terms I outlined.[10]

> We all signed the Contract with America, believe in a balanced budget, and have tried to eliminate unnecessary and destructive regulations. Together our freshman fervor has made government more accountable and closer to the people, and wasting less. We want to eliminate the fraud, waste, and abuse that are riddled throughout our federal government. It's our revolutionary zeal to do these things. For example, I have a bill to impose sunset review on all federal agencies, and close them down if they are no longer doing their job, just as we did in Pennsylvania. Take the Department of Energy for example, which was created to deal with an energy crisis that no longer exists. What do we need it for?[11]

Ed Whitfield of Kentucky encapsulated the views of most of the freshman class by combining both the generational and "anti-big-government" perspectives on the balanced federal budget:

> The major freshman class issue is the total commitment to a balanced budget. Also, reaching a balanced budget will determine which programs are working and which are not. For example, there are 168 federal job training programs, and while the federal government only accounts for 6 percent of education spending, there are 400 federal education programs. The balanced budget is the uniting theme of the

freshmen, and the economic viability of future generations will be tre-
mendously affected by whether or not we are successful.[12]

Ray LaHood of Illinois, Robert Michel's former chief of staff, and thus
a freshman member more seasoned than most to the ways of Washington, entered a rare note of dissent to the Republican endorsements of
both tax reductions and a balanced budget:

> I want a balanced budget, but I could not tell the people in good con-
> science that I can make the hard votes to reduce the deficit, and also
> give you a $345 billion tax cut. I voted for nine of the ten Contract
> items, but I opposed the idea that we could promise people a balanced
> budget and a tax cut.[13]

David McIntosh of Indiana did not share these reservations, but he did
feel that the emphasis on a balanced budget among both the Republican freshmen and the GOP leadership was excessive during the 104th
Congress:

> One thing you should remember is that the focus of the Contract with
> America was broader than the balanced budget. It was more than that, and
> included tax cuts, reforming government, and term limits. Congress needs
> to get back to the larger agenda in the Contract and not focus excessively
> on the balanced budget, which is a Washington-driven exercise.[14]

By the end of the 104th Congress, many more Republican freshman
members probably shared McIntosh's view that an overemphasis on
the balanced budget had derailed the Republicans' broader reform
agenda. To understand fully how and why the balanced budget came to
occupy such a predominant position on the Republican legislative
schedule that it completely overshadowed the passage of the rest of the
Contract with America, it is necessary to examine the House Republican leadership's reaction to the narrow defeat of the balanced budget
constitutional amendment in the Senate in March 1995.

"A Balanced Budget in Seven Years"

The Contract with America committed the new Republican majority to
a balanced budget but was not particularly specific about how this
objective would be achieved, aside from the promise to have an early

House vote on a balanced budget amendment to the Constitution and a line-item veto for the president on appropriations bills. As we have seen, the constitutional amendment failed in the Senate by one vote, while the line-item veto, which was supported by the Clinton White House, was eventually passed by both houses and signed by President Clinton early in 1996.[15] The target date for balancing the budget in the proposed amendment was the year 2002. In Elizabeth Drew's account the 2002, or "seven year," target for the balanced budget was a product of public relations and political strategizing, rather than economic exigencies:

> When the Contract was being drawn up, [pollster] Frank Luntz wanted to use the year 2000, telling the Republicans that it would be wonderful if when the illuminated ball in Times Square went down, signaling the new millennium, all parents in America would know that they weren't passing on more debt to their children. The members said, Wow! Luntz recalled, but then the more budget-educated members said, "We can't do it by 2000." So it became 2002.[16]

Regardless of the political considerations concerning the timing, there could be no doubt about Gingrich and the Republican leadership's commitment to the balanced budget. Despite their opposition to Bush and Clinton's budget packages on the basis that they included tax increases, Gingrich and Majority Leader Armey perceived the critical importance of addressing the deficit in terms of their broader agenda of downscaling the federal government. In conversation with his biographer Dick Williams, the Speaker explained his decision to focus on the budget as the primary item on his legislative program:

> I regard getting to the balanced budget as the fulcrum to move the whole system. . . . It's the only thing that gives you the moral imperative to change the whole structure of the welfare state.[17]

Gingrich further explained the Republican rediscovery of fiscal stringency in terms that differentiated his goals on the budget from those of "Reaganomics" in the early 1980s:

> You did not have in the Reagan team the ability to create a sophisticated positive view of governance, which I'm trying to do now. You have to blow down the old order in order to create the new order. Reagan understood how to blow down the old order, but wasn't exactly

sure what the new order would be. The Bush people were too timid to
blow down the old order.[18]

So even when the balanced budget failed to pass the Senate by one
vote, Gingrich committed the House Republicans to putting together a
deficit-reduction package that would achieve the same objective: a
balanced budget in seven years, by FY 2002. Given that the Republicans had committed themselves to a "middle-class tax cut" and had
pledged that Social Security and defense spending would be exempt
from the budgetary ax, the stringent spending reductions would have to
be found in discretionary domestic spending and the politically sensitive entitlement programs, such as Medicare. The task of finding the
$200 billion in spending reductions to pay for the tax cuts in the
Contract (and particularly the $500–per-child tax credit that was of
critical significance to religious conservatives) and a further $400 bil-
lion as a first installment in the plan to balance the budget by 2002 fell
upon the new chair of the House Budget Committee, John Kasich of
Ohio. In early May 1995 Kasich's committee produced a budget proposal containing slightly less than $1 trillion in spending cuts over
seven years to reach a balanced budget, which passed the House 238–
219 on a party-line vote on 18 May 1995 (see Table 4.1).

The House plan abolished more than 280 federal programs, including the departments of Energy, Education, and Commerce, all long-
time objects of conservative scorn. Discretionary domestic programs
were to be cut by one-third. Within this broad category, education and
training programs were particularly hard hit as funding for the
president's national service program ("Americorps") and his "Goals
2000" education program (setting national standards for schools) was
eliminated entirely. The same fate befell three other conservative bug-
bears: the National Endowment for the Arts (NEA), the National Endowment for the Humanities (NEH), and the Corporation for Public
Broadcasting. Clinton's program of government loans for college students also had its funding drastically reduced. In line with Republican
pledges in the Contract, the House budget also included $353 billion in
tax cuts while reducing the Earned Income Tax Credit for the working
poor. The defense budget was to increase by $67 billion over the level
proposed in the president's budget.[19]

The most controversial portion of the House budget, however, was
the Republican challenge to the giant health entitlement programs:

Table 4.1

Chronology of the FY 1996 Budget Battle

	Budget action
1995	
22 June	House-Senate conference reaches agreement on budget.
29 June	House (239–194) and Senate (54–46) pass conference report (i.e.
11 July	Reconciliation (implementing budget resolution targets) begins in the Senate.
19 July	Reconciliation begins in the House.
1 October	FY 1996 begins. Congressional action completed on only two of thirteen appropriations bills. Stopgap continuing resolution (CR) maintaining funding until 13 November comes into effect.
1 November	Negotiations between President Clinton and congressional leaders begin.
13 November	Clinton vetoes CR and debt limit increase.
14 November	First federal government shutdown begins.
17 November	House (237–189) and Senate (52–47) pass identical reconciliation bill.
19 November	First shutdown ends. CR passed to fund government until 15 December.
28 November	More negotiations between president and congressional leaders.
6 December	Clinton vetoes reconciliation bill.
15 December	CR expires and second federal government shutdown begins.
19 December–1 January	On-off negotiations continue.
1996	
2 January	Senate passes "clean" CR (no strings).
5 January	House passes "clean" CR. Shutdown ends.
28 March	Extension of debt ceiling passes.
24–25 April	After agreement between Congress and White House, House and Senate pass omnibus FY 1996 appropriations bill.
26 April	Clinton signs omnibus appropriations bill. End of FY 1996 budget battle.

Medicaid for the poor, and Medicare for the elderly. Medicaid was to be reconfigured as a block grant to the states with reduced funding, while the popular Medicare program—widely regarded as the "third rail" of American politics because touching it would bring instant political death—was to have a $288 billion, or 50 percent, reduction in its projected rate of growth.[20]

During the House conference with the more cautious Senate in June, the House budget was somewhat modified. The reductions in Medicare were scaled back to $270 billion, and the Education and Energy departments (though not Commerce) escaped the ax. On defense, the House increase was reduced somewhat but was still well in excess of the White House budget.[21] The total figure in tax cuts was also scaled back to $245 billion.[22] Otherwise, the House budget resolution pretty much prevailed in the conference report that passed both chambers on 29 June 1995.

Passing a budget resolution that dealt with numerical abstractions had been fairly easy, but now the House and Senate had to put together an omnibus reconciliation bill making real cuts in real programs that would be binding on the Appropriations Committee and its subcommittees that would actually write the thirteen annual appropriations bills to fund the federal government. A reconciliation bill would, however, serve the Republicans' broader purpose of passing a package that would both show the way to a balanced budget by 2002 and write their broader agenda of reducing the size of government into a single comprehensive bill. The strategy behind packing almost the entire Republican agenda into one huge reconciliation bill is well summarized by congressional scholar Barbara Sinclair:

> The budget provided the primary procedural tool through which Republicans would attempt to enact their agenda. Without it, the "Republican revolution" of a balanced budget in seven years would have had no chance whatsoever; the Republican congressional leaders knew that getting a large number of major and controversial changes through both chambers and past the president as separate bills was a hopeless task. The budget process allowed packaging, it provided protection against the Senate filibuster, and, combined with an adept strategy, it might make it possible to force Clinton to sign the legislation.[23]

For these reasons, the FY 1996 reconciliation bill included not only tax and spending changes but also the Republicans' plans for radical welfare reform. Welfare reform had assumed pivotal importance for Republicans because of their embrace of conservative intellectual arguments that the effects of the welfare system were largely responsible for many of the ills of American society in recent decades. For instance, it was widely accepted among Republicans, and apparently by most Americans in the 1990s, that the main welfare program, Aid to

Families with Dependent Children (AFDC), encouraged teen pregnancy, undermined family values among the inner-city poor, and enmeshed the latter in a stifling culture of dependency from which they found it almost impossible to escape. Some conservative commentators, led by social policy expert Charles Murray, went even further and argued that the welfare system had actually contributed to poverty.[24] By the early 1990s, the consensus on the dysfunctional nature of the welfare system had even expanded to the Democratic Party as presidential candidate Clinton in 1992 made a public commitment "to end welfare as we know it." No significant reform of the welfare system had been undertaken in Clinton's first two years in office, however, as the budget and health-care issues had blocked out most other items on the presidential policy agenda.

The welfare reform bill (The Personal Responsibility Act) that had passed the House as part of the Contract on 24 March 1995 transformed welfare from a federal entitlement program into a block grant to the states, which would now have primary responsibility for welfare. It also barred mothers under the age of eighteen from receiving federal benefits and set a five-year time limit for welfare recipients, after which they were expected to be working.[25] The Senate did not pass a welfare bill until September. The Senate bill was substantially the same as the House measure, except that it added more funds for child care and allowed the states less flexibility in spending their welfare block-grant funds. Senate Republican Leader Bob Dole had made sufficient concessions to pass the bill by 87–12 in the Senate, and the White House indicated President Clinton was prepared to sign a welfare bill along similar lines to the Senate proposal.[26]

The Republicans now set out to package all their proposals to reduce the deficit, including welfare reform, into one massive reconciliation bill that would be passed by both houses. Although this measure, unlike the budget resolution, would be subject to a presidential veto that the Republicans had nothing like enough votes to override, the Republican leaders believed that they had sufficient bargaining counters in the shape of the thirteen annual appropriations bills that had to be passed to keep the government going, and further essential legislation to extend the national debt ceiling, to force the president to deal on their terms.

The final reconciliation bill passed by both houses on 17 November 1995—in the middle of the first federal government shutdown—did indicate a revolutionary change in American domestic policy. Taxes were to be cut by $245 billion for those with incomes less than $110,000 per year (reduced from $200,000 by the Senate after Democratic allegations of a "tax cut for the wealthy"), including the $500 per family tax credit and capital gains and corporate tax reductions. To pay for these—the "crown jewel" of the Contract with America—the Republicans committed themselves to cut spending by $894 billion over seven years. Farm subsidies were reduced, federal student loans were cut back, the earned-income tax credit for the working poor was curtailed, and some tax preferences for corporations were ended. Social Security and Defense were spared from the ax (in fact, defense spending was increased). By far the bulk of the savings—$515 billion, or 58 percent—would come from reductions in three major areas: Medicaid ($163 billion), welfare reform ($82 billion), and Medicare ($270 billion). Medicaid was changed into a block-grant program and its rate of growth was reduced by 50 percent over the seven-year period. On welfare, the entitlement status of poor children and mothers to government help was ended.[27]

By far the biggest savings and the most controversial portion of the entire Republican budget package were in the Medicare program. This massive program, providing federal government assistance to the elderly for health-care expenses, was the largest of all entitlement programs, with rapidly escalating costs as the American population aged and health-care technology accelerated. No serious package to deal with the budget deficit could afford to ignore Medicare, but this entailed a very high political risk because of the overwhelming popularity of the program with voters. According to Maraniss and Weisskopf,

> Since its inception in 1965 as part of Lyndon Johnson's Great Society, Medicare had grown so popular that its budget was compared to a "third rail" that would electrocute anyone who touched it. . . . The GOP needed to squeeze $270 billion from Medicare to fulfill its promise of a tax cut and balanced budget in seven years, a pledge to which Gingrich had bound his colleagues in February. The odds appeared unfavorable. Medicare was perhaps the most popular social program run by the federal government, and its beneficiaries, 33 million elderly Americans, were a potent political force that even the most zealous conservative budgeteers were reluctant to confront.[28]

The potential political problem for the Republicans was magnified by the fact that the amount of money they wanted to take away from Medicare ($270 billion) was uncannily close to the total amount in tax cuts ($245 billion) that they planned to implement. This exchange could easily be portrayed by their political adversaries as punishing the elderly to give a tax reduction to the wealthy (although middle-class Americans would also obviously benefit from the $500 per child tax credit).

The Republican leadership was well aware of this danger. In both the 1982 and 1986 congressional elections, Republican suggestions about "reforming" Social Security had been exploited by Democrats and were believed to have cost the Republicans House and Senate seats. Based on this experience, Republican National Chairman Haley Barbour told the GOP congressional leadership that they should avoid the issue altogether.[29] Gingrich nevertheless believed that by careful choice of language and controlling the message on Medicare, he could win the inevitable propaganda battle. After meetings with Barbour and several leading Republican pollsters, the GOP propaganda effort sought to move the media debate on Medicare away from focusing on Republican Medicare "cuts." To achieve this goal, Republicans were to emphasize that what they proposed were "reductions in the anticipated rate of increase" in Medicare spending and that they were doing this to "preserve" the program and keep it economically viable for future generations. The GOP got some useful ammunition in April 1995, when the Medicare Board of Trustees' annual report, signed by three Clinton cabinet members, warned that the Medicare Trust Fund faced bankruptcy by 2002.[30]

The problem that the Republicans still faced, however, was that a Clinton White House speaking with one voice, and with the inevitable advantage of the presidential "bully pulpit," was in a far better position than a Congress divided into two houses, two parties, and numerous committees to project a unified message on the budget. The Republican commitment to substantial tax cuts also made them vulnerable to the charge that they were trying to balance the budget on the backs of the most disadvantaged Americans while giving a tax break to the better-off.

The Republicans were never able to surmount that allegation. In the late summer and early fall of 1995, while the Republicans were putting their final reconciliation bill together, Republican House incumbents and particularly freshman Republicans in marginal districts were sub-

jected to an advertising barrage from the Democratic National Committee and their allies in organized labor and seniors' groups that explicitly linked the $270 billion "cut" in Medicare spending to the
Republicans proposed $245 billion "tax cut for the wealthy."[31] The
entire Democratic Party, from the White House Press Office to the
congressional Democratic leadership, was singing the same song.[32]
Polls were telling them that the Republican talk of "revolution" and the
media focus on the loquacious Speaker Gingrich and the more strident
members of the freshman class were having an adverse effect on the
Republican Congress's popularity with voters. Congress's approval
ratings and those of Gingrich were falling precipitously, and the
Speaker gave his opponents a golden opportunity when, in a speech to
the Blue Cross/Blue Shield Association in October 1995, he remarked
that the Health Care Financing Administration (the government agency
that administers Medicare, not Medicare itself) would eventually
"wither on the vine."[33] The Democrats replayed these remarks in a
further series of television advertisements, to emphasize that the Republicans had now become too "extreme" and that only the White
House and the congressional Democrats could be trusted to defend
"Medicare, Medicaid, education, and the environment"—all areas in
which the Democrats' polling was telling them that they had a public
opinion advantage over the GOP.

The public relations battle was expanding beyond the reductions in
Medicare and education spending contained in the budget to the Republican assault on environmental regulations. As part of their strategy
of using the budget as their prime policymaking and lawmaking tool,
the Republicans had incorporated several significant policy changes as
amendments, or "riders," to the large appropriations bills that Congress
had to pass to keep the government running and that they thus anticipated would be difficult for the president to veto.[34] According to Elizabeth Drew:

> It was a way of getting around the regular processes of holding hearings
> and "marking up" a bill, subcommittee reporting to committee, commit-
> tee getting a rule and taking it to the floor. If the Gingrich Republicans
> couldn't get something done in one place, they did it somewhere else.
> Because appropriations bills must eventually be passed, putting a policy
> in the form of a rider on a spending bill could have a better shot than
> trying to get it enacted the regular way. The Republicans understood

this, and as in so many instances in the 104th Congress, carried it to new lengths.[35]

The architect of this strategy was the third-ranking Republican in the House GOP leadership, Majority Whip Tom DeLay of Texas, founder and owner of a pest-control company in Houston and a determined foe of federal government environmental and safety regulation, which he regarded as an intrusive and undue burden on business and agriculture.[36] In the FY 1996 appropriations bill drafted by the Appropriations Subcommittee (on which DeLay sat) that funded the departments of Veterans Affairs and Housing and Urban Development (HUD), and the Independent Agencies, DeLay tried to eviscerate the Environmental Protection Agency (EPA) by cutting its budget by a third, its funds for enforcement by half, and including seventeen riders that effectively prevented EPA from enforcing federal environmental laws on toxic waste, wetlands, and clean air.[37] The use of appropriations riders was not confined to the environmental sphere. An amendment to the Labor—Health and Human Services (HHS)—Education appropriation proposed by Congressman Ernest Istook of Oklahoma was intended to "de-fund the left" by prohibiting groups that received federal money from lobbying Congress. Antiabortion riders were also tagged onto various appropriations bills.[38] Ultimately the strategy of overloading the appropriations bills with policy riders proved to be a major strategic error on the part of Gingrich and DeLay. The riders mobilized and energized environmental groups and other Republican opponents outside Congress, alienated northeastern moderate Republicans (alignments on these issues often remained more regional than partisan, even in the 104th Congress), annoyed the more environmentally conscious Senate Republicans, and bogged down the entire appropriations process so that only two of the thirteen appropriations bills that should have been enacted by 1 October (the start of the new fiscal year) were actually completed on schedule. According to Drew, the Appropriations Committee chairman, Bob Livingston, although a staunch budget hawk, became increasingly exasperated by the volume of policy riders on his bills:

> The loading on of policy riders became so extensive that Livingston finally blew. On 13 July, Livingston said, "The more we get sidetracked on policy issues not fiscal issues, the harder it is to get legislation to the

president's desk. He added, "Policy issues probably don't belong in appropriations bills." Livingston tracked down Gingrich at the Reagan Library, where he was speaking, to complain that one bill, for the Departments of Labor, Health and Human Services, and Education, was becoming perilously overloaded. But Gingrich had other imperatives. In an interview Livingston said, "I balked at saddling appropriations bills with amendments that became instead of the tail on the dog the dog itself." Gingrich was displeased with Livingston's attitude.[39]

Realizing how far behind they were on the budget in September, the Republicans had come to an agreement with the White House to pass a noncontroversial Continuing Resolution (CR) to provide stop-gap funding for the federal government until 13 November, by which time they reckoned that their reconciliation bill would be completed. By then they hoped that the president would have capitulated to their essential demands and that they would have a budget agreement that would expedite the passage of the remaining appropriations bills. This proved to be a serious miscalculation on the part of the Republican leadership.

Shutdown and Meltdown

> January to August last year were our best days. When we came back in September, we had the flap over the Speaker and *Air Force One,* we shut the government down, and we declined in our ability to continue to be effective. The Contract was done and we were into the budget debate, and to get the president to the table we shut the government down. That was a disaster as a strategy. The leadership felt it would work, but it didn't and turned out to be an embarrassment to the party, and we've never really recovered from that. The momentum that we had from January to August slowly died, and we've never really recovered.[40]
>
> *Congressman Ray LaHood, Freshman Republican*

> We sent the bills down and the president vetoed them and we got blamed. What we didn't realize is that when you are dealing with a Washington press corps—over 80 percent of whom voted for Clinton—you lose. We learned an important lesson, there, last November and December, when we elevated the president's popularity. It was a miscalculation on the part of the Republicans. We did not think Bill Clinton would allow the government to close.[41]
>
> *Congressman E. Clay Shaw, House Ways and Means Committee*

In their battle with President Clinton over the FY 1996 budget, the Republican leadership believed that they possessed two crucial weapons. The first was the appropriations bills that were necessary to keep the government running. The second was legislation to raise the national debt ceiling so that the government would still have the authority to borrow funds to pay its debts. If it came to a government shutdown or default, the Republican leadership believed that Clinton would get the blame in the court of public opinion, as had happened to Republican Presidents Reagan and Bush during previous brief shutdowns. They also did not reckon that Clinton—whom they generally despised—would have sufficient backbone to face them down. But the president's poll numbers had been gradually improving ever since his decisive and empathetic response to the bombing of the federal building in Oklahoma City by right-wing terrorists in April, and so when the crunch came in November 1995, Clinton's popularity was rising while that of the Republican Congress and its leaders was falling.[42] Defying Congress was no longer necessarily bad politics from the White House point of view.

Talks between the parties began in early November, but the next CR offered by the Republicans to keep the government open included several deep spending reductions that were unacceptable to Clinton. When the September CR expired on 13 November, the federal government shut down except for "essential" services such as Defense and Law Enforcement.[43] On 17 November, both House and Senate finally approved their reconciliation bills.[44] The first shutdown ended on 19 November when the White House and the congressional leadership announced agreement on a CR that committed them both to a balanced budget in seven years according to the data of the Congressional Budget Office (CBO), as opposed to the more optimistic projections of the president's Office of Management and Budget (OMB), which were regarded as unreliable by congressional Republicans.[45] This CR kept the government funded until 15 December, by which time it was hoped that the final details of the budget deal would have been hammered out. The Republicans believed that Clinton had agreed to submit a budget plan of his own as a blueprint for discussions, but no plan emerged. Then, on 6 December, the president dramatically vetoed the Republican reconciliation bill and finally announced his own seven-year budget.[46] When this emerged the following day, it was not based on the CBO figures, as the Republicans had demanded, and the congressional leadership refused to take it seriously. With the deadline fast approaching, the White House submitted another plan on 14 December, but the Republicans again dismissed it as based on rosy economic projections, rather than serious reductions in government spending.[47] Treasury Secretary Robert Rubin had used various maneuvers to fend off default on the debt, so the lack of appropriations remained the Republicans' main weapon, but it was becoming an increasingly blunt instrument as the public blamed Republican intransigence for the second shutdown, which began on 15 December.[48]

Under pressure, Speaker Gingrich appeared to have lost his astute strategic sense and made a number of elementary tactical errors. The worst came during the first shutdown when, in remarks to the press, he appeared to justify shutting down the government on the basis that he and Senate Majority Leader Dole had been ignored by the president while on *Air Force One* en route to the funeral of slain Israeli Premier Yitzhak Rabin.[49] The Democrats and their allies had a field day with this, and it added to the growing public impression of Republican extremism and irresponsibility, which the Democrats were eager to encourage. In negotiations with Clinton, the Speaker also appeared to be unsure of himself, and perhaps too willing to take Clinton's professions of belief in a balanced budget at face value. Time and again during the shutdowns, agreement was announced between the parties, only to collapse once the Republican leaders examined the fine print of what exactly the White House was offering them.[50] On 19 December, after a meeting with Dole and Gingrich, Clinton had promised to negotiate a seven-year balanced budget based on CBO numbers by the end of the year, provided that the Republicans agreed to pass a clean CR and reopen the government. The House Republican Conference with the freshmen at the forefront would have none of it after some comments by Vice-President Gore appeared to indicate the White House had not firmly agreed to negotiate on the CBO data.[51] The president called a news conference and seized the opportunity to remind the public who was responsible for keeping the government closed:

> The most extreme members of the House of Representatives rejected that agreement. These Republicans want to force the government to stay closed until I accept their deep and harmful cuts.[52]

As the polls showed the Republicans being blamed and the media continued to show pictures of empty offices, shuttered museums and national parks, and financially strapped federal employees, the White

House had little political incentive to settle quickly. As a result of the ineptitude of the Republican leadership, they were reaping a political windfall.

When Congress returned right after the New Year, six of the thirteen appropriations bills remained unsigned, and large areas of the federal government were still shut down. Senate Leader—and likely Republican presidential candidate—Dole made it clear in the New Year that he had had enough, and passed a "clean" (without strings) CR through the Senate. After bitter debate in the House Republican Conference, a similar CR was passed by that chamber on 5 January 1996, funding the most popular government functions (veterans' programs and national parks) until the end of the fiscal year (30 September 1996) and the rest until 30 March.[53] Fifteen Republicans, including a dozen freshmen, still voted to keep the government closed. The debt ceiling was finally extended on 28 March, as part of a legislative package that also included some pet Republican projects, like the line-item-veto. Clinton had already agreed to sign this, but attaching it to the debt ceiling enabled the veto to evade a likely filibuster in the Senate.[54]

The budget battle finally came to an end in late April, when both sides realized that they were essentially debating about policy, rather than numbers. The final omnibus appropriations bill funded the areas of government covered by the five regular FY 1996 appropriations bills that were still outstanding.[55] Most of the Republican policy riders were dropped, and Clinton got more funding for his priorities in education and the environment. The Republicans had been damaged enough by the budget battle and were eager to settle before the 1996 election campaign got under way in earnest. A budget battle that had seen fourteen continuing resolutions and two government shutdowns was finally at an end. And the Republicans had lost.

The Freshmen in the Budget Battle: In the Line of Fire

It has already been noted that many of the House Republican freshmen had used the federal budget deficit as the most powerful symbol of the "corrupt" and "unresponsive' Washington culture that they wanted to replace and had made balancing the budget the leading theme of their 1994 election campaigns. As the budget battle proceeded, however, the freshmen found themselves being held responsible by the president and the media—and even by some of their more senior Republican colleagues in both the House and the Senate—for the Republican "intransigence" that had led to the unpopular government shutdown at Christmas and New Year 1995–96.[56] The very revolutionary fervor that the freshmen had promoted and celebrated appeared to have become a liability both for their party and for their own electoral prospects. For the freshmen, the budget battle was the experience that awoke them to the reality of politics in Washington and in the country at large. Some reacted by trimming their sails and getting down to the more mundane business of reelection in 1996, rather than try to remake the world, while a hard-core group remained defiant to the last in refusing to capitulate to the Clinton administration by reopening the government without a budget deal. By highlighting the role of the freshmen, the budget deal also encouraged an intense effort by the Democrats and their interest-group allies to regain control of the House through explicitly targeting the freshman members.

Until the second shutdown, however, the freshmen maintained a remarkable degree of unity on budget issues. Regardless of region or ideology, the Republican House freshmen adhered to the message that addressing the budget problem was the most important issue facing the country. Even moderate members, such as Tom Davis from the Virginia suburbs of Washington D.C., who were taking a considerable electoral risk in voting for spending cuts that had an adverse impact in their districts, strongly supported the Republican budget as the only serious effort being made to address the deficit problem:

> I supported our budget plans, which were far superior to anything the Democrats came up with. I also voted for more cuts in my district than any other member of Congress. This was a real tough time for me, voting for appropriations cuts that might mean the loss of thousands of jobs in my district.[57]

Freshman budget solidarity was particularly evident in the dispute that occurred between the Appropriations Committee chair, Bob Livingston, and freshman Republican Mark Neumann of Wisconsin during the writing of the Defense appropriations bill in October 1995. As mentioned in previous chapters, the combative Neumann was one of the most militant of the freshman Republicans on the budget deficit, which had been his principal motivation for sacrificing a prosperous business career to run for Congress.[58] He was also one of the best-informed Republican members on budget issues, as Appropriations Chair Livingston recalled:

> After the [1994] election, we had a retreat around Christmas time. At that retreat John Kasich who had just moved into the budget chair, presented a seven-year balanced budget. Mark Neumann stepped up with many copies of a softbound budget that outlined in specific terms a balanced budget in five years. If you didn't like the top detail he'd done, he offered four other alternatives. It was an extensive document and the work of a real talent that had influence and a significant role in the overall budget debate.[59]

Despite his respect for Neumann's abilities, the Appropriations chair and the rest of the House Republican leadership began to be exasperated by Neumann's hard-line antispending stance when it concerned the Defense appropriation, one of the few areas of the federal government where the Republicans were reluctant to contemplate spending reductions. Neumann nevertheless voted against a supplemental Defense appropriation supported by Livingston and the House Republican leadership, thereby incurring the wrath of the Speaker and a threat of removal from the Appropriations Committee if he strayed again from the party line.[60] This had little effect on the determined midwesterner, however, and in September 1995 Neumann voted against the conference report on the 1996 Pentagon appropriation, a vote he defended in typical uncompromising fashion:

> I brought down the Defense appropriations bill because they were going to spend $7 billion of my kids' money to send troops to Bosnia. I was punished, and there was a rallying of the freshmen on the issue. If anytime you cross the leadership, you are going to be punished, then they only need my voting card and I might as well stay in the district. All that was stopped because of a revolt of the freshmen.[61]

Neuman's "punishment" was his removal from the National Security Appropriations Subcommittee and reassignment to the less prestigious Military Construction Subcommittee. As indicated, this action provoked an outcry from Neumann's fellow Republican freshmen, who were outraged that their colleague should be punished by the leadership for his ardor in pursuing a balanced budget. Congressman Joe

Scarborough, described how the freshman class rallied in Neumann's defense:

> The freshmen went to the leadership and told them that they expected Mr. Neumann to be returned to the committee or they would vote against every bill. Even freshmen who disagreed with Mark Neumann supported his right as a freshman member to support a balanced budget. They would not allow him to be crushed by anybody.[62]

The matter was finally resolved by keeping Congressman Neumann on the less-prestigious Appropriations panel, but giving him a seat on the Budget Committee as a consolation, and both the freshmen and Chairman Livingston were basically content with that outcome. The incident served, however, as an indication of some latent tension between the leadership's political agenda and the budgetary zeal and determination of the freshman class, a tension that would become more apparent in the bitter debates over strategy in the Republican Conference during the government shutdowns.

One factor that emerged from the budget battle was an even more intense dislike among the freshman Republicans for President Clinton, who had publicly singled them out as "radicals" during the second shutdown. Some freshmen, such as J.D. Hayworth of Arizona, acknowledged Clinton's political skills in exploiting the political opportunity created by the budget crisis:

> Clinton is one of the greatest politicians I've ever seen. He's not enough of a visionary or a thinker to be a true leader, but he has an uncanny ability to get the lexicon of government back and take it out of our hands.[63]

A more common reaction among the freshmen members, however, was disgust at the president for having played politics with an issue that they took so seriously. Dislike of Clinton among some freshmen became almost visceral, as illustrated by the following comments:

> One person closed down the government, and that was Bill Clinton. He didn't keep his word, and broke the law signed on 20 November. We should have fought fire with fire. There's nothing you can do when you're dealing with someone who won't keep his word, and plays games with people's lives, jobs, families, and the country.[64]

> The president's behavior in the budget debate was one of the lowest ebbs in the history of the U.S. presidency. It was dishonest to the core

to scare millions of older Americans with dishonest statements for his own personal political gain. . . . Someone with good character may not be qualified to be president, but someone without good character should automatically be disqualified, regardless of other attributes he or she may have.[65]

The verdict is still out on who will ultimately get blamed for the shutdown. When people are giving me a hard time about it, I just ask them to answer one question: "Is it important for national leaders to keep their word?" That works very well and shuts them up, because Clinton lied.[66]

Bill Clinton may or may not get reelected, but if he is reelected it will be a terrible comment on our value system.[67]

Our leadership did not truly realize Clinton's lack of character, that they were dealing with a man who was not up-front with them. They expected a tough debate but they knew that, as candidate and president, Clinton had called for a balanced budget. But when they got to the table, they found out we had a president whose word was not his bond, and who doesn't really care about a balanced budget.[68]

The other major culprit from the perspective of the frustrated freshmen was the news media, whose coverage of the shutdown obscured their message of fiscal responsibility with images of shuttered museums and national parks, suffering government workers, and "extremist" Republicans:

Remember: 91 percent of the beltway press describe themselves as "liberal" or "moderate," and only 4 percent of them voted for Bush in 1992. That should give you some idea of how difficult it is to get the facts out. Many Americans don't understand that we were proposing to *increase* spending on Medicare, Medicaid, welfare, and student loans. With an objective group of people I'd take my chance on arguing for our budget, but the press did a real number on us. On Medicare, when the Democrats said we were cutting benefits, we put up $1 million for anybody who could prove that we were cutting Medicare. Nobody has taken us up on it. Of course, when they heard this, senior citizens on fixed incomes were scared to death, especially when the media kept talking about "tax breaks for the wealthy," when 89 percent of the tax reductions in our package would have gone to families making $25,000 to $70,000 a year. I read an article the other day that the Medicare

Board of Trustees had reported that instead of going broke in seven years, Medicare will be bankrupt in five. You might see one press article on that, but I've never seen any talking heads saying that this is what the Republicans have been saying for sixteen months. I have to admit that the Democrats have done a good job in getting their lies out, and being shameless in not telling the truth.[69]

There have been nine government shutdowns since 1981, but this one got a lot more attention. Part of it was that the news media inside the beltway got hysterical about the impact on federal employees. In my district eight out of ten people didn't even know there was a government shutdown.[70]

It sure looks different on the inside when you really know what's happening, and then you read the stuff in the papers. The press partisanship is so embarrassingly apparent. To deny the meaning of that fact in the way these proceedings are chronicled is the same as wearing a blindfold and claiming to see the colors in a painting by Jackson Pollock. Thank God for C-SPAN and talk radio.[71]

Not all the freshmen were satisfied in attributing their defeat on the budget to Clinton's duplicity and the manipulation of public opinion by the news media. Some of the more moderate northern members pointed out that the excessive use of policy riders on the appropriations bills had unnecessarily given Clinton and the media additional ammunition to use against the Republicans, and, moreover, that the strategy of shutting the government down was irresponsible and bound to backfire on the GOP:

It would have come out better if we had stuck to economic issues and not tried legislating through appropriations bills, but on some bills they just couldn't resist adding ideological legislation, and that gave Clinton and the Democrats the opportunity to use the presidential bully pulpit to pick and choose their reasons for vetoing the bill. Ninety-eight percent of the bill might be OK, but they would focus on the other 2 percent and accuse us of attacking the environment, the disabled, the safety net, or kids on welfare. It was our own mistake.[72]

The shutdown was a big mistake and a major strategic error. We should have been more thoughtful but instead we put Clinton in the driver's seat. You might say that our reach exceeded our grasp. Many of my freshman colleagues were very naive. The Speaker would pump those guys up so much that when we asked for 80 percent, 30 percent seemed like a big letdown. Our strategy was unsuccessful because we resurrected Bill Clinton. We should probably have toned down the tax cuts and sent the president something that would have made his veto the issue. Sometimes you just can't get what you want by muscling it. They were wrong to think that any political leader will make a decision with a gun placed at his head. They were able to throw it back on us, and throw us off-message.[73]

Several freshman members were inclined to blame the leadership for a flawed strategy. Tennessee's Zach Wamp was one of these:

I don't want to be a Monday morning quarterback, but when we were asked what would happen if they didn't go along with the budget, and the answer was, "We'll shut down the government," it was not thought through well. Once it came time to follow through, it was an unpleasant circumstance that everyone regrets, and now we aren't getting the credit for Congress setting new priorities and getting the budget deficit down to $117 billion. . . . The leadership got outmaneuvered on tactics and we lost because we didn't get the story out.

I don't blame the media for our problems. It was our tactics. I knew when I ran that the national media were more liberal, so why should I complain now that I'm in office? We should have developed our strategy and tactics toward that going in. The country is not looking for complainers. We should also have taken more time to reach out to conservatives on the other side of the aisle, and we should have tried to be less divisive in our rhetoric.[74]

David McIntosh of Indiana also believed that the Republicans had been victims of a failed leadership strategy:

Looking back at it honestly, we made the most important errors prior to our engagement with the president. We signaled over the summer to OMB that we would shut down the government because the leadership believed that we could reach an agreement with Clinton. They should have known that Bill Clinton is a dissembler, and we should have watched his actions, not his words. We should have planned for a long struggle and worked out in August what our definition of a shutdown meant. The second strategic error was to have a debate where we were defending tax cuts while proposing Medicare reductions. We played

into that when it looked like our condition for reopening the government was to increase the amount that seniors paid for Medicare.[75]

Other members mentioned that the Republicans had failed to appreciate that securing control of the House after forty years did not guaran-
tee that the checks and balances of America's Madisonian system of
government would simply disappear into irrelevance. The budget battle
brought home the reality of the separated system to two conservative
freshmen, J.D. Hayworth of Arizona and David Funderburk of North
Carolina:

> We also should have remembered that this is not a parliamentary de-
> mocracy. We don't have executive power here [in Congress]. We
> should never discount the reality of the Constitution and the separation
> of powers. We cannot divorce ourselves from the realities of a constitu-
> tional Republic. It is supposed to be tough. It was designed this way. It
> is maddening, but it does not lead to the concentration of power that is
> harmful to the liberty on which it is based.[76]

> A fragile Republican majority cannot override a Democratic president
> and shut off Senate filibusters. If we want to accomplish more, we need
> more people. We need another election, maybe two more elections. In
> view of what we know now, we should have known that we were going
> to confront the president and that we didn't have a spokesman such as
> Clinton is.[77]

Some freshman Republican members felt that the personality of the
Speaker, who was plummeting in the popularity polls during the budget crisis, was a major liability for the Republicans. A brilliant tacti-
cian and strategist in the 1994 elections and during the first hundred
days, Gingrich, who was not a budget expert and not as accomplished
a communicator as the president, was felt to have made a poor presentation of the Republican case. His tendency to make abrasive off-the-
cuff remarks in public (such as the *Air Force One* incident), and his
allegedly "professorial" manner compared poorly to the PR skills of
the Clinton White House. One freshman member stated this problem
clearly:

> The little guy's view of government is that everyone goes along to get
> along, and will pass anything to get out in time for cocktails. There is a

perception that there is too much going along to get along, and the result is the debt. They liked the idea of people like us standing on principle and saying that there was too much accommodation in Washington. But at the gut level they did not like Newt Gingrich, and the budget message became the Newt message. Maybe someone who comes across as a little more conciliatory, like John Kasich, should have had a higher profile. But we were one-upped by the president, who did a good job.[78]

Gil Gutknecht of Minnesota also believed that a poor communications strategy had led to the Republicans' defeat on the budget:

We lost on the shutdown because of poor communication. Let me make two points: (1) it was not a government shutdown, it was a temporary furlough for nonessential federal employees; (2) we did not make it clear that it was not a political fight as much as a constitutional fight. Article 1, section 8, of the Constitution gives Congress the power of the purse. The impasse came about because the president wanted to tax $150 billion more than Congress was willing to tax, while wanting to spend $250 billion more than Congress was willing to spend. If you put it that way, then 80 percent of the voters agree with us. It's really a battle over how much you are willing to tax and how much you are willing to spend.

But we started explaining rather than stating. Newt acted like a professor, explaining and responding, when what he needed to do was state. We did not do a good enough job of framing the debate, which was really about whether we were going to spend $12.2 trillion or $14 trillion over seven years. When we started talking about the CBO and the GAO [General Accounting Office], we got off-message, while the president had a simple message of saving Medicare, Medicaid, the environment and education. He stayed on-message. We didn't.[79]

The events of the budget battle certainly succeeded in driving a wedge between the leadership and the freshmen that had not existed during the Contract period, when they had both been operating in harmony. During the budget battle, however, the eagerness of the leadership to end a dispute that was costing the Republicans dearly in the court of public opinion ran up against the determined resistance of a group of militant freshmen who were unwilling to countenance any significant compromise on the budget. Of course, the Republican leadership also found it useful to use the threat of the freshmen's militancy as a negotiating ploy—the "crazy uncle strategy," as Gil Gutknecht described it.[80] Appropriations Chair Bob Livingston found this approach to be perfectly reasonable as a negotiating strategy from the leadership's point of view:

> I don't know that I see anything wrong with that. In negotiations you use what you can. In any successful negotiation you use a good cop–bad cop strategy. It's an obvious ploy. The fact is that it didn't work, and we don't have a balanced budget.[81]

David McIntosh, the freshman class's liaison to the leadership, had no doubt, however, that the Republican leadership was trying to blame the freshman class for the leaders' own strategic shortcomings:

> The leadership didn't want to take the rap for a failed strategy, and in a classic Washington maneuver they blamed the freshmen. The freshman class didn't want to back down, and they were told by Newt Gingrich: "I will not back down," but they were let down by Gingrich and Dole, when they decided they had to back down.[82]

It is not obvious, however, that the freshmen were as monolithically militant during the government shutdown as represented by McIntosh and several of the more hard-line members of the class. It is a tribute to the success of the Clinton PR strategy that they were able to depict the entire seventy-three-member freshman class as extremist on the basis of the attitudes of a hard core of twelve to fifteen of the most vocal members of the class. Ironically, all the major participants in the budget dispute found it convenient to depict the freshmen as "crazy uncles" or "bad cops," but in the ultimate showdown vote in January to reopen the government, fifty-nine of the freshmen voted with the House GOP leadership for a clean CR. Zach Wamp and Californian Brian Bilbray were both keen to point out that hard-liners such as Mark Neumann and Mark Souder were not representative of the class as a whole:

> During that debate it was not true that the freshmen were unwilling to negotiate. The freshmen were never consulted. The leadership tried to negotiate, but they were outfoxed by a crafty president, and looking for an excuse to leave the table, they used the freshmen. The Democrats picked up on that, and they began to blame the freshmen for closing

down the government. There are about fifteen freshmen who are ada-
mant about their position on issues, and they are willing to take down a
rule or a bill to stop things and do what it takes to get their way. But I
have watched one bill after another, and I can say that there are fifty-
nine freshmen who understand that politics requires a certain amount of
compromise.[83]

The initial shutdown showed the commitment of some members and
many senior members. But I would like to clarify that the freshmen got
a bum rap. How can you blame seventy-three freshmen for what thirteen freshmen and senior members were up to? Only thirteen of us
wanted to see a government shutdown, but the president felt he could
blame the freshmen.[84]

In contemporary American politics, however, perception is everything,
and there could be little doubt that thanks to their own volubility and
the "media spin" from the Clinton White House, it was the handful of
hard-line budget firebrands who defined the public profile of the freshman class during the budget battle. At a meeting of the House Republican Conference prior to the vote to reopen the government on 5
January 1996, Gingrich, who desperately wanted to reopen the government to limit the escalating political damage to the Republicans (who
were getting blamed for the shutdown by a two-to-one margin in
polls), laid his own leadership on the line to get the conference behind
his decision to sponsor a clean CR to reopen the government. David
McIntosh was told to resign his leadership liaison position if he failed
to vote for the resolution, and the Speaker assured the other freshmen
that he would carefully note those who failed to support him on this
crucial vote.[85] When the resolution passed the House by 401–17, with
fifteen Republicans, twelve of them freshmen, voting no, Gingrich was
true to his word.[86] The Speaker—a formidable fund raiser for Republican candidates—promptly canceled scheduled fund-raising events for
four of the freshman dissidents.[87] The recalcitrant freshmen were unrepentant, however, as can be seen from the comments of Mark Souder,
Bob Barr, and Lindsey Graham:

Nothing [the canceled fund raiser with the Speaker] could have helped
me more and made me look more independent. The critical week was in
November. We put Medicare into the CR and gave Clinton the excuse
to shut down the government by vetoing the CR. He played the senior

trump card, and our numbers among seniors are way down, while we've held our own with other groups. After the plane incident, Bill Clinton found an issue and his footing when Newt lost his. Newt told us in a party meeting that he was getting killed in the polls and that we had to reopen the government and negotiate. John Shadegg (Ariz.), Joe Barton (Tex.), and I voted against the November reopening. We should have kept the government closed and reopened over Christmas. Instead, we shut down again over Christmas and got pummeled.

From November to early January we made five new offers on the budget, but Clinton never moved. In hindsight it looks stupid, but none of us believed that Bill Clinton would change and stand firm. I argued that to get a real budget the shutdown was worth it, but a phony agreement on the table would be worthless.[88]

In my district, constituents kept telling me to "hold the line" or "go further." In Georgia, citizens told me that they sent me to the federal government to shake things up and finally give some attention to serious national problems. I even had letters from federal employees supporting a hard-line approach. I was one of the seventeen who voted against the bill to reopen the government on 6 January. My view is that Clinton was never going to sign on to a balanced budget, and to the extent that our strategy was predicated on that, it was likely to fail.[89]

I was very involved in the budget debate, and I was one of the twelve freshmen who voted against reopening the government. At the time I wondered how Newt Gingrich, Dick Armey, and Tom DeLay would have voted in my situation. I hoped we would stop negotiating another plan if Bill Clinton failed to put a proposal on the table. It's a matter of principle and setting the tone. The overall response in my district was "hang in there." Most people understood that this was not politics as usual and that if America was going to change, conflict had to occur.[90]

Some other budget hard-liners, such as Mark Neumann and Joe Scarborough, supported the Speaker on the CR but fundamentally agreed with the rebels that the Republicans should not have capitulated so readily in reopening the government on 5 January 1996.

People only get branded as "extreme" in this city. Back-home people are so supportive about what we are doing for this country. I think that it's unfortunate that we ended the battle as early as we did. The fact is that we won, and we are on track to a balanced budget ahead of schedule, but I was ready to get back in the trenches, endure the government shutdowns, and fight some more. History will judge who were the people that were willing to stand and do what's right for the country.[91]

We had gone through two government shutdowns and by the end of the second, the president finally came to the table and offered a seven-year CBO budget. At that point we folded immediately because of the tremendous outcry against everything being closed. The polls showed Clinton's approval rating falling from 50 to 42 percent, and we should have gone ahead and closed the deal then, and stuck it out for another week or two. But it was a horrendous time and we had a siege mentality, but unlike everybody else I think that we should have gone the last mile and secured a seven-year deal.[92]

For the congressional Republican leadership, however, the shutdown had become an overly expensive gamble that showed no imminent prospect of a political return. Fearful for the first time that he might actually lose control of the House in the 1996 elections, and battered by ethics allegations from the Democrats (discussed in chapter 6), Speaker Gingrich decided to cut his losses. In doing so he placed his own leadership on the line, and the Republican Conference overwhelmingly backed him. Yet the bond between the House Republican leadership and their freshman "shock troops," which had been so tight during the 1994 elections and the passage of the Contract, although not completely unraveled, had been considerably loosened by the House Republicans' experience during the budget crisis.

Conclusion

The budget debate was widely perceived as a defeat for the "Republican revolution" and for the keepers of the flame of that revolution—the House Republican freshmen. Certainly it ended their momentum and rocked the GOP back on the defensive for the remainder of the 104th Congress. The public relations pummeling from the White House and the press, coupled with strong negative advertising campaigns directed specifically against the freshmen in their districts by the Democrats and allied organizations representing labor unions, seniors, and environmentalists, had a major adverse effect on freshman morale and confidence. Instead of remaking the universe of American government and public policy, their principal priority became electoral survival.

Another consequence of the budget debacle for the Republicans was the loss of confidence in the party leadership, whom many freshmen blamed for not having devised an exit strategy for the budget battle in the event that the Clinton administration proved to be uncooperative, or for coming up with a persuasive message to win over public opinion when the going got tough during the shutdowns. In retrospect, Gil Gutknecht of Minnesota agreed with the focus on the balanced budget but felt that the Republicans had failed at the level of strategy:

> The balanced budget gave us a common standpoint, but we got too bogged down in the minutiae of bills and forgot to emphasize that we were doing this for the future of our kids and our grandkids. I have been a salesman, and I can say that we were selling the feature rather than the benefits. Ronald Reagan saw the big picture and spoke on the value level. We talk about the Congressional Budget Office and people's eyes glaze over. We have to get back on-message. We also have to assume that the national media are not going to give us the benefit of the doubt, that we have to work a little harder to tell our story. We need to do a better job of getting our facts on the table. We have to talk about how a balanced budget can lead to more growth and more jobs, and get people to make that connection.[93]

On the other hand, looking at the budget battle from a longer-term political perspective, while it was apparent that the freshmen had suffered a tactical defeat, in terms of the overall battle of ideas and policy, they had clearly won. Clinton defeated them in public relations terms, but conservatives had so redefined the political debate in Washington that the president and the Democrats were fighting a defensive battle to save as many federal government programs as possible in an overall context of scaling back the size and scope of the federal government. The primary imperative of a balanced budget early in the next century had made it politically impossible for Clinton, or any other Democratic president, to attempt a major expansion of the federal government on the scale of Clinton's ill-fated health-care reform in 1994. This development did not escape the House Republican freshmen, and several of them noted that aside from the public relations aspect, the 1996 budget battle had been a substantial triumph in policy terms:

> We lost a lot of steam in the budget fight, but we still cut federal government spending by $83 billion, and the deficit is at a fourteen-year low.[94]

What has changed is the nature of the game. When I started out three years ago, we were back against the goal line and defending. Now we are playing on their side of the field. The debate had changed, and if you have any doubt, read Bill Clinton's State of the Union address.[95]

Moderate New Jersey freshman Bill Martini made a compelling case that the budget debate and the shutdown had permanently altered the attitudes toward the budget and the size of government in Washington in a Republican direction:

> The shutdown was a complex moment in history, but I'm not sure that we could have done anything differently and politically easier, and also see the results we've gotten which have been very important. I was never one who wanted to shut down the government, but it wasn't Congress alone that shut down the government, and the White House only wanted cosmetic changes. I wasn't happy with the shutdown, but if we didn't bring it to that point and demonstrate intent, we wouldn't be where we are today. We have changed the way Washington thinks, and the American people. Now we have the Democratic Party adopting Republican principles—the balanced budget, small government, and tax relief—and we can take credit.
>
> If it weren't for our commitment, we would have seen what happened in the past. At the beginning of December there would have been a conflict between the White House and Congress, the leadership would have walked into a room and come out with the president to say there was a budget deal, a deal that wouldn't be worth the paper it was written on. And in the next cycle of elections all the incumbents would have been preserved and we would be back in the pattern that got us into this predicament. Sometimes you just can't avoid confrontation.[96]

So while the shutdown demonstrated the limits of the "Republican revolution" of 1994, it also demonstrated the extent of that revolution. Yet as the budget dispute petered out in the spring and summer of 1996, the congressional election cycle began to kick in, and the freshmen were compelled to focus on the imperative of reelection. The decline in the popularity ratings of Congress, and particularly Speaker Gingrich, during the budget debate had given the Democrats a realistic opportunity to retake the House in 1996 and undo much of what the freshmen had been striving to achieve in terms of institutional reform and change in the direction of public policy. In chapter 6 we see how reelection came to predominate in the congressional agenda for the remainder of 1996 and how the freshmen were largely able to survive the Democratic and labor onslaught. The failure of the budget package, however, and the stalling of the Contract in the Senate, appeared to have left the Republicans with a dangerously slim record on which to run for reelection.

It is now necessary to turn to the Senate and compare the experiences of the freshman Republican members in that chamber to their House counterparts. In so doing it will become apparent why the "Republican revolution" had far less impact in the Senate in 1995, and why the Senate was able to take control of the Republican legislative agenda from the House in the final months of the 104th Congress and secure the passage of several important legislative measures.

5

The Neglected Revolutionaries: Republican Senate Freshmen in the 104th Congress

> When I first started in the Senate in 1995, I was asked, "What's it feel like to be part of the new revolution in Washington?" I'd say, "I don't know. I'm in the Senate!"[1]
>
> *Freshman Republican Senator*

The eleven Republican freshmen in the U.S. Senate were the forgotten story of the 104th Congress. While the House freshmen were bathed in press and public attention from the moment of their arrival in Washington, their Senate counterparts got far less coverage and apparently had far less political impact. Part of the reason for this was the greater novelty of the Republican majority in the House after forty years of Democratic rule. The Contract with America, GOPAC, and the leadership of Newt Gingrich had also provided a common platform and purpose for the House Republican freshmen, which was not the case with freshman senators, who generally did not use the Contract as the basis of their campaigns. It was also true that the Republican freshmen in the Senate were far more politically experienced than their House kinsmen and were therefore less likely to identify with the reform ethos that characterized the House freshmen.

This chapter, however, shows that the primary reason for the lower visibility, and apparently more limited influence, of the Senate freshmen lay in the very nature of the Senate, a body that emphasizes comity, reciprocity, decentralization, weak leadership, and individualism in conducting its business. The House, by contrast, emphasizes rules, order, discipline, partisanship, and strong leadership in order to get things done. Numbers are also of crucial significance here. To make an impression in a body of more than 400 members demands some degree of organization and group participation on the part of individual members. In a body of 100 members, an individual senator inevitably has much greater significance.

Yet, although the Republican Senate freshmen in the 104th Congress were muzzled to some extent by the chamber's norms and traditions, their impact was far from negligible. The freshman senators did act as the Senate's "revolutionary conscience" in an effort to get that body to pay greater attention to the kinds of changes in policy and institutional reforms that were being pursued in the House. Moreover, the Senate freshmen, at least initially, worked together to a far greater extent than most previous Senate freshman classes and were the major proponents and agitators for a series of highly significant changes in the Rules of the Senate Republican Conference, which may have considerable long-term significance in enhancing the role of political parties and the party leadership in the Senate. Finally, as the locus of legislative activity shifted from the House to the Senate in the latter phase of the 104th Congress, freshman Republican senators were able to play a role in putting together the legislative compromises that enabled the GOP to recover from the trauma of the budget shutdown and may well have saved the Republicans' control of Congress in the 1996 congressional elections.

This chapter looks at the record of the Republican freshmen in the Senate in the first session of the 104th Congress. In comparing their experiences with those of the House freshmen, a full appreciation for the differences between the two legislative chambers and their roles in contemporary American national government should become apparent.

The Freshman Republican Senators

While the House freshmen constituted almost a third (32 percent) of the House Republican Conference in the 104th Congress, these eleven freshman Republican senators accounted for just over a fifth (21 percent) of the Republican total of fifty-three senators after the 1994 elections.[2] The freshman Senate ranks included only one woman, Olympia Snowe of Maine, and no minorities. As a group, they had considerably more governmental and elective experience than the House freshmen. Six of the eleven—Rod Grams (Minn.), James Inhofe (Okla.), Jon Kyl (Ariz.), Rick Santorum (Pa.), Olympia Snowe (Me.), and Craig Thomas (Wyo.)—were members of the U.S. House of Representatives at the time of their election, while another, Mike DeWine of Ohio, had also served in the House until his election as lieutenant governor of Ohio in 1990. John Ashcroft of Missouri had been a two-term governor of his state from 1985 to 1993, and Spencer Abraham of Michigan had served as a state Republican chairman, an aide to former Vice-President Dan Quayle, and co-chair of the National Republican Congressional Committee (NRCC). Only the two Tennessee freshmen—Fred Thompson and Bill Frist—had never held party or elective office (although Thompson had served in Washington as minority counsel to the Senate Watergate Committee in 1974, before embarking on a successful career as a trial lawyer and movie actor). In sum: this was hardly a group of political novices (see Table 5.1).

Three motivations appear to have been paramount in the decisions of the Senate freshmen to run for that chamber in 1994: the greater ability of individual senators "to make a difference," taking advantage of a political opportunity to advance their careers in what appeared likely to be a good Republican year in congressional elections, and a desire to advance the cause of the Republican Party and their conservative philosophy.

For Tennessee freshman Bill Frist, who gave up a multimillion-dollar practice as a heart surgeon to run for Congress, the influence and visibility of the office of U.S. senator were decisive factors:

> In the U.S. Senate an individual senator can pass a bill or kill a bill, and that's a position I wanted to be in, if I was going to give up a profession that I'd worked toward for twenty years. I ran for the Senate for two reasons: first, I wanted to make a difference; and second, the Senate is a position where you can make a difference once you get there.[3]

Former Missouri Governor John Ashcroft was primarily motivated by the opportunity that the Senate would provide to advance his conservative ideas about government and society at the national level. According to his chief of staff, David Ayres:

Table 5.1

Prior Political Experience of Freshman Republican Senators in the 104th Congress

Senator	State	Public offices held/political experience
Spencer Abraham	Michigan	Co-Chair NRCC[a], 1991–92; Deputy Chief of Staff to Vice-President Quayle, 1990–91; Michigan Republican Chairman, 1982–90
John Ashcroft	Missouri	Governor of Missouri, 1984–92; Attorney General of Missouri, 1976–84
Mike DeWine	Ohio	Lt. Governor of Ohio, 1990–94; U.S. Representative, 1982–90; Republican nominee for U.S. Senate, 1992
Bill Frist	Tennessee	None
Rod Grams	Minnesota	U.S. Representative, 1992–94
James Inhofe	Oklahoma	U.S. Representative, 1986–94; Mayor of Tulsa, 1978–84; Republican nominee for Governor, 1974
Jon Kyl	Arizona	U.S. Representative, 1986–94
Rick Santorum	Pennsylvania	U.S. Representative, 1990–94
Olympia Snowe	Maine	U.S. Representative, 1978–94
Craig Thomas	Wyoming	U.S. Representative, 1989–94
Fred Thompson	Tennessee	Minority Counsel, U.S. Senate Watergate Committee, 1973–74

Source: Michael Barone and Grant Ujifusa, *The Almanac of American Politics 1996* (Washington, D.C.: National Journal).
[a]National Republican Congressional Committee.

Senator Ashcroft had a particular view of how government ought to operate. This was a principled view based on government and its role in society. He thinks that government can crowd other instincts out, like the family and the church. When government tries to do too many things, it affects too many people. Senator Ashcroft wants to change the way government does business and fiscal management. As governor, he experienced dealing with the federal bureaucracy on all those fronts, whether mandating the way programs were run or how money was spent. Senator Ashcroft felt a real call to run in 1994.[4]

Ideology also played a strong role in Congressman Rick Santorum's decision to challenge Democratic incumbent Harris Wofford in Pennsylvania. His communications director, Tony Fratto, recalled:

> The overriding issue was that Rick did not think the state was well served by Harris Wofford. If another prominent Republican who agreed with Rick philosophically and Rick's view of the direction of the party had run, Rick would have supported him. But early on nobody else seemed to be at all interested in challenging Wofford, so Rick saw the opportunity to make a run. Pennsylvania didn't need Harris Wofford for a full six-year term.[5]

Two other Senate freshmen who came straight from the U.S. House—James Inhofe of Oklahoma and Craig Thomas of Wyoming—attributed their decision to run to a combination of political opportunity and obligation to the Republican Party:

> I didn't want to run for the Senate. I always thought that the Senate was kinda snooty, the pay's about the same, and after the 1990 redistricting, I was in a solidly Republican and conservative House district. I told my wife, "Why do it?" Also, Oklahoma statewide is still two-to-one Democratic. But on 30 March 1994 I read a *Wall Street Journal* article that said the Republicans might need just one seat to take over the Senate, and that was my motivation to run.[6]

> It was driven more by the fact that our senior senator was retiring, and the opportunity presented itself to come here. The Democratic candidate was the governor of the state, and the seat would have been hard to hold without me. It was partly because I preferred to be in the Senate, and partly out of a sense of loyalty to the party. So I would have done it even if I had known we would win a majority in the House.[7]

Rod Grams of Minnesota, who had just been elected to the House for the first time in 1992, also decided to risk his political career when the opportunity of a U.S. Senate seat presented itself as Minnesota's Republican senator, Dave Durenberger, announced his retirement:

> I heard rumors that Dave Durenberger was not running again, but I never thought about running for the Senate. It became possible when I had a look at polls that showed I was the best-known candidate with the

best chance of winning. I thought I had an obligation to look at it, and I decided late in the game that I had the best chance. I thought that I would have won my congressional district again. The polling said I would have won, which made it a tougher decision.[8]

Ironically, almost all of the former House members who got elected to the Senate in 1994 had mentioned the frustrations of minority status in that body as a factor in their decision to run for the Senate. None of them had envisaged that the Republicans would be able to take control of the House in 1994. Senator Jon Kyl of Arizona admitted:

> I'm not sure that I would have run if I had known that we would control the House, particularly because I would have had quite a bit of seniority on my committees. But being in the minority had become very frustrating by 1994, and all things considered I'm glad I ran for the Senate. It's marvelous that I have been able to represent my constituents in both bodies.[9]

Unlike their House counterparts, Republican Senate candidates did not run on a party program like the Contract with America. Given the greater diversity between states and the more individualistic focus of the Senate, this would probably have been an impossible exercise in the Senate races. Republican freshman Mike DeWine of Ohio was typical of the 1994 GOP Senate candidates insofar as he paid little or no attention to the Contract. According to his chief of staff, Laurel Pressler:

> No one knew about the Contract. He carved out some things that he thought were important, like welfare reform, crime (which has been a big issue for him throughout his career), and a balanced budget. He decided his agenda outside the revolution. We were doing our own thing.[10]

The other Republican Senate candidates pretty much "did their own thing," too; as they generally emphasized broad themes of change and other issues relevant to their individual states. Fred Thompson of Tennessee emphasized government reform and term limits, and his press secretary, Alex Pratt, pointed out how he symbolized his belief in citizen politics (and attracted widespread media attention) by driving around Tennessee in a pickup truck:

The issues he ran on primarily were government reform and term limits. He believes very much in the concept of a "citizen-legislature" and hopes that term limits and campaign finance reform will put an end to careerism. He believes in bringing in regular folks. Senator Thompson is an extraordinarily effective communicator. Like most campaigners, he had a large van with faxes and phones, and he hated it. He said he wanted to get in his pickup truck and campaign. The staff advised against it, but his top consultant said "just do it," so he did, and he still drives his truck around Tennessee.... I think that Senator Thompson would probably have won without the Republican tide in 1994. He says himself: "Everybody didn't just wake up this morning to become Republicans. It was change that they wanted."[11]

Senator Grams believed that the simple message of scaling back the federal government had been the decisive factor, even in historically liberal Minnesota:

Minnesota is more liberal when it votes at the national level. But the message we tried to deliver in the House in 1993–94 was the same message I used in the Senate campaign. We don't need the federal government wasting money. For our constituents it's a good message to say that we've done everything that we said we were going to do, and that's exactly the way we campaigned.[12]

Rick Santorum's aide, Tony Fratto, felt that in a very close race against Democratic incumbent Harris Wofford, the Santorum campaign's superior grassroots organization had been crucial:

Two weeks out from the election we were up 10 to 14 percentage points. Rick was speaking to the commonsense values of the people of the state, and talking about the real issues as the embodiment of change. It was a winning message until two weeks out, Wofford's ads started showing Rick talking about Social Security and taken completely out of context (they had two guys following Rick everywhere with a video camera). We went from ten points up to four points down, and that changed the whole aspect of the race. We won it in the last four days with great organization. We had a grassroots organization in all the counties, and we worked harder than any campaign I have ever worked in. We also had a coherent message.[13]

Tennessee's Bill Frist also isolated grassroots organization as the critical factor in a campaign that he had researched and planned as thoroughly as the heart operations he had been performing for years:

I went about it systematically. I did nothing but travel the state and visited all ninety-five counties of Tennessee. I talked to people from 7 A.M. to 11 P.M., and every night I was getting the same feedback from the voters. First, they didn't know [Democratic incumbent] Jim Sasser, and second, when they did know something about him, they didn't like him. I was hearing that from Democrats, Republicans, farmers, businesspeople, even people on welfare! After looking at the same polling data for five or six weeks I knew he could be beat if I was a good enough candidate, and I could outwork him. It's not too different from learning how to do an operation. I had good data showing he could be beat, otherwise I would not have run, but run for the open seat [won by Fred Thompson] instead. There was an overall Republican movement in Tennessee in 1994 that would have allowed me to beat Jim Sasser in a close race. The 14 percent margin was because of the attention we paid to the grassroots. I must have made over 900,000 phone calls, and we had volunteers in every city. We really put in the time, energy, and effort at the grassroots level. And we capitalized on individuals who were yearning for change.[14]

It was already evident in their path to the U.S. Senate that the Republican freshmen there would be a somewhat dissimilar group to the House freshmen. They came with much greater political experience, both in Washington and state government, and their campaigns had been much less of a national contest than the House races, with the eventual outcomes being decided more on an individual, state-by-state basis with one or two common national themes. As a consequence, there was no single policy blueprint or manifesto like the Contract that bound the Senate freshmen together, although the six who had come straight from the House obviously had the common experience of serving in a Republican minority that had grown to feel very oppressed by the early 1990s. Some of these members—most particularly Rick Santorum, Jon Kyl, Rod Grams, and James Inhofe—had been enthusiastic followers of Newt Gingrich in his assault on the Democratic majority. They would soon find that that style of roughhouse politics was not conducive to success and effectiveness in the "other body."

Culture Clash: The Freshmen Discover the Norms of the Senate

The Senate and the House are very different bodies, with different rules and a different culture. The Senate was created to represent the states and to act as a "check" on the popularly elected House. It was also given the special prerogatives of ratifying treaties (requiring a two-thirds majority) and confirming federal executive branch and judicial nominees. Even after the Senate moved to direct popular election following the ratification of the Seventeenth Amendment to the Constitution in 1913, it remained very conscious of these constitutional functions and particularly of the need to curb the "impulsiveness" of temporary majorities in the House. While serving as a congressional fellow in Washington, I lost count of the number of times in which congressional observers, members, and staffers would describe the Senate as "the saucer that cools" the overly "hot and impetuous" legislation produced by the House.

In addition to the longer focus and greater freedom given to senators by their six-year terms, the rules of the Senate have been framed to obstruct quick action and to encourage the maximum amount of deliberation and consensus on a particular issue. Until 1917 there were no limitations on debate in the Senate, save those imposed by the senators' collective sense of "fair play." As that genteel notion became antiquated in the twentieth century, Senate rules were changed to allow the possibility of limiting debate through a cloture motion, but as this required a two-thirds vote of the Senate, it was very rarely invoked.[15] Even though the requirement for cloture was reduced to three-fifths, or sixty votes in 1975, the threat of a filibuster still places a formidable barrier to the passage of legislation and greatly enhances the power of minorities, whether partisan or otherwise. The contrast with the House, where floor debate is strictly limited by rules constructed by the majority party, is stark.

In fact, the Senate rules not only give a significant role to the minority party but also give an extraordinary amount of power to individual senators. If a senator's bill is blocked in committee, he can bring it to the floor as an amendment to another bill, with no requirement that it be germane to the subject matter of that bill (except for appropriations bills). An individual senator can also anonymously request that specific legislation not be sent to the Senate floor by the majority leader or minority leader until that senator has been consulted—a practice known as putting a "hold" on a bill. Debate is unlimited, and amendments are unrestricted until a cloture motion is passed, and even after cloture senators can demand further debate and amendment. In fact, most business on the Senate floor is conducted according to "unanimous consent" motions worked out by the party leaders, particularly on procedural matters. But, as the name implies, the determined objection of a single senator can unravel such agreements. Senator Thad Cochran, chairman of the Senate Republican Conference (the third-ranking leadership position) in the 104th Congress, provided me with an excellent summary of the degree of power that the Senate gives to its individual members by comparison with the House:

> Even a minority senator has more power, because of the rule of unlimited debate in the Senate. A single senator can frustrate the passage of legislation, and in concert with others can keep a bill from even being called up by filibustering the motion to proceed, and in some cases forcing the majority leader to postpone consideration. The cloture rules also allow senators to offer an unlimited number of amendments, and even postcloture, opponents of a bill can use this to force further debate. The rules are such that any senator's rights are greater than any House member's rights. And senators can also debate and hold up confirmations; just think of all the officers that have to be confirmed—and the judges!
>
> House members are much more restricted by the rules. There is very little debate in the House as the Rules Committee generally restricts debate on a bill to four hours and decides which amendments, if any, will be offered to the bill, and the hour and the time of the amendment.[16]

In past times the potential obstreperousness of individual senators was tempered, not by the rules, but by the general culture of the Senate. The classic studies of the Senate in the 1950s by journalist William S. White and political scientist Donald Matthews both highlighted the role played by deference and seniority in the Senate of that time. White wrote of an informal "inner club" of senior (predominantly southern) members who really determined what went on in the Senate.[17] Matthews described how the "folkways" of the Senate—principally deference of junior members to seniors, specialization, and reciprocity—mitigated the individualism of senators and allowed legislative business to proceed.[18] In fact, during this period the actual use of obstructive tactics such as the filibuster was rare relative to today and was usually reserved for the most important issues, such as civil rights bills.

But the orderly Senate system of the 1950s was the product of the domination of the chamber by conservative southern Democrats, who controlled the balance of power between the Republicans and liberal

Democrats and, due to the seniority rule, also held most of the committee chairmanships.[19] All this changed from the 1960s onward as liberal northerners came to predominate among Senate Democrats, and the southern Democrats' numbers were reduced by the emergence of the Republicans in the South. The old norms or folkways of the Senate no longer served the interests of activist liberal senators who felt that they had to make their legislative mark in a hurry.[20] Barbara Sinclair provides a compelling description of the changed political environment facing this new generation of senators:

> These senators could not afford to wait, as the old norms had demanded, to make their mark; both their policy and their reelection goals dictated immediate and extensive activism.
>
> An activist style based on participation in a broader range of issues and on the floor as well as in committee became attractive to more and more senators as the political environment changed radically in the 1960s and 1970s. New issues and an enormous growth in the number of groups active in Washington resulted in senators being highly sought after as champions of groups' causes. These developments made the role of outward-looking policy entrepreneur available to more senators. Successfully playing that role brought a senator a Washington reputation as a player, media attention, and possibly even a shot at the presidency.[21]

Similar pressures applied to the generation of activist conservative Republican senators that began to predominate on the Republican side of the aisle in the 1970s and 1980s.[22] In this environment senators had incentives to be much more active and obstreperous in floor debate, using every weapon at their disposal—amendments, holds, filibusters—to achieve their ends. As a result, the use of these devices increased dramatically. During the entire decade of the 1950s there was an average of one filibuster per Congress. In the 103rd Congress (1993–94) there were no less than thirty Senate filibusters.[23]

As we later see, the old norms of courtesy, seniority, and reciprocity still have significant meaning in the Senate, but they certainly no longer possess the power to command a Senate of a hundred individual "policy entrepreneurs." And, of course, the modern Senate, while giving more power and attention to individual senators, is hardly conducive to the easy implementation of any contentious legislation, never mind a national "policy agenda." Ironically perhaps, in the absence of the old "inner club" and "deference," the surviving Senate norms of courtesy and reciprocity may have become even more important to getting any legislative business done.

This was the situation that confronted the eleven freshman Republican senators when they arrived in the Senate in early 1995. The members who had come directly from the House were all immediately impressed by the difference in the number of members between the two chambers, and secondarily, by the influence and attention given to individual members by comparison with the House. The following remarks by Senators Kyl and Inhofe were typical:

> First, we're much closer in the Senate. I remember the first time that the Senate Republicans had a meeting in the Mansfield Room, and all my Republican Senate colleagues could be seated around a table! Compared to the 435 House members, we're a small group. Second, in the Senate you have more power and ability to influence events. Whatever you say or do, people pay much more attention to you, rather than the real anonymity the House provides.[24]

> First, numbers. In the House I was on two committees, one of which had fifty-four members and the other forty-five. It was like a huge mob. In the Senate Environment and Public Works Subcommittee on the EPA, I'm one of only four Republicans.[25]

These views were shared by Senator DeWine's chief of staff, Laurel Pressler:

> The number-one difference, which hit us both, was the numbers. Because there are fewer people, you are able to control the agenda a little bit better. That is true in the Senate, whether you are in the majority or the minority. The House is very majority driven, whereas in the Senate an individual senator can drive the agenda more. One senator can pretty much stop legislation, and everything works around unanimous consent agreements.[26]

By comparison with the formality and strict majority party control in the House, the 1994 Senate freshmen who had served there were immediately struck by the informality of the Senate rules. These greatly enhanced their influence as individual members, but simultaneously made it next to impossible to advance a partisan Republican agenda like the Contract with America, which sailed through the House in less than one hundred days. Senator Jon Kyl, a strong ally of Newt Gingrich during his House career, found that the same rules that enhanced his individual influence also meant that the Senate minority could not be ignored in similar fashion to the House Democrats for most of the 104th Congress:

> Third, and most important, the reason that the Senate does not pass things as the House does is not so much because of a more moderate philosophical orientation but because of the rules, or the lack of rules, in the Senate. In the House everything works in relation to the rules. In the Senate there are no rules. To do anything you need either unanimous consent or a cloture motion, which requires sixty votes, and it's very difficult, unless your party has over sixty votes, to get sixty senators to agree on a vote. Here the leadership is under the constraint of having to please the minority, which either objects to everything we do or offers to make a deal on terms that are not good. So the leadership has to make concessions all the time to the minority.[27]

Senators Rod Grams and Craig Thomas were also immediately struck by how the differences in the rules and the absence of a strong, partisan Rules Committee weakened the control of the majority party leadership over the Senate agenda relative to the House:

> There are fewer people. The rules are a lot different. The only thing they have in common is that you vote yes or no on the final bill. In the Senate I have a lot more influence and power because the body operates on unanimous consent. Any one senator can stop legislation. The House is geared more toward timing. There's a time limit on debate and the leadership can bring up a bill any time. The House is run for the majority. The Senate is run for the minority, which can stop a bill from even coming to the floor. They can object to the motion to proceed, and you have to invoke cloture to override a filibuster. This gives the minority a real opportunity to influence legislation.[28]

> It is probably less different for me than, say, a California senator, because I represented the same constituency [the state of Wyoming at large] in the House. In the House there's a defined operating procedure, and the Rules Committee assigns the process. Here there's no such assignment, and you can be influential even if you are only one person. Because of the smaller numbers, it's easier to have an impact or input here. So I'd say that the main differences

were the process and reduced numbers. Of course, we also have more resources, but we also are expected to do more things, and there are more demands on your time.[29]

According to his chief of staff, David Ayres, Senator John Ashcroft of Missouri, who had never served in a legislative body, was initially shocked at the unstructured and "chaotic" nature of the Senate:

> Senator Ashcroft tried to come with low expectations, but he was surprised by the chaos, the lack of planning, and the lack of control over events, especially the scheduling. It took quite a bit of getting used to, because as governor he had been able to dictate his schedule. As governor, you are a schedule maker; here you are a schedule taker; and things are coming at you at a fast pace. We had a very good transition, better than most governors have. Governors tend to get frustrated by the legislative process, and the fact that decisions never seem to be reached. In the legislative process you're at the beginning of government. As an executive you're at the end, and you have a single, clear choice to either veto or sign the bill. It's conclusive.[30]

The differences in the rules and procedures of the Senate also meant that many aspects of the Senate "culture" or "folkways" described by White and Matthews in the 1950s have persisted into the 1990s. Indeed, comity and cordiality in particular have become even more important virtues in such an unstructured body as the contemporary Senate. New Republican senators reared in the partisan bear-pit of the late 1980s and early 1990s House of Representatives found the transition to the norms of the more sedate and polite Senate initially irksome. Rick Santorum of Pennsylvania, who had delighted in joining Republican diatribes against the Democrats while serving in the frustrated House minority, was a case in point. His spokesman, Tony Fratto, explained the young senator's frustration with the Senate:

> In some ways Rick Santorum was better suited for the House than the Senate. The House is fast paced, with a Rules Committee that controls debate time and has the ability to move legislation quickly. It's more open to frank dialogue, and the debate is more hard edged. The Senate has a slow pace. It's easier to hold up legislation, and the debate is more deferential and cordial, which makes it harder to get to the heart of certain issues. And that change has sometimes been difficult for Rick.

He's the kind of guy who prefers to cut to the chase. He prefers to stand up and say what he really means, and you don't get that in the Senate.[31]

Senator James Inhofe of Oklahoma, the president of the Senate freshman class, had also been a hard-line conservative firebrand while in the House, but he more quickly accommodated to the exigencies of the Senate and confessed that he now preferred the greater comity of that body:

In the House, if you are philosophically opposed to someone, you always have to hate 'em. It's so polarized, and the hatred goes back and forth. For example, in the House I never had a conversation with Henry Waxman because I disagree with everything he believes in. In the Senate the first one I took on on the floor was Bob Byrd. I thought that we had a knockdown, drag-out debate, but he said to me as we were walking back through the basement: "I thought that was a very nice debate, but in the Senate we do it differently. Instead of being hostile we do it in a friendly way." That's a difference that transcends floor appearance. You don't do that in the House. Maybe after sixty that's more meaningful, and when I was Rick Santorum's age, I was just as defiant as he is. In the Senate, because of the number of members and the decorum and the historically friendly environment, I enjoy my time more and can be friendlier.[32]

Tennessee freshman Bill Frist, who had the least political experience of the freshmen, decided to spend his initial months in the Senate observing how the chamber worked, rather than concentrating on partisan debate:

As an administrator I had run the Vanderbilt Transplant Center where we had over a thousand people, so I had a lot of administrative experience at running a department and managing people. As far as being a legislator, I was an outsider but I had more business experience in managing people than 90 percent of the people here. There is a different culture here. The Senate has its own rules, parliamentary and civil rules. When I got here, I carefully sat back and watched the proceedings, which was different from my freshman colleagues. I anatomized and dissected the proceedings of the system. I was gathering information, just like in medicine. Other freshmen, who came from the House, came out swinging. My approach was to figure out how the system works, take my time, and do things well.[33]

Another difference between the Senate and the House is the role played by the committee system. The flexibility of the Senate floor procedures generally means that committees are less important to the legislative process in the Senate than in the House. Members serve on three full committees, as compared to a maximum of two in the House, and because senators are obliged to cover the whole gamut of policy issues, they are generally less likely than House members to be specialists in particular areas of policy and legislative activity. Rick Santorum's communications director described how looser floor procedures in the Senate undermined the status of committees:

> Committees matter less here. It doesn't matter if you are on the Finance or Armed Services committees, for example, because you can get up and offer an amendment to a finance or defense bill on the floor and hold up the Senate. And there's no Rules Committee.[34]

Santorum's fellow former House members, Rod Grams and Jon Kyl, both found their committee work more valuable in the Senate, simply because the smaller membership gave them a bigger say than in the House:

> There are fewer of us than in the House. There you had twenty-two Republicans on a big committee. Here the ratios are eight to seven, which is a lot fewer, and you have more input and a better chance to shape the bill in committee. Trent Lott told me that there are only 100 of us trying to do the same thing as 435 House members. In the Senate we're spread thin.[35]

> The committees are smaller in the Senate, and so I have more impact. I have enjoyed my committee work much more in the Senate than in the House.[36]

The freshman senators did not all have such a positive view of their committee work, however. John Ashcroft, who had never served in Congress, chafed at the seniority system that placed him below the former House members on the seniority ladder on his committees and was wary of how the "incrementalist" nature of the committee system had contributed to the extended federal government that the "Republican revolution" was pledged to dismantle. As his chief of staff, David Ayres, explained:

The Senate does not value state experience in working out seniority because any congressional service is superior to being a state governor. All the former congressmen who moved to the Senate have seniority over Senator Ashcroft.... Senator Ashcroft has not really been that engaged in his committee work. Of course he goes to the mark-up of legislation, but as far as the hearings are concerned, he's not very focused on that. The senator has a clear idea from the 1994 campaign about what people wanted done on issues like welfare reform, term limits, juvenile crime, tax relief, and fiscal restraint. Congress tends to be focused on reauthorizing very narrow programs to benefit small segments of the public. The senator has not allowed those to distract him from the clear agenda of Missourians, so he has paid more attention to floor activity and legislative initiatives on the issues I mentioned. Maybe later in his term he will get more involved in committee activity.[37]

Another freshman "outsider," Fred Thompson of Tennessee, found the committee work exasperating for a sightly different reason: the incredible demands that it placed on his already crowded schedule. According to his spokeswoman, Alex Pratt, "time demands" was the most frustrating aspect of Senate life for her boss:

He sits on four committees and chairs three subcommittees. Sometimes he is scheduled to vote at 9 P.M. at night, or they have thirty stacked votes, where the staff have to explain how you vote on your way down to the chamber. You have to keep your promises and make deals. You also have a responsibility to meet with your constituents, and to be conscientious and deliberate on issues. You have to deal with the press, and you are on the road every weekend. You have Steering Committee lunches and policy committees and the Wednesday Club. The senator says that you do not have enough time to do anything, and that you do everything half well. You have to do five-minute interviews on issues that you haven't even looked at. The senator does extensive preparation himself. He has no speechwriter and does everything himself. He would like to see more constituents and spend more time on issues, but sometimes he will have three hearings in one day.[38]

The freshmen I spoke with were almost unanimous in their view that freshman members had a surprising degree of power in the Senate, particularly in comparison to the large and more formal House. Most of them commented that the most rewarding part of serving in the Senate was the feeling of effectiveness, an effectiveness they had been denied as House members:

As a freshman in the House, you're relegated to the back row, in the Senate you can't tell the difference.[39]

In the House there's more confrontation. Members are more aggressive and push ideas. It's controlled by the majority and has to pass the legislation the majority wants. The Senate is more collegial and that slows down the process. Bills come out of the Senate that are more moderate in tone than the House, but you hope that things might be changed in conference. The Senate is more rewarding because you see more of your work reflected in what's being done.[40]

Rick Santorum's communications director, Tony Fratto, also gave an interesting example of how his boss had been able to manage the Senate floor debate on welfare reform after the resignation of Senator Bob Packwood because of his expertise on the issue—an opportunity he would probably not have been given in the House:

Rick was able to step right in and manage the bill, and he did a creditable job. Today he'll be on the floor all day long in the welfare debate, because he knows the issues inside out. In the Senate there's an opportunity for freshmen to do that, but the House freshmen rarely have that opportunity.[41]

In concluding this section, which has dwelt on the differences between the chambers in terms of membership, rules, and culture, I have excerpted some interesting comments by Senator Craig Thomas, who asserted that from his experience, despite the greater civility of the Senate, individual senators are not really intimate with each other. They act basically as political loners, instead of relying on groups for social or political support:

In the Senate it's easier to be acquainted with everyone because we're fewer, and there's a little more sense of camaraderie and civility on a personal basis. I was in the House for five years and there were still a lot of Democrats that I didn't hardly know who they were. Despite the smaller numbers in the Senate, members are a little more independent, and they don't form caucuses or groups. Also, everyone takes off when the Senate is not in session. So you don't develop real close personal ties because we are off on our own missions. In the Wyoming legislature, we had only forty-day sessions, but we all lived at the same motel, we all went to the same receptions, and we were all in our seats on the floor during the session, so we all knew each other. We even saw each other a lot of the time out of session, so we formed more lasting, real friendships. Here you don't develop friendships. It's more of an arm's length kind of relationship.[42]

The Senate Republican freshmen, however, did bond together and attempt to act as a pressure group in the chamber in the early months of the 104th Congress. And, as we see in the next section, they *were* able through concerted action to effect change in the Senate Republican Conference and the Republican Senate leadership.

The Impact of the Senate Freshmen

Although the new Republican senators in the class of 1994 garnered nothing like the high public profile of the House freshmen, they made a more rapid impact on the internal politics of their party. Before the 104th Congress met, the second-ranking Republican in the Senate, Majority Whip Alan Simpson of Wyoming, was challenged for his position by the ambitious Senator Trent Lott of Mississippi. Lott, who held the fourth ranking leadership position of conference secretary, was opposed by Majority Leader Dole, and by the third-ranking Republican, his fellow (and more senior) Mississippi Senator Thad Cochran. But all but one of the eleven Senate freshmen supported Lott (the exception being Craig Thomas, from Simpson's state of Wyoming), who won by a one-vote (27–26) margin.[43] While Simpson was ideologically somewhat more moderate than Lott, the real reason for his defeat was simply his long association with Washington and the political status quo. Lott, who had served in the House as the Republican Whip to Bob Michel before his election to the Senate in 1988, was more closely identified with the "revolutionary" tone being set by Gingrich (to whom he had been politically close) and the House GOP. His upset triumph over the popular Simpson with the help of the freshmen demonstrated that the Senate was not impervious to the current of change sweeping both party and country after the 1994 elections.

In the initial months of the 104th Congress, the Senate freshmen established a clear profile of themselves as a group and made a concerted effort to work together on issues of common interest, particularly issues concerning political reform such as term limits and campaign finance reform.[44] Senator Thad Cochran, the chair of the Senate Republican Conference, remarked on the distinctiveness and political impact of the freshman senators:

> They are a very reform-minded group. They came bent on making changes in the laws, procedures, and rules that affect the way the Senate operates, such as limiting the terms of elected leaders, secret written ballots in the conference on committee chairs, and the adoption of a party platform and agenda, which will come into operation in the Senate Republican Conference in 1997. . . . Senate consideration of term limitations would not have happened without pressure from the recently elected Republican senators, especially Fred Thompson and John Ashcroft. All of the freshmen decided that was one of the Contract items they wanted to push. Campaign finance reform was another issue that had support from a lot of new members.[45]

Freshman Class President James Inhofe of Oklahoma also noted the cohesiveness of the group on particular issues:

> There are various fiscal items that we are together on. Olympia Snowe is the moderate of the group. She doesn't have the same conservative feelings as the others. Fred Thompson is a trial lawyer, and he doesn't share all our positions on tort reform. Apart from that, we agree on the balanced budget, term limits, and deregulation.[46]

Arizona Senator Jon Kyl also emphasized the ideological bond that held the Senate freshmen together:

> Of course I work with people that I have a lot in common with. We're a large group that came together during the early days of the revolution and we have a lot in common. We meet every week, and we work together on special orders on the floor. Most of us are conservatives. In terms of clout, we asserted ourselves most clearly on changing the rules of the Senate Republican Conference by sticking together and getting the sophomores to vote with us.[47]

Senator Grams of Minnesota reiterated the point that the freshmen had served as the conscience of the "Republican revolution" in a hesitant and skeptical Senate by pushing hard for institutional reform and a balanced budget:

The freshman class has brought about a lot of changes here. Without the freshman class we would have no majority in the Senate, and we've gotten little credit for being able to change many things in the debate and the mood. We're reducing the budget because the freshmen are here. We pushed hard for term limits and the balanced budget. Older senators can't push term limits because they've been here so long, and it would have been hypocritical for them to get out front on the issue. But the freshman class supported it, and the others got behind us. The freshman class has had a big impact although we've been quieter as compared to the House, but we've got things like rotating chairs, getting conference approval for chairs, and the reorganization of the conference.[48]

Senator Santorum's aide, Tony Fratto, also argued that this particular group of Senate freshmen had had an unusual impact on the institution:

In the Senate the freshmen work together in a lot of ways, but they don't need to form the kinds of groups that they do in the House. On the floor of the Senate everybody is recognized, and even one senator can have an effect on legislation in some way. A number of the freshman senators' chiefs of staff meet weekly, and there's a good rapport between the freshman senators. They know and like one another. You see their names cosponsoring legislation quite a lot. During morning business many freshmen have a "freshman focus" where they get together to debate an issue, which has never been done in the Senate before. This is the first group of freshmen in the Senate that has arrived with an identity. A lot of them—like Kyl, Santorum, and Snowe—knew each other in the House.[49]

By contrast, Will Feltus, the staff director of the Senate Republican Conference, was rather dismissive of the overall influence of the Senate GOP freshmen and stressed that as the 104th Congress had proceeded, their cohesiveness had diminished and their influence had faded:

Their principal impact is that they made us a majority in the Senate. In the beginning they organized themselves into a freshman caucus, and they were more visible early on as a group. But we haven't seen so much of them in the second session. The height of the freshmen's influence in internal Republican politics was during the attempt to censure or discipline Mark Hatfield. But that was a complete fizzle, and it taught some of the more activist freshmen to be more patient in bringing change.[50]

During the 104th Congress, the freshman senators met once a week to discuss issues and plan strategy. While these meetings were well attended and useful earlier in the Congress, with the passage of time and as the freshmen became more integrated into the Senate, interest and attendance began to fall off. When asked in the summer of 1996 if the freshman class still worked closely as a group, Class President James Inhofe conceded:

> Not as well as when we got here. We have a freshman meeting once a week, but the attendance is not as good as it was. It's due to scheduling difficulties more than anything else.[51]

Senator Thomas of Wyoming agreed:

> Especially when we first came, there was a class cohesiveness. We were brought together by the common idea of being freshmen. There's still a camaraderie and common bond, but the longer we're here the more we have separated into regional areas or committee areas, and the class bond goes away. During the first year we were pretty close because we felt we had a common mission, but that has reduced some, which is too bad. If we had melded with the sophomores, we would have had a group of about seventeen, which would have been a good, solid bloc in the conference. Now we're not at odds, but we don't do as much together, and I notice that there's not such a good attendance at class meetings.[52]

In addition to weekly meetings, the Senate freshmen tried to work together on the Senate floor. Since the mid-1980s, the Republican minority in the House had routinely coordinated their forces for the "one-minute" and "special orders" speeches at the beginning and end of the day's legislative business, to castigate the Democrats and to advance their own policy proposals. Most of the House veterans who arrived in the Senate in 1994 had participated in these activities. Senator Grams was typical:

> It was a lot of fun. Of course we were in the minority, but for two years we formed a "theme team," whose main purpose and success was to make a clear distinction between Republican and Democratic proposals. We proposed a Family First bill in 1993 which included a tax cut and a balanced budget. We looked for areas where we could define ourselves,

but we didn't distort Democratic proposals and offer no alternatives, the way the Democrats are doing now in the House.[53]

Class President Inhofe decided to bring the "theme team" concept—renamed the "freshman focus"—to the Senate floor, where participants would not be bound by the rigid time limitations of the House:

> As chairman, I've tried to do what we did over in the House and use "theme teams," where we all cooperate and get together and go to the floor to speak on a common theme. It's working well, and we've all been pretty cooperative in that regard. In the House we had to use the theme team concept in one-minute speeches, but in the Senate you can go down and get the floor and hold it. The opportunity to dominate is easier.[54]

Freshman cooperation also extended to the staff level. In a body where the workload has to be divided among 100 members, as opposed to 435, and the demands on members' time are ferocious, the role played by personal staff is obviously much more important than in the House. Senior staffers for freshman Republicans continued to work closely with each other during the 104th Congress. David Ayres and Laurel Pressler, chiefs of staff, to Senators Ashcroft and DeWine, respectively, testified to the degree of integration among the freshmen and their senior staffers:

> The freshman Senate class has a weekly meeting and the freshman senators' AAs [administrative assistants/chiefs of staff] and LDs [legislative directors] meet once a week. These meetings serve a couple of purposes: (1) they can compare experiences, be supportive of each other, and use the meetings as sounding boards for ideas; and (2) they can unify around policy proposals and work on a common agenda.[55]

> They have meetings every week, and I host a meeting of the chiefs of staff every Thursday morning down the hall. It's tough in the Senate because of the schedule. They've done a lot of "fly-arounds" together to help other candidates. Senator DeWine has also been pretty involved in the "freshman focus" on the floor.[56]

The "fly-arounds" referred to by Ms. Pressler were another innovation by the freshman senators. These public relations and fund-raising trips involved groups of Senate freshmen appearing together in one another's home states, and as the 1996 elections approached, in states with competitive U.S. Senate races. The point of this exercise—the brainchild of Michigan Senator Spencer Abraham, a public relations expert from his days at the NRCC—was to bring the freshman message of balanced budgets and political reform to the masses "unfiltered by the Washington media" and to help elect more like-minded Republicans to the Senate.[57] Class President Inhofe, frustrated by the power of the minority to obstruct the Republican agenda in the Senate, was an enthusiastic participant in the fly-arounds:

> Because of the cloture rule, it takes sixty votes to have a majority that could vote through everything that the House passed. That has motivated us to go out in our freshman fly-arounds and try to elect more Republicans to the Senate. I think we can reach sixty this year, and I'm not satisfied with just holding the majority.[58]

There was a general consensus among the senators and staffers that the most significant success achieved by the freshmen members was the changes in the rules of the Senate Republican Conference. The catalyst for those changes was the decisive vote of veteran Oregon senator and Appropriations Committee chairman, Mark Hatfield, against the balanced budget constitutional amendment. As mentioned in chapter 3, the amendment had been approved by the House during the "hundred days," but fell just one vote short of the required two-thirds majority in the Senate in March 1995. Several freshman senators were particularly upset that someone holding such a powerful position in the Senate Republican leadership as Senator Hatfield had voted against a measure that commanded such overwhelming support within the party (the Oregon senator was the only Republican to vote against the amendment). A movement was immediately started among freshman members, with important support from some more senior members including Conference Secretary Connie Mack of Florida, to "discipline" Senator Hatfield by removing him from the Appropriations chairmanship. Rick Santorum, John Ashcroft, and Rod Grams were particularly outraged:

> The balanced budget amendment was the crown jewel of the Contract with America, and it was something that would have had more impact than anything else this Congress could have done. But on that most

important vote, a member of the leadership voted the other way. Senator Hatfield voted his conscience on this most important vote, but he was also a member of the leadership of his party, and you can't reconcile the two. . . . All Rick wanted to say was that we have to reconsider how we treat the leadership. On a leadership vote, you can't be a member of the leadership and not vote for them. Rick believes that our policy in the future should make clear that on big ticket items members of the leadership have got to be with us.[59]

Senator Ashcroft does not believe in the seniority system. He's not deferential in that respect. When several senators attempted to take the Appropriations Committee chairmanship away from Senator Hatfield because of his vote against the balanced budget amendment, Senator Ashcroft spoke out in conference. His point was that no senator should be expected to vote against his conscience, but if senators have been elected to leadership positions by the party, they should adhere to the principles and approach of the party. If they don't, they shouldn't take a position of leadership.[60]

I agreed with the attempt to disciplin[ing] Senator Hatfield. I respected Senator Hatfield's right to vote any way that he thought, but, on the other hand, there is a difference between voting to represent the people of Oregon and voting to reflect the members in the conference. . . . We wanted to throw out a signal, rather than try to change his vote. He has the right to vote that way, but should he be chairing committees? The values that were controlling legislation were not reflecting the majority values of the conference.[61]

The Hatfield affair was an excellent illustration of the differences between the Senate and the House. While Speaker Gingrich had successfully asserted his authority over the committee chairs in the House, despite the evident discontent with Hatfield the Santorum-Mack initiative in the Senate failed because most of the senior Republicans, and particularly Majority Leader Robert Dole, made their opposition absolutely clear. Dole did not, in fact, allow the proposal to even come to a vote in the Senate Republican Conference.[62] The Conference staff director, Will Feltus, saw the incident as a lesson for the Senate Republican freshmen in understanding the peculiar culture of the Senate:

The more senior members were against it. A lot of the freshmen had a blood lust after Mark Hatfield. But after two weeks trying to win people over, they saw it wasn't gonna work, and it never came to any kind of vote before the conference. It comes back to the issue that the Senate doesn't want to run itself the way the House runs itself. Many of the freshmen came from a House background, and the Senate has been frustrating for them. Nobody really knows how the Senate works. There aren't any rules, and the leadership has little or no leverage over members.[63]

Rick Santorum also learned that the combative, partisan attitudes that had served him well in the House were not the keys to success and effectiveness in the Senate:

> More than anybody else, the difference between the House and Senate has been a problem for Rick Santorum. There is a tradition here of not saying what you really mean, and a lack of willingness to say what's on your mind. The problem is that sixty-five senators were thinking what Rick Santorum's thinking on the most important vote in this Congress. . . . I don't know if Rick handled it as delicately as he should have. It's the kind of thing they don't like facing, which is unfortunate. Senator Mack was aligned with Rick, and a lot of other senators said, "I agree with you, but you shouldn't have said it out loud and turned it into a fight."[64]

In the wake of the controversy over Senator Hatfield, however, the Senate Republican leadership was compelled to address the discontent among the junior Republicans by setting up a task force, chaired by Senator Mack and including freshman senators Santorum, Thompson, and Kyl, to look at the conference rules on party loyalty and committee chairs. In May 1995 the task force circulated draft proposals that included term limits for committee chairs, giving the Republican leader authority to fill committee vacancies, establishing a Republican legislative agenda for each Congress, and the confirmation of committee chairs by the conference.[65] According to Senator Kyl,

> We wanted to address three issues: the seniority system, term limits for committee chairs, and limiting the number of committee and subcommittee chairmanships a senator could have.[66]

In July 1995 the Senate Republican Conference officially adopted several of the Mack task force's proposals in a series of significant rules changes. Committee chairs were henceforth limited to a six-year term, as were all the party leadership offices except majority leader and president pro-tempore. A Republican legislative agenda was to be established by a three-fourths vote of the conference at the start of each Congress. Republican committee members were also given the power to select the committee chair by secret ballot followed by a secret "confirmation" vote by the whole Senate Republican Conference. And, finally, members were limited to one full committee or subcommittee chairmanship, except for members of the Appropriations Committee.[67]

While the reforms adopted were not as dramatic as several that had been suggested in the original Mack task force package, they were still significant changes all based on the concept of loyalty among senators toward a party program, quite a revolutionary notion in the highly individualistic Senate. Conference chairman Senator Thad Cochran of Mississippi believed that the impact of the changes would be far-reaching and was already reflected in the outcome of the contest to succeed Senator Dole as majority leader in May 1995, when he was defeated by (the allegedly more conservative) Senator Lott:

> One of the reasons why the freshmen pushed the idea of having a legislative agenda and having committee chairmen approved by a secret ballot is that it gives the threat of retaliation some credibility. I recall the discussion in the conference, when it was said that members of the leadership refusing to go along with issues considered very important by members of the conference cannot be tolerated. It looks back to the attitude reflected in the Democratic Caucus in the House in the early 1970s, when they decided that they could have a vote in the caucus where members who didn't vote with the majority of the caucus could lose their committee chairmanships and even be denied membership in the party. The Republicans have never really behaved that way, but now in the House and Senate, and especially in the House, the new leadership selects the committee chairs, a revolutionary development that has spilled over into the Senate. It had laid the groundwork for an aggressive leadership that has the support of a majority of the caucus and can even pick the Senate committee chairmen next time.
>
> In the leadership race, I saw so many chairmen line up to support Senator Lott. All the committee chairmen except two (who didn't announce their vote publicly) voted for him over me. Even moderates like John Chafee and Jim Jeffords, who is in line to be a committee chair. These changes have made the leadership much more powerful by giving them a capacity to insist on party loyalty and discipline.[68]

Despite Senator Cochran's fears of the explosive potential of the new rules in changing the nature of the Republican Party and the Senate, there remained good reasons to suspect that unless the Senate's own lax rules on debate were changed (requiring a two-thirds vote of the whole Senate), changing the rules of the Republican Conference alone would not have much more than symbolic significance in mitigating the individualism and indiscipline of senators. In concluding this section on the impact of the freshman senators, however, it is interesting to make the point that if Senator Cochran is correct, then despite all the hoopla and publicity given to the House freshmen, their much less visible Senate counterparts would ultimately have the greater long-term influence over their chamber and the Congress as a whole.

The Contract and the Budget

While the Contract with America sailed through the House on schedule by the end of April, the procedural hurdles in the Senate effectively brought the Republican legislative agenda to a halt. The relatively uncontroversial items in the Contract—the Congressional Accountability Act and the unfunded mandates legislation—passed the Senate fairly quickly due to overwhelming support on both sides of the aisle, but after the narrow failure of the balanced budget constitutional amendment in March, the remainder of the Contract stalled in the Senate as the attention of both chambers became concentrated on the budget and reconciliation package.

The rapid implementation of the Contract with America was always highly improbable in the Senate, since the latter simply gives too much dilatory power to determined minorities and individual senators to allow a party program to be readily passed there.[69] As Rick Santorum's aide, Tony Fratto, accurately put it:

> To have an agenda like the Contract with America with a lot of items you can tick off, probably would set you up for failure in the Senate because the Democrats would be even more unwilling to let us accomplish those things. You can't get things done like that in the Senate. In the House you can use the rules to limit amendments and debate time. In the Senate you have to take things as they come because you have to get unanimous consent even to have your bills considered, with the exception of appropriations and reconciliation legislation.[70]

Senator Craig Thomas of Wyoming, however, and Senator Ashcroft's chief of staff, David Ayres, both argued that despite the protestations of more senior senators, the concept of the Contract and a partisan agenda had influenced the Senate:

> We had something similar over here, but it was a little different. Phil Gramm, who chaired the campaign committee, had five or six issues, but we didn't feel attached to the Contract with America. I do think the Contract gave the Senate freshmen and sophomores the opportunity and the obligation to change direction here, and despite the lack of closure, there has been substantial progress. We have changed the whole basis of debate here from how much you spend to how much you are going to cut. We've seen a turnaround and a fundamental change.[71]

> It [the Contract with America] was marginally helpful during the 1994 campaign because it kept our candidates focused on a common agenda. It was helpful that they said the same things and were campaigning on the same themes. It gave us a road map for what issues to pursue, and in the first months here, it was tremendously helpful.[72]

In the preceding comments, the mention of the influence of Senator Phil Gramm of Texas and the lesser effectiveness of dilatory tactics on budget-related legislation indicate two factors that were to be extremely important in determining the Senate's course of action on the FY 1996 budget package. The fiscally conservative Texas senator was widely regarded as Senator Dole's leading challenger for the Republican presidential nomination in 1996. The fear of Gramm's breathing down his neck and outflanking him on the right by playing to Republican conservatives on Capitol Hill and beyond compelled the pragmatic veteran Senate majority leader to set aside his inherent skepticism regarding ideological "quick fixes" on budgetary matters and, at least initially, embrace the radicalism of the new House majority.[73]

The second factor was even more important. As mentioned in the previous chapter, in order to get the most contentious Contract items through the Senate, they would have to be packaged together into the reconciliation and appropriations measures for FY 1996, which were not amenable to filibustering and other delaying tactics by the Democratic minority. The Senate Budget Committee chairman, Pete Domenici of New Mexico, initially proposed a seven-year balanced budget plan in April that included massive reductions in Medicare and

Medicaid and discretionary domestic programs, but included no tax cuts, as pledged in the Contract and in the House budget.[74] Domenici compromised somewhat under pressure from Phil Gramm, but the final budget resolution that emerged from his committee on 11 May 1995 included only $170 billion in tax reductions, compared to the $353 billion already approved by the House as part of the Contract.[75] On the Senate floor the Republican leadership beat back a flurry of Democratic amendments and a more radical tax-cutting amendment by Phil Gramm that was supported by a majority of Senate Republicans (including Dole).[76] The Senate budget passed 57–42, with all fifty-four Republicans in favor on 25 May.[77] In conference with the House, the final figure for tax cuts was agreed to be $245 billion.[78] Majority Leader Dole had moved in the direction of the House because of his presidential aspirations, and his support was decisive in persuading Domenici and other, more skeptical senior Republican moderates.[79]

After the compromise budget resolution had been passed by both chambers at the end of June, work began on the reconciliation and appropriations bills that would turn the budget targets into real cuts in taxes and spending. At this stage the Senate finally began serious action on some Contract items that were to be packaged into the reconciliation bill to expedite passage. Welfare reform was a case in point. The greater influence of moderate Republicans in the Senate and the need to get Democratic support to preclude "killer" amendments and filibusters on the original bill (before it went into the reconciliation package) resulted in a less drastic measure than the House proposal passed during the "hundred days," particularly in the areas of increased spending for child care.[80] The Senate welfare bill passed 87–12 on 19 September, and President Clinton hinted that he might sign it as opposed to the more draconian House measure.[81]

The final Senate reconciliation package, passed on 28 October 1995, offered lower cuts in Medicaid, education, and in the earned-income-tax-credit than the House, reflecting the greater influence of Republican senior moderates such as Rhode Island's John Chafee and Nancy Kassebaum of Kansas. Senate Democrats also used the Senate's "Byrd Rule," which forbids the addition of nongermane items to a reconciliation bill unless sixty senators vote to waive the rule, to delete several additions to the FY 1996 reconciliation bill (including parts of the welfare legislation) on the Senate floor.[82] The Senate also reduced the upper-income limit for the $500 per child tax credit to $110,000 (compared to the House's $200,000).[83] In conference, the Senate prevailed on the $110,000 limit, while the final welfare proposals reflected the more stringent House version. In other areas the conferees split the differences. By the time the package was finally passed by both houses on 17 November, Washington had already been hit by the first government shutdown.[84]

During the agonizing budget battle of November 1995–January 1996, with its concomitant government shutdowns and late-night negotiations, the Senate generally stood on the sidelines until close to the very end, as the Clinton White House and the House Republicans (including the freshmen) dictated the pace of negotiations. It was clear, however, that the seasoned Washington political operators who represented the Senate Republicans in the negotiations—Dole and Domenici—were far readier to compromise with the Clinton administration but felt unable to move in that direction before Gingrich and the House leaders did likewise. As it became apparent in late December that the shutdowns were damaging the Republicans (and by association his presidential prospects), Dole finally decided to act. On 2 January, saying "enough is enough," he got an unconditional (or "clean") CR passed by the Senate to reopen the government, thus forcing the House Republicans into a corner, which led to their own clean CR and final surrender on 5 January.[85] As we see in the next chapter, this date marked a turning point in the 104th Congress, when the revolutionary zeal of the House exhausted itself against a brick wall of White House obstruction, and the more compromise-oriented Senate picked up the legislative initiative for the remainder of Congress. As the politics of revolution was supplanted by the politics of reelection, it was the Senate—after a change of leadership—that took the lead in the series of legislative compromises with the Clinton White House that characterized the 1996 session and probably salvaged the Republican majorities in both houses in the November elections.

Despite the fact that it was the Senate Republican leadership that initiated the Republican climb-down on the budget, the freshman Republican senators were generally unrepentant about the budget battle, and several (like many of their House brethren) were inclined to blame their defeat on the duplicity and communications skills of the Clinton White House:

> The president is clearly a better politician than any of us collectively, and he was able to sell the American people the myth that it was our

fault that the government was shut down. Oklahoma is next door to Arkansas, and I'd watched him as governor and I knew what a rogue he is, and how he got away with it, so when he started demagoging us on Medicare, I wasn't surprised. I felt that it all might have happened differently if, before Christmas, we had passed a reconciliation bill and gone home after we'd done our job. If he vetoed it, he would have taken the blame for shutting down the government. Instead, we caved in and came back.[86]

We should not have assumed that the president was actually negotiating. It was more politics than policy. The president was weighing everything from the point of view of looking to get back in 1996. America's interests were shortchanged because the Democrats were not willing to accept minority status, and policy be damned. So they tried to delay and kill the Republican agenda. [Minority Leader] Daschle would take that line in debate and shape it. The House Republicans believed that they could negotiate and pass a good budget, but when you look back you can see that the president and the Democratic leadership were posturing for political reasons. For example, when they described a Medicare increase as a "cut." They did everything they could to paint the Republicans as mean and draconian, when they were more generous than the president in 1993.[87]

Aside from castigating the president and the congressional Democrats, however, several other senators believed that the Republicans had made fundamental strategic errors. According to his chief of staff, David Ayres, Senator Ashcroft believed that Republicans had made a major tactical error by taking on the difficult and dangerous Medicare issue:

Senator Ashcroft was discomfited by the approach that the party decided to take with regard to Medicare. We spent the August recess in 1995 talking about health care, and we were pushed to go out and talk about the reform of Medicare. The senator has no doubts that the political strategy of the first year was destined to be a failure, because it was a flawed approach that clearly derailed us. We should have gotten some of the other things done that needed to get done in this session and held back on the difficult issues that we couldn't tackle in this Congress or until we get a Republican president. We gave President Clinton a clear opening on the political front and derailed our own agenda. The president used it well.[88]

Senator Craig Thomas felt that the Republicans should have adopted a more graduated strategy instead of precipitating a single do-or-die battle with the government shutdown:

> With hindsight, we maybe should have adopted a more gradual approach. Our mistake was to end the first shutdown without getting enough from the other side. Shutdowns are not a popular thing, and the public sees it as a teenage food fight with no real merit.[89]

At least most of the Senate freshmen (except Senators Inhofe and Thompson, who had won special elections to fill vacant Senate seats in 1994 and had to run again for a full six-year term in 1996), did not have to face the electorate in November 1996 with the shadow of the shutdown and "Mediscare" still hanging over them, whereas their House counterparts had to get reelected to maintain Republican control on Capitol Hill. Ironically, it would be the activities and legislative initiatives of the Senate that ensured most of the House freshmen returning in November 1996.

Conclusion

The Senate freshmen in their outlook on the budget battle had more in common with their House counterparts than their more cautious and skeptical senior Republican colleagues in the Senate. Many of them had come from the House and had had their baptism in national politics in the ferociously partisan atmosphere that characterized that chamber in the early 1990s. As House members, they had been disciples of Newt Gingrich and had become used to relentless and combative partisanship, and so it is hardly surprising that they had more enthusiasm for the Contract with America and the "Republican revolution" than most of their more senior Republican colleagues in the Senate. Senator Jon Kyl had no hesitation in admitting that he identified with the House freshmen and their crusading zeal:

> I do identify with the House freshmen, and I have regretted that too many of those in power here do not identify with their political agenda. The Senate Republican Conference is behind the House Republican Conference in its evolution, but the revolution here is almost complete, and after the next election, with another new class, it will be complete.

On the other hand, House members do not understand the rules of the Senate and have a lack of appreciation of how things work here. They say "pass a bill and make him veto it," but it's not so easy to pass a bill, because unless sixty members agree to a vote, you can't send it to the president to veto. That impediment has to be taken into account.[90]

Senator Thomas of Wyoming, another House veteran, also felt strongly that the House GOP freshmen, whatever the excesses of their revolutionary zeal, had had a positive effect on Washington:

With the House freshmen, it was inevitable that there would be some shock treatment after forty years of the same theme. It has been abrupt, but their function is to cause things to change. It's possible that they've overreached, that they have aroused more revolutionary expectations. They have been a little unwilling to make accommodations in the legislative area, and perhaps a little naive. But on balance, they have created an atmosphere where things can be done. Of course, they have made enemies, and the Democrats have done a good job in creating hostility toward them, but they're a good thing, and once we get the proper message, we can go out to the voters and change that.[91]

None of the senators that I spoke to, however, admitted that they would have been happier staying in the House. In fact, most of them, whether from inside or outside Congress, greatly valued the influence and attention given to senators as individuals, compared to the necessity for teamwork, discipline, and hierarchy in the House, and felt that the obstructionism, chaos, and need to compromise in the Senate was a price they were willing to pay for that individual influence. Even the iconoclastic Rick Santorum, who had the hardest time adapting to the norms of the Senate of all the Republican freshmen, ultimately found serving in the Senate to be a more satisfying experience:

He enjoys it, and he's getting into it. When he first went to the House, the House fit his personality as it was at that time. There was a lot to do and the place was really a mess. But he likes the Senate more. He sees that he has greater impact on issues and that people listen more to what you have to say. He has the place figured out finally. I couldn't tell you how many times Rick trekked up to the House Rules Committee with amendments but was not permitted to introduce them on the floor for a debate and a vote. The six-year term makes an incredible difference, and I'm glad that we're not having to deal with an election this year. It takes an incredible amount of energy dealing with an election every two years.[92]

The two Tennessee freshmen, Senator Bill Frist and Senator Fred Thompson, had not served in the House and did not bring the same level of combativeness to the Senate. Both believed, however, that even as freshmen with one year's service in the Senate, they had demonstrated how an individual senator could be effective. According to Senator Thompson's press secretary, Alex Pratt, the two Tennessee freshmen working together had been an even more effective combination:

> Once when he [Senator Thompson] and Senator Frist found out that Tennessee was going to lose an item in the budget, they fought together, successfully, to keep it. In the Senate it is possible to say: "This will not happen" like that. In the House the member is dependent on wooing the committee chairmen, and God forbid that the chairman be of the opposite party! Here that doesn't make for tensions the way it does in the House.[93]

For Senator Frist, the least politically experienced of the Senate freshmen, the controversy over the confirmation of Clinton's nominee for surgeon general—a fellow Tennessean physician, Dr. Henry Foster—was a defining moment in terms of exerting influence and demonstrating independence from the party leadership:

> Other freshmen, who came from the House, came out swinging. My approach was to figure out how the system works, take my time, and do things well. The Hank Foster nomination was a defining issue for me, where my party went one way and I went another. I knew Hank Foster. We served on an ethics committee in Tennessee and we were medical associates. I knew that he had the highest ethical standards, but here even superficial research was made part of the public record to defeat him. But I took a stand different to my Republican colleagues, and it became a defining issue for me. I am an independent thinker. I'm not going to part with a majority of my party on every vote, but I'm also not going to be strong-armed or pressured to change a vote I think is right. Nobody did strong-arm me on the Foster vote, and nobody tried.[94]

Senator Thomas remained troubled by the lack of party discipline and order in the Senate and the degree of independence held by committee chairs that got in the way of the Republican agenda. These were the types of frustrations that led to the significant changes in Senate Republican Conference rules after the Hatfield incident in the summer of 1995:

> Sometimes in the Senate there's not enough discipline, and having agreed our general direction, we need a dictatorship on the details! We need to set out the way we are going as a group, and someone has to enforce that. In the House there's more willingness to work as a group. In the Senate there ought to be a leadership decision on the agenda and on timing, and the committee chairs should be asked to try to adhere to that. There was more of that in the House. In the Senate the leadership is setting agendas, but the committee chairs see themselves as fairly independent, and it's hard to advance an agenda or find any time for that agenda. That's one weakness of the organizational structure of the Senate. The Senate chairmen seem to feel that they can be very independent from the main body.[95]

With one or two exceptions, these views did not resonate among more senior GOP senators. The outgoing Republican Conference chair, Senator Thad Cochran, was very concerned about the possible long-term impact of the changes in Conference rules:

> I don't sense that it is in the long-range interests of the party to become more ideological. It narrows our appeal, and to govern effectively you have to have confidence that those who are elected by the people have a broad appeal. You can't just appeal to the most ideologically pure in the electorate because, if we insist on ideological purity among leaders and committee chairs, we will alienate a majority of the electorate. It may not happen right at first, but eventually look what happened to the Democrats after they narrowed their appeal, rather than broadened it. If we follow the same course, we'll be back in the minority again. I believe in politics as an act of addition, not subtraction.[96]

Those rule changes stand as by far the most significant achievement of the Senate GOP freshmen and, as noted earlier, if the new rules turn out to be as momentous as some suspect, then the Senate Republican freshmen will have had a greater long-term impact on their chamber than the more policy-oriented House freshmen. This chapter has tried to make the point that the essential difference between the chambers was not in the ideology or disposition of the freshman Republican classes, which were fundamentally similar, although the Senate freshmen were obviously more politically experienced. The difference lay in the relationship between the freshman members and the party leadership. In the House many of the freshmen had been recruited by Newt Gingrich and reflected his outlook on policy and tactics. The Speaker cultivated the freshmen and paid attention to them, and as a consequence, they were his strong allies in centralizing control in the House and keeping the committee chairs in check. While that alliance was strained by the budget battle, it never broke down entirely during the 104th Congress.

In the Senate the freshmen were proportionately less of the GOP Conference (a fifth as compared to a third), so the leadership was less obliged to pay attention to them. Committee chairs were also more senior, confident, and independent in the Senate. The really crucial difference, though, was that Majority Leader Dole came from a totally different generation and had a different outlook than the Senate freshmen, and although they respected his experience and political skills, they did not have the intimacy and influence that their House counterparts had with Speaker Gingrich. As we see in the following chapter, this would change somewhat when Senator Lott replaced Senator Dole as majority leader in June of 1995.

The saving grace for the Senate freshmen was that they did not need to be intimate with the party leadership to have an impact because of the lax floor rules of the chamber. Freshman senators soon found that they could have far greater impact as individuals than in the House. They also shared the belief of their House kinsmen that although they might have lost the budget battle as a result of bad strategy and tactics, they had won the wider battle for the political direction of the country. Of course, that change in direction would be in serious jeopardy if the Republicans proved unable to hold onto the House and Senate in the 1996 congressional elections—an outcome that began to look highly possible in the immediate aftermath of the budget battle. The Republicans' struggle to hold onto their majorities on Capitol Hill and the impact that had on the freshmen is the subject of the next chapter.

6

The Struggle for Reelection

The end of the second government shutdown and the admission of defeat in the budget battle with President Clinton suddenly concentrated Republican minds on the need for reelection in November 1996. For most of 1995 the Republicans and political observers in general had assumed that the GOP would have little trouble in holding onto both houses of Congress in the 1996 congressional elections. The Democrats were still shattered by the shock of their 1994 defeat, and the large number of Democratic retirements announced in 1995 appeared to preclude a serious Democratic opportunity to grab back control of the House and presaged further Republican gains in the Senate, perhaps getting the GOP close to the magic number of sixty Senate seats required to invoke cloture. Moreover, after 1994, the Republicans also seemed to have a better than ever chance of securing complete control over the federal government by defeating the gravely wounded President Clinton.

A series of events, beginning with the Oklahoma City bombing in April 1995 and culminating in the government shutdowns at the end of the year, changed the political equation for the 1996 campaign considerably. The Oklahoma tragedy enabled President Clinton to perform the presidential role of national empathizer and healer, at which he excels, and the perpetration of the blast by right-wing extremists raised some doubts among voters about the "revolutionary" rhetoric being deployed by some of the hotheaded members of the Republican Congress and their supporters. The improving economic situation during 1995 also led to a gradual rise in the president's approval ratings, but it was the brilliant exploitation of the government shutdowns at year's end that decisively placed Clinton in the driver's seat for reelection while raising serious doubts regarding the Republican Congress in the minds of the voters. The budget battle also had highlighted the impact of the freshmen, but in a highly unflattering light as "extremists" or "radicals," and their mentor Speaker Gingrich's popularity ratings (never very high) fell to truly dismal levels in the wake of the budget debacle.

With the Democrats rejuvenated by this sudden reversal in the president's fortunes, it appeared that the first Republican Congress since 1954 might turn out to be another brief interlude (like the Republican Congresses elected in 1946 and 1952) in a long-term period of Democratic domination, with the change in the direction of public debate that the Republicans had achieved being arrested or even sent into reverse. Sensing the possibility of victory, Democratic-supporting interest groups, led by organized labor, began a large-scale advertising assault against the Republicans, particularly the electorally vulnerable House freshmen. The possibility of defeat, both at the individual level and regarding Congress as a whole, concentrated the minds of the Republican leadership and the freshmen on finding a way to reverse the tide of adverse publicity. In this chapter we see the various steps they took to recover themselves, starting with the radical lobbying and gift reforms that hearkened back to the original Republican image as reform-minded outsiders cleaning out the Augean stables in Washington. Under the leadership of their new majority leader, Trent Lott of Mississippi, the Senate Republicans also took the lead in passing a series of popular measures that showed the Republicans trying to govern responsibly, rather than irresponsibly as in shutting the government down. At the same time, the individual level freshman members worked hard to exploit their financial advantage over their Democratic challengers and to use the congressional appropriations process to provide projects and programs for their districts. Suddenly, in 1996, the Republican revolutionaries of the previous years were beginning to resemble the incumbent freshman members of the pre-1994 era as they strove mightily, district by district, to secure their reelection.

This chapter looks at the battle for control of the House and Senate in 1996 and the extent to which the Republican freshmen compromised their reforming zeal in order to get reelected. First, however, it is necessary to look at the final series of institutional reforms carried out by the Republicans, which were largely ignored in the fury of the budget battle, but which carried considerable implications for the institutional conduct of Congress.

Lobbying, Gift Giving, and the Failure of
Campaign Finance Reform

Many of the freshman Republicans had emphasized the concept of a citizen legislature in their election campaigns in 1994. Although term limits had been the most prominent item in that concept, it also encompassed an effort to bring the legislative branch closer to the voters by undertaking significant reforms in the way Congress conducted its business and precluding future scandals similar to those that bedeviled the Democratic Congress in its final years. The Republicans could certainly point to the opening-day reforms described in chapter 3—abolishing proxy voting, term limitations on the Speaker and committee chairs, reforming the committee structure, and the Congressional Accountability Act—as significant changes in the manner in which the U.S. House organizes itself. On the other hand, these matters of Capitol Hill "housecleaning," while important in institutional terms, were unlikely to be noticed by most voters. For the latter, and especially the supporters of Ross Perot who had supported the GOP in 1994, reforms dealing with the sensitive areas of lobbying and campaign finance were likely to have a far greater impact.

A widespread national consensus existed among both press and public that the campaign financing system for congressional elections, established in the wake of the Watergate scandal in 1974, had become corrupted by the large donations made to congressional candidates (and particularly incumbent members) by political action committees (PACs)—donations that allegedly gave undue influence over members of Congress to lobbyists representing those PACs in Washington. In addition to the PACs, most of the public apparently believed that Washington lobbyists used gifts and favors to members of Congress to maintain an iron grip on the legislative branch. Again, this view was particularly associated with Ross Perot and his supporters in the electorate.

While the freshmen might have expressed similar sentiments to Perot on these matters on the campaign trail, once they arrived in Washington, advocacy of major lobbying and campaign finance reform became a much more difficult matter. Senior Republicans, including the Speaker and the party leadership, were not particularly enthusiastic about campaign finance reform once the system had, at last, begun to work in their favor. Reform agitation also implicated senior Republicans in the alleged "corruption" of the Washington system that reform was intended to address. Freshman Republican and citizen legislature advocate Mark Sanford of South Carolina described how freshman Republicans who wanted serious reform of lobbying and campaign finance found themselves caught between the populism of their constituents and the reluctance of their more senior Republican colleagues:

> Every time you talk about these issues you are talking about limiting someone's career and how they raise money, and that's getting real personal. But if you go back to the guy with the pickup truck in my district, and I tell him that if someone gives me $15,000 that it doesn't influence my decision making in any way whatsoever, he's going to yell, "Bullshit!" We've got to get back to the simple, commonsense level someone like that operates on.[1]

As noted in chapter 3, the Republicans had tried and failed to pass a constitutional amendment on term limits during the "first hundred days." The defeat of term limits did not lead to an abandonment of reform in the area of lobbying members of Congress, however. After Senator John McCain of Arizona (the strongest Republican advocate in the Senate of lobbying and campaign finance reform) had secured the support of the Republican freshmen, the Senate in July 1995 passed a strict ban on privately paid "recreational" (as opposed to "informational" or "official") travel, and any gifts or meals worth more than $50, with a $100 annual limit on gifts from any one person.[2] Later in the year, again under freshman pressure in the Republican Conference, the House followed suit with an even tougher gift ban (sponsored by Speaker Gingrich) being written into the chamber's rules on 16 November. House members were now precluded from accepting any gifts or meals except from family and friends. Recreational travel paid for by lobbyists was also banned, and exceptions were made only for promotional products, such as caps and T-shirts, from members' home districts.[3]

In addition to the gift ban, the 104th Congress passed the first major reform of lobbying practices since 1946. The bill, signed by President Clinton at the end of 1995, changed the law affecting lobbying in several significant ways. First, the scope of the law was extended from members of Congress to cover those lobbying congressional staffers and executive branch officials. All lobbyists were required to register with the clerk of the House or the secretary of the Senate, to submit forms detailing their clients and contacts, and to file reports detailing their activities every six months. Lobbyists for foreign entities or U.S. subsidiaries of foreign entities would be required to register for the first time. In sum: by contrast with the widely disregarded 1946 law, all those lobbying the federal government now had to report on their activities and expenditures.[4] Again, freshman Republicans played a key role in getting a reluctant House GOP leadership to go along with the measure.[5]

But while the Republicans were generally commended in the media for the lobbying and gift reforms, on the most salient and important reform area, campaign finance, neither the freshmen nor the leadership in either chamber were any more successful in forging a consensus than their Democratic predecessors had been. Given their lesser dependence on PAC contributions, it was hardly surprising that the Senate showed more enthusiasm for major campaign finance reform than the House. The major Senate proposal sponsored by Senator McCain, freshman Republican Fred Thompson, and Wisconsin Democrat Russell Feingold was a fairly radical measure that would have banned PACs completely and imposed "voluntary" spending limits with free television and radio time and reduced mailing fees to candidates who complied. The bill actually commanded support from a majority of senators, but fell six votes short of the sixty required for cloture on 25 June 1996, largely due to the opposition of the new Senate Republican leader, Trent Lott, and a long-time Republican foe of campaign finance reform, Senator Mitch McConnell of Kentucky.[6] Only eight Republican senators supported cloture, including just two of the eleven freshmen: Fred Thompson and Olympia Snowe of Maine.

In the House, a bill similar to the McCain–Feingold measure was sponsored by long-time GOP reform advocate Christopher Shays of Connecticut, freshman Republican Linda Smith of Washington, and Massachusetts Democrat Martin Meehan. Among the freshmen, Ms. Smith, a former Washington state legislator who had won her congressional primary as a write-in candidate and who had the closest ties to Ross Perot of any of the freshman Republicans, was by far the most persistent and militant advocate of campaign finance reform, an approach that did not entirely endear her to more senior Republican colleagues.[7] The House Republican leadership generally shared these misgivings. Many, like House Appropriations chair Bob Livingston, took umbrage at the "self-righteousness" of some of the freshmen on the issue and bemoaned their advocacy of the public financing of campaigns, a position long-associated with the "good government" group Common Cause, to which many Republicans were philosophically opposed:

> Linda Smith is not typical. She's a Perot person who fits well with the Reform Party. On campaign finance reform people should stop and reflect that it's a strong indicator of a philosophical division between government control of campaigns and individual representation. The Common Cause position would give the government control of every facet of a campaign including fund raising, and that would give you elitist, centrist candidates who are exactly the type of people who make up the membership of Common Cause. Reformers who emphasize disclosure, on the other hand, aren't concerned with the amount of money in campaigns but want to make sure that the voter knows who's backing candidates. Anything that deviates from that philosophical division, or a person whose agenda departs from those two positions, is demagoging the issue in my opinion. Such a person doesn't understand the philosophical division and doesn't want to.[8]

Livingston's philosophical objection to the prohibition of PACs and the introduction of public financing was shared by Rules Committee Republican David Dreier:

> I don't see raising PAC money, for example, as evil. You can't juxtapose campaign finance reform with taxpayer funding of campaigns. I am a vigorous opponent of that. Money in campaigns is not evil as long as you have full disclosure. You've got a well of cynicism from the fourth estate, but you can argue that PACs help to get people involved and participating in politics. They are probably something like Madison had in mind in *Federalist No. 10,* when he talked about people coalescing around a common interest.[9]

Other members of the leadership were concerned that the Smith–Shays proposals would eliminate the newfound Republican advantage from PACs and thereby enhance the Democrats' chances of recapturing the House. Science Committee chair and Gingrich confidante Bob Walker shared this concern:

> A handful of them have pushed even further and, in some cases, our freshman colleagues' willingness to talk about changes has gone overboard. Some of the suggested campaign finance reforms would endan-

ger Republicans and enhance the positions of the Democrats. Those changes would leave the Democrats with union support, while we would lose our base support.[10]

A House Republican leadership task force on congressional reform, chaired by sophomore Peter Hoekstra of Michigan, rejected the Smith–Shays proposals in its January 1996 report. Under pressure from freshman members, however, the group did feel obliged to recommend some changes in the status quo in order to demonstrate Republican concern on the issue. They recommended lowering the limit on PAC contributions to candidates from $5,000 to $1,000 and a doubling of the limit on individual contributions to $2,000. The GOP task force agreed with the Smith–Shays proposal in one regard: candidates should be required to raise over half their funds in their own districts.[11]

A countervailing force to the need to follow press and public opinion by seriously addressing the reform issue, however, was the advantages that Republicans were now reaping from PAC donations due to incumbency, and the heavy spending by Democrat-supporting groups, particularly organized labor, against vulnerable Republican incumbents.[12] These factors had mitigated much of the enthusiasm for campaign finance reform among the freshmen, who, facing tight races, were the recipients of much of this PAC largesse.[13]

Despite these reservations, Speaker Gingrich, who had promised publicly to address campaign finance reform after a meeting with President Clinton in New Hampshire in June 1995, decided that the Republicans had to show some willingness to address the issue. In May 1996 the Speaker went further than the Hoekstra report and urged an outright ban on PAC contributions, even though the Republicans were now the primary recipients of PAC dollars. Needless to say this commanded nothing like a consensus within the divided House Republican Conference.[14] While the radical Smith–Shays measure had been killed off by the failure of its Senate counterpart in June, the leadership decided to bring a campaign finance reform measure to the floor during "reform week" on 18 July. This bill retained the Shays bill's limit on raising funds outside a candidate's district, raised the individual contribution limit to $2,500 while lowering the PAC limit to the same figure, and raised the maximum annual amount individuals could contribute to candidates, PACs, and parties from $25,000 to $72,500 (indexed for inflation). The proposals also banned "leadership PACs," which members of Congress use to raise money for distribution to their fellow partisans, and allowed candidates to exceed the contribution limits if they were being outspent by an opponent's personal funds. Finally, in a strike against organized labor's heavy spending against the Republicans, the GOP proposal would have required union members to provide written agreements before their dues could be used as political contributions.[15]

The last item guaranteed united Democratic opposition, the raising of the maximum limits for individuals infuriated the media and supporters of the Smith–Shays proposals, and senior Republicans saw little need to change the status quo. As a result, "reform week" transpired to be an almighty flop as the Republican leadership pulled its bill from the floor on 17 July, realizing that it faced a humiliating defeat.[16] In the following week the bill was modified some more to take account of GOP objections—the individual contribution limit went down to $1,000 (indexed for inflation) again, and the aggregate individual limits went down to $50,000—but it still was insufficient to win over Democrats, militant GOP reformers, northeastern Republicans who feared further provoking organized labor, or senior Republicans who were skeptical of the whole enterprise.[17] When the bill finally came to the floor on 25 July it was easily defeated 162–259, with sixty-eight Republicans voting against, including twenty-five freshmen (more than a third of the class).[18]

With the fizzling out of campaign finance reform, the institutional reform efforts of the freshman Republicans more or less came to a close. The approach of the election had diverted their attention to other matters, and the decision to address campaign finance reform so late in the Congress, rather than in the first flush of revolutionary zeal, had guaranteed that the enterprise would fail despite the determined efforts of dedicated Republican reformers such as John McCain and Chris Shays, and enthusiastic freshman members such as Fred Thompson in the Senate and Linda Smith in the House. Campaign finance reform became caught up in the politics of reelection and maintaining control of the House in the face of the Democratic-labor onslaught, which came to predominate over the politics of reform in the second session of the 104th Congress. The last word on the issue goes to the disappointed reformer Chris Shays, who saw the defeat of reform as a sign that the freshman Republicans were "sadly" becoming acculturated to the ways of Washington:

One year ago the freshmen were a major force for reform, now I would say, somewhat sadly, that they have been absorbed by the system. Reform reached its limits after one year and now they seem to have abandoned and rejected reform—especially campaign finance reform. I'm not even sure that we could pass the accountability legislation, the gift ban, and lobby reform today. None of that would have happened if it hadn't been done early on. The longer you're here, the more you're influenced by contacts and lobbyists who become your friends, and then you're not so keen to want to change things.[19]

Back to Grassroots Politics: "All Politics Is Local"

From the previous section it is clear that if 1995 was the year of ideological "revolution" and reform of Washington as far as the Republican freshmen were concerned, in 1996 the traditional House imperatives of fund raising and close attention to district concerns became paramount. The budget battle had clearly demonstrated the limitations of the Republicans' ideological message of budget balancing and returning power to the states and local governments, and while the Republican record on institutional reform was reasonably impressive, the danger remained that the freshmen's reputation as bold reformers would be superseded by their actions during the government shutdown. Indeed, the statements and actions of some of the more militant freshmen during the budget debate had identified the entire class with a "hard-line," "radical," or "extremist" position. Shortly after the end of the shutdown, a poll conducted by Louis Harris and Associates for *Business Week* at the end of January 1996 found that while 49 percent of the respondents still found the House GOP freshmen to be "a new breed of politicians who are trying to keep their promises," 45 percent considered them to be "extremists."[20]

The Democrats and organized labor were certainly well aware of the opportunity that the budget battle had given them to regain control of the House in November 1996. The AFL–CIO had been running television and radio ads in several Republican-held House districts since the summer of 1995, and in March 1996 the federation's new president, John Sweeney, announced that the unions would spend $35 million in a special "educational" effort to oust the Republicans, with most of the money to be raised by a special assessment of union members.[21] Most of these funds were specifically directed against freshman Republican members, forty-four (or 62 percent) of whom were targeted by the AFL–CIO, as opposed to only 14 percent of senior Republicans.[22] Republican reform advocate Chris Shays commented on the degree to which the approaching 1996 elections and the labor offensive diminished the freshman Republicans' enthusiasm for reform:

> Because the freshmen came here to change things, but public perceptions of them didn't turn out the way they expected, they are feeling shell-shocked and battered. It's hard for a freshman member to go back into the district on a Friday, turn on the TV set, and watch commercials saying: "Representative So and So wants to cut Medicare, Medicaid, and Food Stamps." They've been brutalized by labor. And when labor has six people working full-time for your defeat and going around your district spreading lies, the freshman member will say, "How can I be for campaign finance reform when I need more money, not less, to defend myself?"[23]

For Arizona freshman J.D. Hayworth, one of the most heavily targeted Republican incumbents, campaign finance reform had become secondary to the broader goal of holding on to the House:

> Some people are so caught up in dogma that they are willing to unilaterally disarm. If you want the genuine flavor of reform, they should stay with us, because if you let the other guys back, it will be like the Romans to the Carthaginians. You'll never see reform, but you'll see flourishing unions, and those guys are cynical, tough, ward heelers. It's tough to conduct things in a spirit of comity, when you see how political debate is conducted at such Orwellian depths.[24]

Congressional Democrats, after a year in the doldrums, also began to get their act together by papering over their ideological differences, rallying behind the president and taking every opportunity in both House and Senate to deride the Republicans as extremists and introduce legislation designed to divide or embarrass the Republican majority.[25] A particular target of labor and Democratic attacks was Speaker Gingrich, whose own comments and actions during the budget debate had hardly endeared him to the American public. The Speaker's public approval sank to abysmal levels during the budget debate and was augmented by a prolonged investigation by the House Ethics Committee of charges brought by Democratic Minority Whip David Bonior relating to the tax-exempt status of GOPAC, the Speaker's organization to recruit and train Republican candidates.[26] In a deliberate effort to damage the Republicans electorally by discrediting Gingrich, Bonior filed a barrage of charges against the Speaker to the Ethics Committee throughout 1995 and 1996, eventually resulting in the appointment of a special counsel to investigate and report on Gingrich's ties to GOPAC.[27] District by district the Democrats also sought relentlessly to tie Republican incumbents and candidates to the unpopular Speaker.[28] To a large extent the strategy succeeded, since Gingrich was forced to lower his public profile; furthermore, in March 1996 he carried out a "reallocation of duties" that turned much of the day-to-day running of the House over to his deputy, Dick Armey.[29]

Gingrich's ambivalent relationship with the freshmen had become evident during the budget debate, when his eagerness to reopen the government had angered some of the more hard-line conservatives in that group.[30] His actions during that period had also aroused doubts about his judgment and leadership among the class as a whole (see chapter 3). But, ironically, with one or two exceptions, the Democratic and labor assault on their leader probably served to strengthen support for the embattled Speaker among the freshmen, as Congressman Hayworth's comments above indicate. There was also the fund-raising factor, for while the Speaker had become deeply unpopular among voters in general, he remained very popular among Republican grassroots activists and was a most formidable fund raiser for Republican candidates, including the House freshmen. In January 1996, when Gingrich was at a low ebb in the polls following the government shutdown, he netted $3.2 million at fund raisers for GOP candidates, including twenty-five freshmen.[31]

Whatever their personal feelings or sense of gratitude toward the Speaker, however, many freshman members in marginal or Democratic-leaning districts targeted by the AFL–CIO felt the pressure to demonstrate some independence from the controversial Gingrich. Iowa's Greg Ganske began spending heavily on television advertising to counter the union ads in the spring of 1996, in an effort to demonstrate to his constituents that he was "Not a Newtoid."[32] Around the same time, a number of freshman members began regularly voting against approving the journal of the preceding day's House session to magnify their percentage of votes cast in opposition to the Speaker.[33] In general, the historic levels of Republican unity displayed in the first session of the 104th Congress showed a marked drop-off by the middle of the 1996 session, with northeastern members (including freshmen) being particularly likely to defect on issues such as the environment and gun control.[34]

The "mellowing" of the freshmen was a generally noted phenomenon in the aftermath of the budget debacle, as the more traditional conservatives and moderates within the group began to assert themselves against the vocal and militant minority of hard-liners that had defined the class up to that point.[35] One indication of the change was the election of a more low-key, pragmatic, and consensus-oriented Californian, George Radanovich, as class president for the second session of the 104th Congress, over the younger, more vocal, and more militant Joe Scarborough of Florida. Like many of the less visible freshmen, Radanovich had spent his first year trying to secure his House seat, before he turned his attention to broader matters:

> In my first year I wanted to get a firm foundation, so I spent more time in the district clearing my campaign debt, raising money, and scaring off opposition. Once I had a safe seat, I had more time to spend on other projects. I ran for class president because Roger Wicker [of Mississippi] was standing down after having agreed to do it for only one year.[36]

Congressman Radanovich tried to refocus the freshman class on issues of common agreement and concern, and he set up a series of four "task forces" on "vision/message," "incumbent retention," "legislation," and "communications" to achieve this end:

> I would get back to the balanced budget issue, and not get bogged down in superfluous issues like the minimum wage. We need to talk about restructuring society and keep the dialogue within that realm. We need to stress the themes that keep us focused on our objective.[37]

At the district level, freshman members adopted a variety of approaches tailored to their individual constituencies. Many, such as Wisconsin's Mark Neumann, were unrepentant about their uncompromising attitude to the budget debate and campaigned for reelection on the basis of their integrity and fealty to the promises they had made in 1994.[38] Maryland's Bob Ehrlich, although less outspoken than Congressman Neumann, shared his Wisconsin's colleague's approach to reelection:

My approach has always been, "This is what I think. If you like it, vote for me, and if you don't, don't." The country will still go on if I'm not in Congress. A congressional career is not so important to me that I am willing to say or do anything to stay here. When I get letters saying, "I will not vote for you," I reply, "Please do not vote for me, and don't expect me to lie to you." Some people are taken aback by that, but while I am honored to be here, my life is not identified with being in the U.S. Congress.[39]

Californian Brian Bilbray emphasized how the freshmen had actually kept their promises to reform Congress:

We can say that we were sent to Washington and we started the process of changing Washington. We've done things that other people only talked about. We brought things like the gift ban and proxy voting. My God! The ice isn't delivered to each office anymore![40]

Joe Scarborough of Florida and Oklahoma's J.C. Watts also stressed integrity and fidelity to promises as the key themes in their reelection races:

After all, all they [the freshmen] have done is what they said they were going to do. I go to town-hall meetings and I tell them, "This is what I'm going to do, and if you don't like it, you can vote for somebody else." That is such a new concept: that a politician tells you exactly what they're going to do, and then does exactly that. This is where the Contract with America is a positive for us, and, in fact, the Contract may be more important in 1996 than it was in 1994, because we can say we promised A, B, C, and D, and look at what we did. The only challenge will be to neutralize the Democrats on the issue of Medicare. In my congressional district, I did it by holding Medicare town-hall meetings all over the district, and demonstrating that the facts on that issue are on our side.[41]

The American people admire and respect the fact that someone gets out there and fights. It's like the old fighter who gets up off the canvas and wins the fight. That's the American way. We believe that a majority can be wrong, and you have to keep fighting. Sooner or later someone is going to say, "He's right. He makes sense." We've already saved the American people $83 billion, and the deficit is lower today that it has been for fourteen years. In the fall we can say, "We wanted something done and we did it."[42]

Other freshmen began to pay more close attention to "traditional" pork-barrel politics in an election year. While many freshmen had associated the delivery of programs and projects for individual districts with the "corruption" of Congress under Democratic rule, they were not impervious to similar activities in the heated preelection atmosphere that surrounded the House following the budget debacle. For freshman members targeted by labor or in tough reelection fights, "bringing home the bacon" assumed an additional importance, and the appropriations bills for FY 1997 were stuffed with projects in the districts of GOP freshman members at the urging of the Republican leadership.[43] Several agencies and programs survived the budgetary ax because GOP members, under electoral pressure, had found them to be highly popular in their districts.[44] Ohio freshman Steve LaTourette from suburban Cleveland cited the National Endowment for the Arts (NEA) as an example:

> On Arts funding, I don't want to give tax dollars to someone who urinates in a bottle over a crucifix and calls it art, but the NEA funds the Cleveland Orchestra to visit schools in my district, so kids can experience the Cleveland Orchestra.[45]

As mentioned in the last section, the Republican House freshmen had not been shy about building formidable reelection warchests by exploiting the advantages of incumbency. Prior to 1994, incumbency had particularly benefited Democrats in raising money from political action committees (PACs). As soon as the Republicans gained control of the House in 1995, the GOP leadership was determined to reverse that situation, and House Majority Whip Tom DeLay led the effort to put pressure on business PACs to change their pattern of giving to the benefit of the new majority. In return for generous donations, lobbyists and PAC representatives were given access to Republican leaders and committee chairs and consulted on legislation.[46] Freshman members were also encouraged by the National Republican Campaign Committee (NRCC), chaired by Congressman Bill Paxon of New York, to begin setting fund-raising targets for 1996 and tapping their 1994 donors right away.[47]

These efforts paid off in spectacular fashion. In 1993–94, Democrats held a 65–34 percent advantage over Republicans in donations from the top 400 PACs, but in the first six months of 1995, this changed to a 53–47 percent Republican advantage.[48] The Republican freshmen had also followed their leaders' advice to a T, despite some strong hostility toward PACs among certain members of the class. By the end of March 1996, freshman Republicans running for reelection had raised an average of $384,000, compared to their Democratic challengers' average of $68,500. In terms of PAC donations, the Republican freshman advantage was even more pronounced—a nine-to-one advantage in average PAC donations of $139,000 to $12,500 over their Democratic challengers.[49] Although improved Democratic fund raising after the government shutdown had opened up the possibility of a Democratic Congress and heavy "independent" expenditures by organized labor in targeted districts partly compensated for this advantage, the boot was now firmly on the other foot as far as the partisan advantage in campaign spending was concerned.

In the wake of the public relations disaster of the government shutdown, the House Republican freshmen were thus obliged to return to the kind of grassroots politics of constituent service, the pork barrel, and campaign fund raising that had characterized their Democratic predecessors. It would not be fair or accurate to describe this as an entirely voluntary development for a class that had regarded itself as bold political reformers, and some of whom felt very strongly indeed on the issue of campaign finance reform, but the sudden possibility of defeat and a Democratic House compelled the freshmen to engage in frenetic fund-raising activity and pay stronger attention to their districts. The exigencies of reelection thus were a large part of the explanation for the much lower profile of the Republican freshmen in Washington in 1996: first, because they were too busy dealing with district- and reelection-related matters to expend their energies on grand revolutionary designs for reshaping the American federal government; and second, because their public profile during the budget debate had gotten too high for their own good. Not just in the areas of campaign finance but across the whole policy spectrum, the freshmen's enthusiasm for reform had greatly diminished as they were thrown on the political defensive. The demands of electoral survival were now paramount.

A Change in Strategy: Trent Lott and the New Spirit of Bipartisanship

The spring of 1996 was not a happy time for the Republicans in Congress. In the wake of the budget battle, they had completely lost momentum and were under heavy fire from both the Democrats and the labor unions. The major beneficiary of the budget battle was President Clinton, who, with the help of a booming economy and Republican ineptitude, was now enjoying a substantial lead in the opinion polls over his Republican challenger, Senator Dole. Dole had easily won the Republican nomination during the front-loaded primary season in March 1996, when it became clear that his principal opponents would be millionaire publisher Steve Forbes and right-wing television commentator Pat Buchanan, neither of whom was regarded as a plausible Republican nominee. The Senate majority leader also succeeded in part because of the overwhelming degree of support he had from party elites—including the Republican members of Congress.[50] In the end, Dole won the nomination because he was the candidate acceptable to all the Republican factions—traditional Republican conservatives, supply-siders, the religious right, and Buchananite populists—but the Forbes and Buchanan challenges had brutally exposed Dole's weaknesses: his age, his image as a Washington insider, and his reputation as a pragmatic Capitol Hill "deal maker," uninterested in and unsympathetic toward the broader ideas and themes of the 1994 "Republican revolution." The outsiders—Steve Forbes with his radical plan for a flat tax and the abolition of the IRS, and Buchanan with his melange of protectionism, anti-Washington rhetoric, and traditional social conservatism directed at white working-class voters—both in their different ways were closer to the revolutionary spirit of 1994 than Dole.[51]

The other problem for the prospective nominee occurred back on his home turf, the U.S. Senate. Once it became clear that Dole would be the Republican nominee, the Senate Democrats deliberately began to obstruct Senate business by systematically reintroducing a series of amendments to bills on the Senate floor that were intended to divide the GOP and embarrass Dole.[52] Tapping into the working- and middle-class economic anxiety reflected in the Buchanan candidacy, and the Republicans' persistent public image as the party of the advantaged (reinforced, of course, by the government shutdown), Democrats now demanded Senate floor votes on issues that were popular with voters but not with Republicans—particularly a rise in the minimum wage and a bill sponsored by Democratic Senator Edward Kennedy and Republican Nancy Kassebaum of Kansas to allow employees changing jobs to retain their health insurance coverage. The strategy succeeded brilliantly in keeping Dole entangled in Washington, dealing with essentially "no-win" issues.[53]

Meanwhile, on the House side, the shell-shocked Republican leaders had still not recovered any sense of direction, and instead of dictating the course of events they were now at the mercy of external forces, such as the Senate Democrats, the labor unions, and restive conservative interest groups. Against the judgment of Speaker Gingrich, the National Rifle Association (NRA) forced a successful House vote to repeal the popular ban on assault weapons contained in Clinton's 1994 crime bill (which Dole made clear he had no intention of introducing in the Senate) and only succeeded in embarrassing many endangered northeastern Republican moderates.[54] The NRA played a further role in the House's rejection of the major provisions in Clinton's antiterrorism bill, which had been largely endorsed by Dole and the GOP Senate.[55] A determined minority of mainly freshmen members also continued to agitate against leadership-backed compromises on the budget, culminating in a vote on a six-year Dole-inspired Republican deficit-reduction package in June, where nineteen Republicans, including sixteen freshmen, voted against the leadership on the grounds that the package included unacceptable increases in spending. The leadership was able to prevail only after intense lobbying of wavering freshmen.[56] Congressman Mark Sanford, who eventually backed the leadership, discussed how the freshmen were torn between their 1994 "mandate" and the changed political atmosphere of 1996:

> It's impossible to detach yourself from the presidential nominee, but maybe you should. In the first year here you deal with policy, and in year two with politics. That seems to be the cycle Congress runs on. If I confine myself to my mandate and look at the little guy with the pickup truck, and think about adding $4 billion to the deficit, I'd vote no [against the budget package]. My conclusion, though, is that until you control all three bodies of the federal government, you can't do anything about the deficit.[57]

Yet for all this agitation on the right wing of the freshman class, it also became apparent that many northeastern Republican incumbents (including freshmen), under severe pressure from organized labor, were finding it politically impossible to resist the Democratic demand for a minimum-wage increase.[58]

As the Democrats and the news media utilized every opportunity to brand the Republicans as extremist, they now faced the additional danger of being branded as incompetents by the public. Given the failure of most of the Contract measures to pass the Senate or obtain the presidential signature, the Republican congressional leaders found themselves dangerously short of a substantial record of legislative accomplishments to present to the voters. Of course this accusation was somewhat unjust, since in addition to their substantial institutional reforms and forcing Clinton to agree to a seven-year balanced budget with substantial spending reduction, the Republican Congress had also passed (and Clinton signed into law) both a radical farm bill promising the eventual phasing out of government supports for agriculture and a massive and extremely important telecommunications bill transforming the role of government in regulating the "third wave" of communications technology.[59] But these measures, though important, were not at the very center of the Republican legislative agenda, like welfare reform, immigration reform, and the balanced budget, and it was here that the Republicans' failure to deliver was earning criticism from commentators on all points of the political spectrum in the spring of 1996.[60]

The Republican leadership in the House had attempted to deal with the situation with a widely advertised "reallocation of duties" in March 1996 as the unpopular Speaker Gingrich announced that he was handing over day-to-day management of the House to his deputy, Majority Leader Dick Armey, while Gingrich would concentrate on national campaigning.[61] Given Gingrich's unpopularity with voters and Armey's reputation as a conservative ideologue, this arrangement did not immediately appear to make much strategic sense, although it probably appeased discontent among conservative freshmen, who had come to trust Armey more than Gingrich.[62] Conservatives David McIntosh and David Funderburk typified the discontent with the leadership among the more conservative freshmen:

> Right now the leadership has fallen into the classic error of Washington politics of re-fighting the last battle, and if you do that in campaigns, you lose. We've used a defensive strategy in 1996, based on our 1995 defeat in the budget debate. The result has been a failure to set the agenda going into the next election in 1996 and shape a majority in the House and Senate. We should pass bills that define us against Bill Clinton, but instead we're passing bills that are more likely to muddle the distinctions.[63]

> We [the freshmen] have been branded as "goats" because we "don't understand compromise" and cut deals. We haven't been represented in the best way by our leadership, which is more susceptible to compromise. The leadership has been saying one thing and doing another. Gingrich realized he couldn't do everything, and he decided to sit back and be the idea man, and leave Armey as the legislative manager and implementer.[64]

Among the more moderate members of the class, however, there appeared to be less hostility toward the leadership, although in the midst of the heated debates over the minimum wage, there was some concern that with the top three leadership positions all being held by southerners—a Georgian and two Texans—there was a lack of sensitivity to the concerns of more northern members. Ray LaHood of Illinois felt quite strongly on this issue:

> It's a serious problem. The leadership should be more reflective of the country geographically and philosophically, and of the Conference. We're not all conservatives and we're not all southerners. There's a big difference in points of view and a big difference in expertise, and I know other members feel the same way.[65]

LaHood, and two other prominent moderate members, Tom Campbell of California and Steve LaTourette of Ohio, were keen to stress, however, that Speaker Gingrich, in contrast to his public profile as an intolerant and indignant ideologue, had gone out of his way to be responsive to their concerns. In contrast to the conservative members, they were effusive in their defense of their embattled leader:

> On the other hand, the Speaker has attempted to be tolerant of different points of view, and he has been very open-minded. He has an open-door policy, and he is very approachable, although in the end he has the authority to decide what to do. He's a good listener and he wants to hear all sides. Of the 435 members of the House, Newt Gingrich is one of the hardest-working members we have here. He works longer hours and is totally dedicated and immersed in his job. So I give him high marks for being a strong Speaker who is open to both sides.[66]

The media perception of the leaders as extremists is quite wrong. The leadership has held together a diverse Republican majority, and they know that we will have a majority only so long as they have the skills to hold it together. For example, Newt Gingrich did not want a vote to repeal the assault weapons' ban, but he had no choice after a discharge petition was started and the NRA was gathering signatures.[67]

The Speaker has taken a very bad public relations beating. In fact, Newt Gingrich is very pragmatic in private, and his personal manner would surprise most people who say they don't like Newt Gingrich. The Speaker said it was immoral to shut down the government, and he rose and introduced legislation to get the CR up and running, and some of the most conservative members of the conference didn't respond. On the minimum wage I wrote a note and told the Speaker that the best speech he had ever given was to the House conference meeting where he got up and said, "Look, you very conservative members are a majority of the conference, but you need the moderate members to make you a majority in the House of Representatives, and if you don't find common ground you'll again be a minority in the House." That was something that had to be said, and the Speaker said it.[68]

On the Senate side, the major change was Dole's decision in early May to resign from the chamber to concentrate on his presidential campaign.[69] Dole had tried to remain as majority leader and set the legislative agenda from the Senate, but the obstructionism of the Democratic minority had created an embarrassing situation for the nominee as they purposely blocked all of his initiatives on the Senate floor.[70] Dole was succeeded by his deputy, Majority Whip Trent Lott, who easily defeated his only challenger, his fellow Mississippi senator and GOP Conference chair, Thad Cochran. Lott, who had served with Gingrich in the House during the 1980s, was regarded by Washington commentators as more ideologically aligned with the "radical" agenda of the House Republicans, although his political career also revealed a strong pragmatic streak that was hardly characteristic of the public profile of the House freshmen.

In fact, with Dole's resignation and Gingrich still badly wounded in the polls, Lott became the de facto leader of the demoralized congressional GOP.[71] Certainly leadership was needed, for by midsummer the Republicans were drifting badly and looking toward their presidential nominee for direction—direction that the pragmatic Washington insider Bob Dole was unable to provide. This perception was held by the freshman members in both Houses, who were highly concerned by the apparent lack of an agenda from Bob Dole or any other national Republican leader. Conservative freshman Lindsey Graham of Georgia expressed his frustrations with the party's presidential nominee:

> We'd better come up with an agenda. Bob Dole had failed to express how the United States would be different with him as president. I can answer, but Bob Dole can't answer. It's got to be an agenda close to why we got elected in 1994. He needs to take stands on issues. Hell, I don't know where he stands now. Bill Clinton is beatable, but I couldn't have gotten elected in 1994 unless I stood for something.[72]

Graham's exasperation was shared by Senate freshman John Ashcroft of Missouri and his chief of staff, David Ayres:

> Now we have to juxtapose that period where we knew where we were going, when the Contract drove the Senate business as well (whether the senators admit it or not), with the present, where we are having this constant debate and quarreling over what issues to focus on: whether we should put distance between ourselves and the Democrats, or minimize the differences. Part of the problem is that we haven't decided what our approach or our agenda is. We need a battle plan, and the best thing the House did was to put that battle plan forward as a road map for us. Now we are looking at the presidential campaign to provide leadership and an agenda. We need again a very issue-oriented, idea-oriented approach.[73]

In fact, it was the pragmatic rather than the programmatic route that was espoused by Senator Lott and House Republican leaders, as the remainder of the 104th Congress was characterized by a series of compromises with the Clinton White House designed to give the beleaguered Republican incumbents a record to run on in the fall campaign. Although the Dole presidential campaign was hoping that Congress would send measures to Clinton that he would veto in order to demonstrate the president's "ineffectiveness," the congressional leaders felt obliged to guard their own flanks and take some credit for major legislation.[74] Thus, the summer of 1996 saw a flurry of major legislation being passed before Congress adjourned so that members could go home and campaign, including a radical welfare reform; a rise in the minimum wage; the Kennedy–Kassebaum bill on health insurance portability, immigration reform, and a renewal of the Safe

Drinking Water Act.[75] The Republican congressional leaders also reached agreement with the administration on a stopgap budget for FY 1997 that maintained most of the president's spending preferences. On each of these measures the Republicans were required to give some ground to ensure passage through both houses and a presidential signature.

Their greatest triumph was on the welfare bill, where they were able to put pressure on Clinton, who had vetoed two earlier versions of welfare reform, by finally sending him a slightly modified version of the Senate bill without the Medicaid cuts and including some money to the states for children, but still including the transformation of AFDC into a block grant, the five-year cutoff, and the "workfare" requirements from the earlier bill.[76] The president, saddled by his commitment to "end welfare as we know it" and unwilling to concede any of the center ground in the presidential race, signed the measure after some agonizing. Both Clinton and the GOP Congress therefore gained from the passage of welfare reform at the expense of the hapless Bob Dole.[77]

On the minimum wage, unrelenting Democratic and labor pressure finally forced the Republicans to back down and accept a compromise package linking an increase of ninety cents an hour in the minimum wage to a package of business tax breaks.[78] On the Kennedy–Kassebaum health insurance "portability" measure, agreement was held up for weeks as the House argued for the inclusion in the bill of provision for tax-free Medical Savings Accounts (MSAs): policies that would allow individuals to supplement high-deductible health insurance plans with savings accounts for lesser medical expenses. Democrats feared that such accounts would siphon the healthy and wealthy out of traditional insurance plans and thereby leave more expensive premiums for those remaining. In the end a compromise was reached in conference to establish a limited MSA program, capped at 750,000 policies.[79] On immigration reform, a bill combining restrictions on both legal and illegal immigration had been divided late in 1995 when it became clear that there was significant opposition to restricting legal immigration in Republican ranks.[80] The final bill that passed in late September 1996 and was signed into law by Clinton dropped many of the more draconian Republican proposals and concentrated on toughening the exclusion and deportation of illegal immigrants.[81] The drinking-water bill became very important to the Republicans because of the terrible publicity they had received on environmental issues following Tom DeLay's deregulatory riders in the 1995 budget, and was passed and signed by Clinton in the late July blizzard of legislative activity that also included the health insurance, welfare, and minimum-wage bills.[82] Environmental concerns also surfaced in the decision to compromise with the White House in the FY 1997 appropriations bills. The GOP leadership, desperate to wind up business and allow its members to get home to campaign, agreed to an additional $6.5 billion in domestic spending demanded by Clinton and provided additional funds in the electorally sensitive areas of the environment and education.[83]

In all of the above measures, the Republicans, while gaining several of their objectives, had been forced to make substantial concessions to Clinton, who, with a commanding lead in the presidential campaign, had recovered the initiative in Washington and with the aid of the Senate Democrats was once again able to set the legislative agenda in the wake of the government shutdown. By compromising with Clinton, the Republicans, of course, were vindicating the president's claims to represent the center ground in American politics and depriving their presidential nominee of valuable ammunition to use against the incumbent. The only areas where the Republicans were able to embarrass Clinton somewhat were forcing the president to veto a ban on "partial birth abortions" (a particularly gruesome surgical procedure), and to sign a federal Defense of Marriage Act (or DOMA) that prohibited federal recognition of gay unions and infuriated many of Clinton's liberal and gay supporters.[84] Neither measure made enough of a public impact to assist Dole substantially, however.

By compromising with Clinton in the final, critical weeks of the 104th Congress, the Republicans had left behind the unrelenting revolutionary spirit of the 1995 session, and the freshmen, instead of being in the conservative ideological vanguard, were largely swallowing these compromises in a last-ditch effort to save their seats. The deals on the above legislation were negotiated by the congressional party leadership alone, particularly by Senate Leader Lott. Unlike 1995, the freshmen had no seat at the table, and aside from a relatively small group of conservative dissenters, generally kept quiet as the bills were passed and signed and then rushed to take credit for them with their constituents. The political education of the freshmen that had begun during the budget battle of 1995 was completed in the late summer and fall of 1996. The final section of this chapter discusses the 1996 campaign and the success of the House Republican freshmen in retaining their seats.

The General Election Campaign and Results

The Republican general election campaign in 1996 was an exercise in dissociating the presidential race from the battle to hold on to Congress. This was true not only of congressional candidates seeking to distance themselves from the losing presidential campaign of Bob Dole, but also the Dole campaign's seeking to isolate itself from the "extremist" image of the congressional Republicans and especially the unpopular Newt Gingrich. Thus, at the Republican National Convention in San Diego in July, there was little talk of "revolution" and the Contract with America, and there was a minimal presence by the Republican congressional leaders at the convention's podium during prime-time viewing hours except on the second night of the convention when Congresswoman (and House GOP conference secretary) Susan Molinari delivered the keynote address (aimed more at extolling Dole and appealing to women voters, not at defending the record of the GOP Congress). On the same evening, the youthful and telegenic House Budget chair, John Kasich, and Congressmen J.C. Watts (the only House freshman to address the convention in prime time), Henry Bonilla of Texas, and Texas Senator Kay Bailey Hutchison also made prime-time appearances to demonstrate the party's concern for women, minorities, and baby boomers, rather than to defend Congress. Although Speaker Gingrich was named "permanent chairman" of the convention, his appearances at the podium were brief, and what remarks he did make were directed at softening Congress's harsh public image.[85]

But as Dole conspicuously failed to offer a really serious challenge to Clinton in the polls, Republican congressional candidates returned the favor by increasingly separating themselves from the Dole ticket. Instead of the united partisan effort of the Reagan-Bush years, in 1996 the Republicans more closely resembled the Democrats of that period as they sought to minimize the impact of a likely presidential landslide for the opposing party in their districts. In short: if 1994 had been about "nationalizing" congressional elections, 1996 was about localizing and individualizing each race as far as the Republicans were concerned. The main focus of the partisan battle in 1996 was for control of the House. With the economy booming, the world at peace, and Bob Dole proving to be a less than stellar presidential candidate, Clinton seemed assured of reelection to the presidency. In the Senate races, barring a complete electoral disaster, the Republicans also appeared likely to prevail. Of the thirty-four Senate seats up for reelection, nineteen were held by Republicans and fifteen by the Democrats. Moreover, of the thirteen "open seats" created by retirements, eight were held by Democrats, and four of those were in the South—Alabama, Arkansas, Louisiana, and Georgia—the GOP's region of fastest electoral growth nationally, and therefore highly vulnerable.

In the House, with the Democrats needing a net pick up of only twenty seats for control, the situation was much more serious for the Republicans. Generic ballot tests throughout 1996 had shown a slight Democratic advantage in most polls, and the Republicans were still reeling from the electoral assault by organized labor and the fallout from the government shutdown. The major advantages the Republicans had were again in the areas of open seats and candidate recruitment. As in the Senate, there were more Democratic retirements, 29–21, from the 104th Congress than Republicans, and nineteen of the twenty-nine Democratic retirements were, again, in the Democrats' weakest region, the South. Moreover, in terms of experience in elective office—the best measure of candidate quality—the Democrats had also fallen short in their candidate recruitment.[86] In fact, many of the Democratic retirements and recruitment decisions had been made in 1995, when the Republicans were riding high and prior to the GOP public relations disaster of the government shutdown.[87] While this gave a distinct advantage to the Republicans, the battle for the House remained tight throughout the fall campaign.

The contest to control the Congress, of course, focused on the seventy-three Republican freshmen, forty-three of whom (59 percent) had won with less than 55 percent of the vote in 1994, and seventy of whom were running for reelection in 1996.[88] These races were also the main focus of labor's $35 million television advertising campaign to unseat Republicans. Forty-four freshman Republican members were the targets of at least one AFL–CIO television advertisement, and of the twenty-four Republicans who were labor's prime targets, twenty-one (or 88 percent) were freshmen.[89] Several freshman members, such as Michigan's Dick Chrysler and Bill Martini of New Jersey, who represented northern districts with a strong labor presence, were particularly conspicuous targets of the unions' efforts.[90]

Of course, as indicated earlier, the Republicans were not exactly defenseless regarding financial resources for the fall campaign. The freshmen had outraised their challengers by 9:1 in terms of PAC donations by the end of March 1996, and even though the Democrats closed the gap, the median House freshman Republican had raised $850,000 by mid-October to the median Democratic challenger's $400,000, and twenty-two of the freshmen had raised more than $1 million.[91] From April 1996 onward, the Republican National Committee and the National Republican Congressional Committee were airing ads to answer the labor barrage, with the NRCC ultimately outspending its Democratic counterpart by $27.4 million to $10.3 million.[92] While Republican National Chairman Haley Barbour had been criticized by many freshmen for not responding to labor earlier, the consequence of his strategy was that the Republicans had a large amount of cash available to be spent in the critical final weeks of the campaign in order to try and save the Republican House.[93] Finally, thirty-one business organizations came together in a group known as "The Coalition" to help Republicans who were under fire from labor with a $7 million ad campaign in thirty-three House districts, and the Christian Coalition spent $10 million and distributed 46 million "voter guides" to help the Republicans.[94]

Republican candidates were well aware that the floundering Dole presidential campaign had become something of a liability, so they began to take some pains to distance themselves from the nominee.[95] An editorial in the conservative *Weekly Standard* magazine publicly urged Republican candidates at other levels to dissociate themselves from Dole to save the Republican Congress.[96] Many Republican congressional leaders, national party strategists, and leaders of interest groups aligned with the Republicans, such as the Christian Coalition's Ralph Reed and Americans for Tax Reform's Grover Norquist, had written off the Dole ticket long ago and were concentrating their efforts on saving the Republican House.[97] These protagonists were well aware that one of the most compelling arguments in their arsenal was to argue for a Republican Congress to put a check on a reelected Bill Clinton, about whom most Americans still harbored ambivalent feelings. To make this point explicitly, however, would be to concede publicly that Dole could not win, and there was a risk that a massive landslide for Clinton might drag down the Republican House anyway. After the fund-raising scandals regarding the Clinton campaign broke in the last two weeks of the election, however, the Republicans began to air national advertisements urging voters not to give the reelected Clinton a "blank check." At the same time the national polls began to show movement toward the Republicans in the House races.[98]

Whether it was the late abandonment of Dole, the Clinton fund-raising scandals, or the late advertising blitz that did the trick, once the dust had settled on 3 November 1996, it became apparent that the Republicans had held on to both houses of Congress while Clinton was beating Dole 49–41 percent in the national popular vote for president. The Republicans had a net loss of 9 seats but still held the House by 227 seats to 207 for the Democrats, with one Independent. In the Senate the Republicans actually made a net gain of two seats increasing their margin of control from 53–47 to 55–45. The Republicans held all their open Senate seats, picked three Democratic open seats (two of them in the South), and lost one incumbent, Larry Pressler of South Dakota. In the House, eighteen Republicans were defeated, including twelve freshmen (67 percent). Of the 213 Republicans running for reelection, 195, or 92 percent, were reelected. Of the seventy freshmen running for reelection, fifty-eight were reelected at the slightly lower return rate of 83 percent. Of the twenty-one freshmen who were heavily targeted by organized labor, seven (or exactly one-third) lost.

The freshmen who lost had long been on the "most vulnerable" lists of both parties. Two—Frank Cremeans and Fred Heinemann—were defeated by Democratic incumbents they had defeated in 1994. Jim Bunn, Heinemann, Steve Stockman, and David Funderburk had been tainted by bad press publicity for misstatements or hints of scandal. The average winning percentage of the group had been 51.5 in 1994, and all of the twelve except Funderburk and Andrea Seastrand represented districts that were carried by Clinton in the presidential election.[99] Finally, these incumbents attracted some of the best-financed challengers in the 1996 election cycle, and despite the tremendous incumbent advantages in fund raising, five of the twelve freshman losers—Michael Flanagan, James Longley, Heinemann, Dan Frisa, and Bunn—were actually outspent by their challengers in 1996.[100] Finally, nine of the defeated twelve were from the Northeast/Great Lakes or the Pacific Coast, the Republicans' weakest regions in the 1992 and 1996 presidential contests (see Table 6.1).

Overall, the Republicans were able to hold on to Congress because a significant number of voters bought the "blank check" argument made by the Republicans in the closing weeks of the campaign and split their tickets between President Clinton and Republican House candidates. Ninety-one Republicans were elected in districts that were carried by Clinton, and thirty (including six members of the GOP class of 1994)

Table 6.1

Members of the 1994 Republican House Freshman Class Defeated in 1996

	District	Scandal/ controversy	Winning % 1994	District vote for president, 1996 (%)	Labor target[a]
Jim Bunn	Ore, 5	Y	50	Clinton, 47–41	Y*
Dick Chrysler	Mich. 8	N	52	Clinton, 49–40	Y*
Frank Cremeans	Ohio 6	N	51	Clinton, 44–43	Y
Michael Flanagan	Il. 5	N	54	Clinton, 63–30	Y
Dan Frisa	N.Y. 4	N	50	Clinton, 56–36	Y
David Funderburk	N.C. 2	Y	56	Dole, 52–40	Y*
Fred Heinemann	N.C. 4	Y	50	Clinton, 49–45	Y
James Longley	Me. 1	N	52	Clinton, 52–32	Y*
Bill Martini	N.J. 8	N	50	Clinton, 58–34	Y*
Steve Stockman[b]	Tex. 9	Y	52	Clinton, 48–45	Y*
Randy Tate	Wash. 9	N	52	Clinton, 51–36	Y*
Andrea Seastrand	Calif. 22	N	49	Dole, 44–44	Y

Sources: Michael Barone and Grant Ujifusa, *The Almanac of American Politics 1998* (Washington, D.C.: *National Journal*, 1997); and Jonathan D. Salant, "Finances Take Priority in This Year's Race," *Congressional Quarterly Weekly Report*, 26 October 1996, p. 3084

[a]All of the defeated members were the targets of at least one advertisement by the AFL–CIO. Asterisk (*) denotes defeated freshmen who were the targets of "Video Voter Guides," the most intensive AFL–CIO television ad campaigns.

[b]Stockman won a three-candidate election on election day, but due to court-ordered redistricting he had to fight a runoff election on 10 December, which he lost to Democrat Nick Lampson.

were elected in districts where Clinton won an outright majority of the presidential vote.[101] This was also reflected in election-day exit surveys of voters, where it was found the 50 percent of voters "feared a Democratic Congress would be too liberal" as opposed to only 42 percent who "feared that a Republican Congress would be too conservative."[102] It also appeared that Clinton voters in 1996 were twice as willing to split their tickets as Dole voters, and Republican House candidates also won a seven-point margin among the 8 percent of the electorate that voted for Ross Perot.[103]

It was a close-run thing for the Republicans though. In the total national popular vote for House, they eked out a narrow 48.9 to 48.5 percent plurality, as opposed to the 52–45 percent margin they had enjoyed in 1994. They also won a majority of House votes only in the South (55 percent) in 1996.[104] Indeed the open seats in the South proved crucially important to the GOP as they won seven of the nineteen seats vacated by retiring Democrats and made a net gain of five seats in the region overall, while losing seats in every other region of the country. And while only twelve freshmen were defeated, a further twenty-seven won reelection with less than 55 percent of the vote, and the 1994 Republican freshmen, unlike their Democratic counterparts after the 1974 elections, did not appear to have enjoyed a significant rise in their reelection percentages: the "sophomore surge."[105] The Republicans may also have been helped by the fact that despite misgivings about revolutionary rhetoric and extremism, the public broadly approved of the "reforming" reputation of the 104th Congress—most clearly represented by the freshmen—and were hesitant about handing control of the House back to the Democrats after just a two-year hiatus. On election day 1996, Congress enjoyed a 35 percent approval rating in the polls, compared to 19 percent for the Democratic Congress on election day 1994, and a plurality of Americans (44–39) believed that the 104th Congress had been "more of a success than a failure" and that it had "achieved more than the average Congress."[106]

The final factors involved in freshman and Republican survival were the legislative compromises on major legislation at the end of the 104th Congress and the increasing independence of vulnerable Republican members, particularly the freshmen, from the party leadership. The legislative compromises partially defused the Republicans' image of "extremism" and provided the 104th Congress with a clearer record of legislative accomplishment.[107] The increasing independence of the Republicans in the second session of the 104th Congress is evident from the drop in the number of party unity votes—in which a majority of one party votes against a majority of the other—from 73 percent in 1995 to 56 percent in 1996. The drop in support for the party position was most noticeable among freshmen from vulnerable northern districts, and while increasing independence from the party did not save all of them, eight of the twelve freshman Republican members with the largest drop in their party unity score were reelected with a mean percentage of 53 percent.[108]

In short: avid fund raising in 1995, a move to the center in 1996, and the increasing attentiveness of freshman members to the views and priorities of their districts, rather than a national policy agenda, (just) saved the House for the Republicans in 1996.

Conclusion

The year 1996 was a lesson in political reality for the Republican Congress and particularly for the Republican freshmen in the House. Unprepared for defeat in the budget battle and the counterattack from the left, they appeared dispirited and disoriented in the early months of 1996, as Bill Clinton came roaring back to popularity thanks to the government shutdown and a strong economy. This was an outcome that neither the militant freshmen nor the party leadership had foreseen, believing that their commitment to political reform and a balanced budget would outweigh all other considerations with the voters. In addition to these problems, the freshmen found themselves saddled with a wounded and profoundly unpopular House Speaker; a weak presidential candidate, about whom few freshmen could muster much enthusiasm; and a $35 million national advertising campaign directed specifically against them by organized labor.

The freshmen realized by the early summer of 1996 that in this situation it was now every man for himself in a battle for electoral survival, and they fell back on the more traditional freshman member's role of constituent ombudsman and service provider. The defection of dozens of freshmen on the minimum-wage issue was the first major sign that they were going to strike out on their own regardless of the cost to the party's ideological priorities, and while a determined minority continued to remonstrate with the leadership over budgetary compromises, most freshmen got their heads down and tried to lower their Washington profile and raise their district profile.

The replacement of Dole as Senate leader by the more energetic and pragmatic Trent Lott provided the opportunity for the Republican congressional leadership to make a fresh start on a more compromise-oriented approach toward the White House and Senate Democrats that yielded major benefits in terms of legislative accomplishment and demonstrated the efficacy of a much-maligned Congress. The passage of the gift and lobby reforms also demonstrated that despite their inability to address the campaign finance reform issue, the Republicans had accomplished significant and popular political changes in the institutional workings of Congress. The resort to pragmatism in 1996 had been an electoral necessity for the congressional Republicans, but as the final chapter demonstrates, their reforming zeal of 1995 had still left a significant impact on Washington and American national politics.

7

Conclusion

"What difference did they make?" is the obvious question that has to be resolved in the conclusion of this work on the freshman Republicans of the 104th Congress. The issue can be approached in two different ways: first, "what difference did the freshmen *believe* that they had made?" and second, the observer's conclusion, "what difference did they *actually* make?" In the spirit of this volume, I allow the members to speak for themselves in the first section of this concluding chapter and finally offer my own assessment of the impact of the freshman Republicans and their success in fulfilling their mission of government reform and changing the direction of public policy in the United States. It will be obvious to the reader by now that the freshmen did make a considerable impact in both of those areas, although it was much more limited than most of them would have preferred. No other freshman class—even including the "Watergate Babies" of 1974—had gained so much attention and influence in Washington, D.C., nor acted as such a cohesive entity within the House itself. On the other hand, sooner or later the checks and balances of the American political system, the political culture's antipathy to "radical" or "programmatic" politics, the near-impossibility of implementing major political change from Congress, and the imperatives of the electoral cycle were going to catch up with the freshmen. For some it was a learning experience, but for the more radical members of the class this was an inevitable disenchantment. As we see, however, almost all the freshmen believed that even given the setbacks, they had irreversibly changed the direction of American politics.

A Worthwhile Endeavor?

One of the most revealing questions asked of the freshman Republican members of the House (and Senate) in the spring and summer of 1996 was whether or not they had actually found serving in Congress to be an enjoyable experience. The most militant members of the class, those most imbued with the freshman ethos as outsiders seeking to change the direction of the country for its long-term good, were the most likely to express resentment at the burdens of the job and dislike of Washington as a whole. For Mark Neumann, being in Congress was an unpleasant duty that he was undertaking for the sake of saving the country:

> No [I don't enjoy being here], but it's part of my responsibility. A lot of people might think it's fun being here, but for me it's more like a pain in the rear. When I was in business, I built 120 homes a year, I could watch my kids, and if I wanted to do something, I simply left and did it. I made five times the amount I do here, and I worked when I wanted. Now I am under the control of people here who do schedules, and away from my family. Frankly, if I'm not reelected, my life would be a whole lot better. This is not a fun place to be, and if it is, I haven't figured it out.[1]

Congressman Neumann's sentiments were largely shared by another of the more militant freshmen, Joe Scarborough of Florida, although he stressed that he still found the job "rewarding" because of the opportunity to change the direction of policy:

> It's not fun. There's nothing fun about this job, but it is the most rewarding job I could have in the world. I was talking with another freshman on the way up to Admiral [Jeremy] Boorda's funeral about the pressures, and he said that the two or three times where he actually got treated well—like on a military base—did not make up for the time away from his family or his business. If I didn't feel that I was part of an important movement, I would be home by now, and if I ever feel that we're not moving fundamentally, that's where I'll be. I can't imagine being on the back benches of the minority for more than two years.[2]

Discontent with the strain of the job was not confined to the more conservative members of the class. Moderate Steve LaTourette also mentioned the strain on his family and the dispiriting effects of his constituents' hostility toward the institution of Congress:

> There are two main difficulties. I have to leave my family at home, and when I'm home, it's not really home anymore. My friends and my extended family think I'm dead! The second problem is that in my local

community I encounter some attitudes that make it disheartening work: people who think that all members are on the take and take family junkets and so on. Maybe that was true in the past, but I want people to know that most House members work hard and try to do the right thing.[3]

J.C. Watts of Oklahoma and Van Hilleary of Tennessee both mentioned the budget battle and the attitudes of the president and the news media as a particularly disheartening experience:

[I am surprised] how shameless people in Washington are: distorting the truth, and blatantly lying about what it is that we have proposed. Where I'm from, you play by the rules and tell the truth, step up to the plate and lose or win. Here I've seen blatant lies being told, for example, saying that we're "cutting" Medicare when we're raising benefits. That should give you a good idea how out of touch government is with the American people.[4]

I enjoyed it immensely up through November [1995]. Since then, the demagoguery of the president and the dishonesty of the labor unions have made life less enjoyable. Because of our success in turning the direction of the country, it's been worthwhile.[5]

On the Senate side, freshman Republican Jon Kyl was somewhat ambivalent about whether he enjoyed the Senate more than the House, because of the obstructionism and compromise endemic to the former chamber:

It's more enjoyable [in the Senate], though you have a different set of frustrations. The ability I have to make changes is much greater here. But with an increase in success comes an increase in the frustration level. Unfortunately, Bob Dole taught the Democrats how to bring the Senate to a halt, when he stopped the Clinton health-care bill.[6]

Most of the members interviewed were much more enthusiastic about the experience of serving in Congress, however. David McIntosh and Lindsey Graham were among the more conservative members of the class, but even despite the budget setbacks, they were keen to emphasize how rewarding it had been to change the direction of policy and the political system:

I'm having a great time. I'm blessed with a great wife, who enjoys helping me and loves to campaign in the district. It's a partnership that has strengthened our marriage. I'm reenergized when I go back home and people come up and say "keep going" and "keep fighting." I've been here less than two years, and it has helped to have been part of the freshman class. And although we lost last year's budget battle, we helped to give the system a prod. It has been worth the time and effort to aim a shot in the right direction.[7]

I have thoroughly enjoyed it. In fact, it's been overwhelmingly enlightening, and I have a great sense of accomplishment to be part of a new group that's trying to change the direction of the country, and I'd like to see it through and be in Congress when we get a balanced budget. As a job, I've had better. The opportunity to do well for our country is wonderful, but as a career? No thank you![8]

Class President George Radanovich of California was rather less enthusiastic, but still emphasized fighting for the freshman policy agenda of institutional reform, a balanced budget, and the devolution of power to the states, local communities, families, and individuals as the most fulfilling part of the job:

It's been an enjoyable experience. Of course it has changed my life flying across the country all the time. I set myself a ten-year term limit, assuming I get reelected. It begins to get old some days, but I want to get my vision installed. I'm sure there will come a time when I couldn't stand it.[9]

One of the most conservative freshmen, Bob Barr of Georgia, was also very upbeat about the job of congressman and was especially thankful to the House Republican leadership for giving freshman members so much influence over the direction of policy:

It's fundamentally satisfying to work on legislation and see results, and I feel the utmost confidence about what I've accomplished for my constituents, who have an awareness that their representative is voting on matters of national importance. I'm having a significant impact on national policies, and a lot of it is due to Newt's vision, which has given us the opportunity as freshmen to have input.[10]

Ed Whitfield of Kentucky was similarly positive, although he chose to emphasize the institutional reforms of Congress as the most significant achievement of the freshmen:

I have enjoyed it. It is important for the American people to benefit
from a strong two-party system, and that we try to reform Congress as
an institution. We had an audit for the first time in forty years, and
we've been able to reduce staff by a third, and get rid of twenty-eight
committees and subcommittees. We also now apply to ourselves the
same laws we apply to everyone else. I would rather lose the election in
1996 than back down one inch from what we're trying to do.[11]

Among the freshman Republican senators, one of the genuine outsiders
of the 1994 Republican congressional intake, former heart surgeon
Senator Bill Frist of Tennessee, had no doubt that as an individual
member of the Senate he *had* been able to make a difference:

I've had a great time. It was clearly the right thing to do. The question
that I couldn't answer when I started was whether I could make much
of a difference on issues. After two years here, I would say there is no
question that an individual can make a difference in the direction of the
country. I'm not frustrated. It took me eight years to become a heart
specialist. We have been able to pass a balanced budget, and product
liability and welfare reform, which are revolutionary concepts for the
country. And we've changed that in twelve months. So I can't be too
frustrated. We've made real progress![12]

It is interesting to note in passing that while the House freshmen all
mentioned the significance of being part of a broader group or movement, Senator Frist described his achievement in the individualistic
terms characteristic of the Senate, even though he had only served
there for a little over a year.

The answer to the first of the "what difference?" questions requires
little further elaboration. It is evident from their own words that despite
the frustrations of Washington and the disruption of their social lives
and careers, the overwhelming majority of the freshmen believed that
they had succeeded in changing the political direction of the country.
They were particularly proud to have taken some important steps to
reform Congress as an institution and to move the nation closer to a
balanced budget. And even in the politically difficult spring and summer months of 1996, the freshmen, while adopting a lower public
profile, were largely unchastened and unrepentant regarding the events
of the previous year. Their confidence in the rightness of their cause
was undiminished, even if they had been forced to reconsider their

short-term tactics. There was no sense of defeat or despondency about them. They had no doubt that they *had* made a difference and that Congress and the country were the better for their presence.

The Republican Freshmen, the Republican Congress, and the Context of American Politics in the 1990s

Explaining American electoral politics in the 1990s is not an easy task. The 1970s and 1980s, with their electoral volatility and endemic divided government, revealed the decreasing relevance of the traditional realignment paradigm premised on strong parties and strong party loyalties when both of these conditions were absent. A closer approximation to American political reality in the 1968–90 period was to talk in terms of two different electoral alignments at different electoral and governmental levels: a presidential realignment favoring the Republicans on issues related to national security and the Cold War, which could be traced back to the McCarthy era in 1952; and a congressional alignment favoring the Democrats grounded in the 1930s during the New Deal and consolidated during the 1960s.[13] The end of the Cold War unraveled the "two alignments" thesis, however, and enabled the Democrats to become competitive once more in presidential politics. At the same time, the Republicans have become competitive in elections to the U.S. House (they had been able to secure the Senate during the 1980s) for the first time since the 1950s. Although a case could be made for a new "split-level" electoral alignment with Democratic domination of the presidency and Republican domination of Congress, as we approach the millennium, in neither case was a definitive new congressional nor presidential majority fully established by 1996.[14] With Bill Clinton winning two presidential elections with pluralities, and the Republicans enjoying only very narrow congressional majorities, American electoral alignments were still in flux.

Aside from the electoral picture, however, three developments characterized American politics in the 1990s, and they go some way toward explaining the influence and behavior of the Republican freshman class in the 104th Congress. First, the clear ideological realignment at both the elite and mass levels in favor of reducing the size of the domestic state. Second, the widespread public concern with the "failure" of American political institutions to deal with urgent national issues and the linkage of this failure to the "corruption" of the political process by an alliance of incumbent officeholders and powerful outside interests. And third, a widespread public perception that major American social institutions and values were being threatened by social and economic forces, which gave rise to a defensive conservatism on issues related to family and religion in large sectors of the electorate.

The onset of perennial huge budget deficits under the Reagan and Bush administrations had delegitimated liberal arguments for a further expansion of the domestic state and focused the American political debate on the necessity of economic retrenchment. President Clinton's first term demonstrated the ideological and electoral hegemony of this approach, as the first Democratic president in over a decade ultimately gave more priority to demonstrating his deficit-cutting credentials than establishing bold new government programs. When Clinton did turn toward a potentially major extension of the domestic state with his health-care proposal in 1994, he met with total and humiliating defeat. As we have seen, Clinton was able to salvage his presidency only by adopting Republican rhetoric and policies on economic issues in 1995–96.

The deficit was also the prime piece of evidence cited by critics of the political system for the system's apparent inability to deal with urgent political issues in the early 1990s. Ross Perot brilliantly succeeded in linking the two concerns in 1992 and won 19 percent of the national popular vote for president. But the perception that America's national political institutions had become rotten was reinforced by a series of embarrassing and well-publicized scandals—Jim Wright, Toney Coelho, Dan Rostenkowski, the bank scandal, the post office scandal, Bob Packwood—that engulfed Congress in 1988–94.

Finally, scandal and corruption in Washington were also linked by many commentators (by no means all of them on the political right) to a decline in traditional social values. Easy divorce, the welfare system, rising crime, high abortion rates, and the focus on sex in popular entertainment media all appeared to place traditional American social institutions under threat. One aspect of this was the political mobilization of conservative Christians into the Christian Coalition by the Reverend Pat Robertson and Ralph Reed, who was to become one of the most influential figures in national Republican councils during the 104th Congress. Another indication of the continuing anxiety on these issues was the adverse public reaction to the very liberal sexual views of Clinton's first surgeon general, Joycelyn Elders, and the president's determination to address these issues with his various "pro-family" initiatives in the 1996 campaign.

The three above-mentioned phenomena largely explain the beliefs and behavior of the Republican freshmen in the 104th Congress: the centrality of the balanced budget issue; the belief in the need to reform Congress and lead a revolution in the direction of American national government; and concern about the perceived civic and moral "unease" in American society in the mid-1990s. These themes also explain why the freshmen felt some affinity with Perot and got elected in large part due by winning over Perot voters—who stayed with them, by and large, in 1996. Of course, the freshmen subscribed to the Contract with America and the "Republican revolution," but it was the emphasis on the deficit, political reform, and their status as "outsiders" that distinguished them from the rest of the Republicans in Congress. This distinctiveness also earned them particular attention from the news media and contributed to an astonishing sense of cohesion among the group, which, initially at least, overcame both regional and ideological considerations.

The freshmen, in fact, were not so politically inexperienced as they were often portrayed by themselves and the press. Most of them had either held public office or been candidates for public office prior to 1994. They were also not a representative group of American society, with very few women or minority members among the group. In reality, the social profile of the class came pretty close to that of the Republicans in Congress as a whole.

Social profile or not, the freshmen certainly were regarded distinctively from the moment of their arrival in Congress. On their own, they constituted about a third of the Republican Conference, and together with the sophomore class of Republicans from 1992—with whom they had strong ideological affinities—they accounted for over half of the total number of House Republicans. It was this factor that contributed to their extraordinary influence with the House leadership. The freshmen enabled the Republicans to win their first majority in the House in more than forty years, and they were the chief bearers of the message of the 1994 elections. From the start, the leadership paid assiduous attention to the freshmen, giving them an unprecedented number of positions on exclusive House committees, awarding them subcommittee chairmanships, and consulting them closely on policy and tactics, with two freshman members, David McIntosh and Sue Myrick, attending leadership meetings as representatives of the freshman class.

For most of 1995, the freshman Republicans led a charmed life as the Contract sailed through the House within the hundred-day time limit, and they marched largely in lockstep behind the dominant Speaker Newt Gingrich, who had allowed them to play such an integral role in setting the House agenda, to the occasional discomfort of more senior House Republicans. In addition, pressure from the freshmen persuaded Gingrich to adopt a radical gift ban and tougher regulation of lobbyists as a mark of the GOP's determination to reform Congress. But as the Contract stalled in the Senate, all attention became focused on the Republicans' massive FY 1996 balanced budget package. For the freshmen, the balanced budget was of primary importance; in fact, the budget issue alone not only symbolized everything they felt was wrong with the American political system but was also the central reason why many of them had taken the decision to enter politics. As a result, they were the most unyielding Republicans when it came to negotiating with the Senate and the White House on budget policy, and they—and the Republican leadership—underestimated the ability of the Clinton White House to turn the budget issue to its own advantage by focusing on politically popular programs, such as Medicare, and by using the White House bully pulpit to make sure that the Republicans got blamed for the government shutdown at the end of 1995.

Unable to compete with Clinton, the freshmen found themselves being blamed by the Democrats, the news media, and their own leadership for intransigence in failing to bring the shutdown to an end, and while this only exacerbated their already dim view of the first two institutions, the break with the leadership was a shock, and their confidence in Newt Gingrich would not be fully restored for the remainder of the 104th Congress. Having failed to prevail on the budget, the freshmen found themselves directionless for the second session of the Congress. Capitalizing on their political victory in the budget battle, the Democrats and the labor unions began an all-out advertising barrage directed specifically against the House Republican freshmen. Inside Congress, the Democrats in the Senate also recovered the initiative by sponsoring popular legislation on the minimum-wage and health-care insurance reform, which went against the grain of the "Republican revolution," but which the Republicans found politically hard to oppose. The once all-powerful Speaker was incapacitated by massive public unpopularity and an ongoing ethics investigation, and to cap everything, the electorally vulnerable freshmen found themselves saddled with a weak presidential nominee, a man with whom they had little cultural or ideological affinity, at the top of the 1996 GOP ticket.

Somewhat ironically, the actions of the Senate Republicans bailed out the House and saved the Republican Congress in 1996. The substantial contingent of eleven freshman Republican senators had made far less immediate impact on their chamber than their House counterparts, largely because the rules and traditions of the Senate do not encourage group activity or the rapid implementation of a new political agenda. While having less influence on policy, however, the changes adopted at the instigation of the freshmen in the Senate Republican Conference rules enabling the Conference to "discipline" committee chairs, may well have a very significant long-term impact on senatorial behavior and the distribution of power within the Senate. In any case, when Trent Lott succeeded Bob Dole as Senate leader (with virtually unanimous freshman support), he soon realized that without some record of legislative achievement, entailing some compromises with Clinton and the Senate Democrats, the Republicans might be in very serious electoral trouble in the fall.

The spurt of legislation toward the end of the 104th Congress helped to salvage the Republicans' reputation and probably saved many of the House freshmen. While several of the diehard members of the class—most of them, with the honorable exception of Mark Neumann, representing very conservative districts—continued to resist compromise and defied their electors to remove them, many of the vulnerable freshmen abandoned the politics of broad policy change characteristic of 1995 for a politics of reelection in 1996. They had already discovered the advantage of amassing a large warchest of PAC contributions in 1995, and in 1996 they became increasingly concerned about dissociating themselves from an unpopular leadership and the suspicion of radicalism or extremism. More attention was paid to constituent service and programs benefiting their districts. Many freshmen, in fact, began to vote intentionally against their party in unimportant procedural votes in the House, simply to inflate their overall scores on opposition to the leadership. The final key to the Republican comeback in the fall of 1996 was the freshmen's successful "localization" of their races, and the deliberate separation of themselves from the failing Dole campaign, by emphasizing the dangers of awarding a reelected Bill Clinton a Democratic Congress.

One clear conclusion from the experience of the House Republican freshmen is that ideological fervor and commitment to a national policy agenda are still likely to be intermittent and ephemeral phenomena on Capitol Hill. Much of the "revolutionary" behavior of the freshmen and the Republican majority in 1995 was reversed or modified in 1996, as the full impact of the American governmental system and the two-year House election cycle became apparent. Given a four-year term, the freshmen might have been able to afford to be militant revolutionaries for another couple of years. But with reelection looming in 1996, they found themselves compelled to fall back on the same incumbency protection tactics that characterized congressional elections in the last two decades of Democratic rule. Of course, this is hardly surprising because the whole design of the American governmental system is intended to preclude short-term ideological majorities from getting their way. Whatever else was wrong with the American system of government in the 1990s, in this regard it was still working very well. In fact, given the relative narrowness of their majorities in Congress, it is remarkable that the Republicans were able to achieve the major change in the policy direction of the country that they did in 1995–96.

The freshmen also learned to be politicians. It is interesting to note that the members of the class who were defeated in 1996 had long been identified by both parties as some of the weaker links—either due to the Democrat-leaning nature of their districts or personal notoriety—in the class. The budget battle taught many of the freshmen that politics, particularly American politics, is the art of the possible. Ideas and zeal alone will not win the battle; a measure of guile and picking battles you can win is also critical, as the more seasoned political operators, Clinton and Trent Lott, discovered. The freshmen realized that the system does not lend itself to radical change, or if it does, only for brief and intermittent periods. In reaction to the ineptitude of Clinton's first two years, the Democrats' perceived reversion to big-government liberalism with the health-care plan, and the accumulating evidence of an arrogant, corrupt, and unaccountable Congress, the country was ready to try a fresh start with the Republicans in 1994. The Republicans fulfilled their mandate by undertaking a substantial overhaul of Congress's practices and internal procedures that was generally well received by the public. In fact, their continuing image as outsider reformers remained a major electoral asset for the freshman Republicans right up to the 1996 elections, even though the exigencies of electoral survival had led the Republican leadership to avoid making any serious attempt to deal with the most urgent area of reform: campaign finance.

The Republicans also fulfilled their "mandate" by showing that the House could "work" legislatively and passed the Contract within the specified "hundred days." Their dominance of the national political agenda in 1995 confirmed the major shift to the right on economic and social policy in America during the 1990s. Where they erred was to become too fixated on the specifics of reducing the budget deficit. While the decision to tackle Medicare showed political courage, the Republicans tried to have their cake and eat it too, by combining the Medicare reductions with tax cuts, and given the opposition of Clinton and their relatively narrow congressional majorities, this was simply not politically possible. Instead of putting together a package that would be politically difficult for Clinton to veto, the Republicans tried to drive him into submission by shutting down the government and refusing to raise the debt ceiling. By doing so, they fell into the trap of "radicalism" and "political extremism" and lost the center ground of American politics to the president. Only the Republicans' belated move toward the center at the end of the Congress saved the day. In a sense, the Madisonian system worked perfectly. The Republican House changed the political agenda and the terms of political debate, but the Republicans had no mandate for the kind of radical dismantling of the federal government expected by many freshman Republicans, and the events of 1995–96 revealed this as the new congressional majority was checked by the Senate and the executive branch.

From the experience of the Republican freshmen in the 104th Congress, what conclusions can we draw about American politics in the 1990s? First, there has clearly been an ideological realignment toward generally promarket policies, balanced budgets, and a more limited federal government. The Republican Party, which has been espousing these themes since the New Deal, has not surprisingly benefited electorally from this change, as is reflected in the new Republican congressional majorities. For forty years, the Democrats held on to Congress by servicing their districts and bringing new government programs to their constituents. By the early 1990s, the conservative critique that this incremental expansion of government was largely responsible for ballooning federal budget deficits had become conventional wisdom among the public. The Republicans also gained from the perception that Congress had become "corrupted" under the Democrats, a perception that appeared to be confirmed by the late 1980s and early 1990s scandals. Finally, with the assistance of allied groups like the Christian Coalition, the GOP also managed to capitalize on concerns in large sectors of society about changing social and sexual mores. In 1994 the Republicans managed to put the Democrats on the defensive on all these issues, and the result was their dramatic takeover of Congress.

The modern American political system does not lend itself to long-term party alignments, however, and the very fact of the Republican congressional victory in 1994 made it less likely that the GOP would be able to win the presidency in 1996.[15] Both major parties are dominated by committed activists on either side of the ideological spectrum, but the electorate does not identify with parties or, by and large, with ideological positions. In this broad middle-class, suburban, center ground, where Ross Perot mined votes in 1992 and the congressional Republicans did likewise in 1994, a demand for change to address national problems exists, but not for "radicalism" or more specifically for change that might drastically undermine government programs such as Medicare or federal aid to education, which bring real benefits to middle-class voters. For this large segment of the electorate, it has become habitual and rational to split their allegiances between different levels of electoral competition, and that is just what happened in 1996. While they might have supported much of the thrust of the "Republican revolution," they were wary of a really drastic and sudden assault on the domestic state, particularly after the freshman Republicans showed their teeth and shut down the government. Bill Clinton, for all his faults, was a safe bet to keep the "radicals" from going too far.

The whole direction of the political system in the late 1990s undoubtedly favors the Republicans, and the Democrats are in the position of Republicans during the New Deal era, who can prevail only by saying "me too." Also, like the Republicans of the New Deal/Cold War eras, they may well have a slight advantage in presidential elections as long as the GOP controls Congress, simply to keep the "radicals" in check. Of course, the Republican congressional majority might also unravel on a number of fronts. For instance, there *is* an inherent tension between the social conservatism that the party has espoused in recent decades and the unbridled free-market policies to which it is committed. Nothing is more subversive of traditional social values than unrestrained capitalism. Support for free trade has also become harder for Republicans, who are responsive to lower-middle-class and blue-collar concerns about the global economy—concerns tapped by Patrick Buchanan in his campaigns for the GOP presidential nomination in 1992 and 1996. While these potential divisions are serious, they may not, in fact, have that much effect on the Republican congressional majority for two reasons. First, internal divisions and contradictions are not necessarily impediments to assembling a congressional majority, as the Democrats demonstrated for forty years. In fact, by broadening a party's support base, they may actually be a positive advantage and an indication that a party is approaching national majority status. Second, the cultural conservatives and populist anti-free traders are far stronger and more dangerous to the Republicans at the presidential level, where these types of issues have a larger resonance, and where party splits and policy contradictions *are* likely to have a very damaging effect. Again, witness the Democrats in 1968–92!

What may well emerge from the apparent state of flux in the first half of the 1990s are the underpinnings of a new alignment or electoral order in American politics with Republicans favored in congressional elections and Democrats in presidential politics. Of course, it is not being argued that the Republicans will run Congress for forty years or that the Democrats will establish a "lock" on the presidency as impressive as the Republicans did from 1952 to 1992. The point is merely that, other things being equal, the expanded Republican coalition is likely to have the advantage in congressional elections and the narrower Democratic coalition in presidential politics. The exuberance and influence of the Republican freshmen in the 104th Congress is thus likely to be a temporary and untypical phenomenon symptomatic of a period of transition. If the Republicans are to keep control of Congress, the politics of 1996 is more likely to be typical than the politics of 1995: a politics of accommodation, compromise, and attention to state and district concerns, rather than a politics of radical agenda change and implementation. We should also expect that a stable Republican majority will be far more internally divided and much less cohesive than the freshmen of 1995–96. In these circumstances we would also expect to see congressional committee chairmen and individual members become far more independent, and the gradual erosion of the temporarily all-powerful Speakership erected by Newt Gingrich in the 104th Congress. In short: a Republican-dominated Congress in its internal structure and institutional norms, if not in policy outputs, is likely to bear an increasing resemblance to the Democratic regime that was overthrown in 1994.

Events early in the 105th Congress appeared to corroborate this analysis. After being reprimanded by the House for several ethics violations in January 1995, Newt Gingrich clung on to the Speakership by a thread and was but a shadow of the formidable figure who dominated Washington in 1995. In the FY 1998 budget negotiations and tax and appropriations bills, committee chairs such as John Kasich (Budget), Bill Archer (Ways and Means), and Bob Livingston (Appropriations) played a much more prominent role than they did in the 104th Congress. The freshman Republican intake of 1996 was little heard from, and while the more militant sophomores of the class of 1994, such as Mark Souder, Lindsey Graham, David McIntosh, and Joe Scarborough, constituted the nucleus of opposition to the Speaker within the House Republican Conference, they were certainly not in control of the general direction of the House, as had appeared to be the case in 1995.[16]

In such a loose and volatile political system as modern America one should, of course, be wary of essaying such ambitious predictive schemas. A sudden national security crisis or an economic depression could well unravel this nascent alignment. The Republicans might also fail to handle their internal contradictions or define themselves too narrowly, as in 1995, and lose control of the House, where they have not yet established a clear predominance. But in 1998 and 2000, with the norms of the electoral cycle running against the party controlling the White House, the Republicans should considerably pad their margins of victory in both chambers, unless they try too hard to force the pace and get too far ahead of the electorate. They might even get hold of the presidency, although we have good reason to think that if this is the case, Republican control of all three branches of the federal government would expose the party's internal contradictions and would prove to be rather short-lived.

The issue remains open as whether the extraordinary influence of the Republican freshmen in the 104th Congress was symptomatic of a revolutionary change in Congress as an institution and in the political system more broadly. The evidence to date indicates that the freshmen accomplished significant and necessary change in Congress, particularly in the area of lobbying reform and congressional accountability, but that over time the old institutional norms of decentralized power and the predominance of localism over national agenda-change will reassert themselves. On the second issue, it is more likely than not that the huge Republican freshman class of the 104th Congress, in its behavior and attitudes, *was* symptomatic of a broader popular and congressional realignment toward economic conservatism. Ironically, however, if the GOP is to consolidate that majority over the next decade, the party will have to conduct itself in a manner almost directly opposed to that of the freshmen of the 104th Congress.

What About Congress?

The essential issue raised in the first chapter of this book was whether or not the new Republican majority would be able to arrest or even reverse the low public esteem of Congress as a political institution. From Figure 7.1, it is evident that to a certain extent the Republican Congress was able to do this. Although a majority of the public continued to disapprove of Congress, the margins were significantly lower during the 104th Congress, and the truly dismal disapproval ratings of the early 1990s have not been repeated. As mentioned in the previous section, the public elected the Republican Congress to address what it most disliked about the institution, namely, the perception of corruption and unresponsiveness, and to the extent that the Republican Congress addressed this with measures such as the Congressional Accountability Act, lobby reform, ending proxy voting, and the gift ban, they met with public approval. In fact, this is one area where the perceived outsider status of the Republican freshmen and their strident articulation of the demand for political reform assisted their reelection and probably worked to the benefit of the Republican Congress as a whole.

But while public disapproval of Congress may have bottomed out, its prestige as an institution compared with the presidency and the Supreme Court remains poor.[17] The long-term structural forces—the presidential bully pulpit in the electronic media and the antipathy of national educational and media elites toward the pluralistic politics of legislatures—alluded to in the first chapter are thus still operating to weaken Congress's position relative to the other major institutions of American government. Newt Gingrich and the

Figure 7.1 **Congressional Approval: 103rd and 104th Congresses**

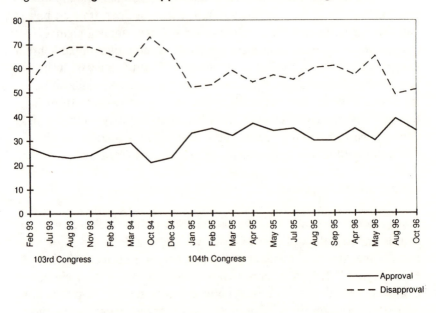

Source: The Gallup Poll Monthly, October 1996.

Republicans actually gained points with the public in making the House less pluralistic by centralizing authority in the party leadership, weakening the committee system, and repudiating the incrementalist policymaking characteristic of the Democratic regime. With the benefit of presidential unpopularity and an apparent mandate from the 1994 elections, Gingrich was able to set the national policy agenda from Congress, as Jim Wright had been able to do in a more limited fashion against a weakened President Reagan in the wake of the Iran-*contra* scandal. But from the time of the Oklahoma City bombing in April 1995, President Clinton became increasingly able to utilize the stature and visibility of his office to undermine public support for the Republican Congress. With a ruthlessly efficient political operation ensuring that the White House (and the congressional Democrats) were all following the same message and playbook, Clinton was easily able to best a discordant, divided, quarrelsome Congress in the high-stakes battle over the government shutdown at the end of 1995. After that, the Republican Congress was essentially tamed, becoming more preoccupied with its members' electoral survival than changing the national policy agenda.

The reversion of the 104th Congress to the model of the Democratic Congresses of the 1980s in its second session essentially confirmed the inferior position of Congress in the modern American political system and suggests that this situation can only be temporarily and intermittently reversed, in circumstances when two conditions are met: first, when the incumbent president is politically weak or incompetent (Reagan in 1987–88, Clinton in 1994–95), and second, when Congress has strong, centralized, internal leadership to fill the vacuum (Jim Wright in 1987–88, Newt Gingrich in 1995). For various structural reasons—the weakness of the parties, the demand for national policymaking and rational expertise, and the prerogatives of the presidency in foreign policy—long-term national political leadership from Congress is almost impossible to maintain. In fact, so ubiquitous is the faith in presidential direction that even the 104th Congress blithely awarded a Democratic president a line-item veto on appropriations bills, potentially one of the greatest increases in presidential power in American history. The modern American political system's structural bias in favor of divided government, discussed in the previous section, makes national political leadership from Congress even harder to obtain, when the electorate has almost deliberately selected a president of the opposite party to preclude that possibility. Finally, while part of the aura of the presidency might have become eroded in the aftermath of the Cold War and the absence of a perpetual threat to the country's national security, America's continuing broad international engagement as *the* major world power and guarantor of the global order makes it likely that presidents will continue to gain power from their leading role on the world stage.

The Republican 104th Congress's reassertion of congressional authority was thus a brief interlude created by the special circumstances of 1994–95, and while Congress will continue to have brief periods of predominance in the political system when such circumstances permit, it is highly unlikely to become the norm. In fact, in the absence of the extremely lopsided congressional majorities necessary to override a presidential veto, efforts to lead the national government from Congress against a powerful president may well result in making Congress look ineffectual and contribute to a party's loss of a congressional majority, as almost happened with the Republicans in 1996. Congress can delay and obstruct measures, and it can articulate the national mood, but except in highly unusual circumstances, it cannot lead. The modern American political system is simply unwilling to tolerate leadership from a divided, discordant, and pluralistic legislative branch and is broadly antipathetic toward legislative norms and practices. In this situation, even politically weakened presidents speaking in one voice with direct access to a national audience have inherent advantages, as the congressional Republicans found to their cost in 1995–96.

Notes

Notes to Chapter 1

1. For a rare defense of Congress by a former member, see Fred. R. Harris, *In Defense of Congress* (New York: St. Martin's Press, 1995).

2. Woodrow Wilson, *Congressional Government: A Study in American Politics* (Baltimore: Johns Hopkins University Press, 1981).

3. Alexander Hamilton, James Madison, and John Jay, *The Federalist Papers* (New York: New American Library, 1961), pp. 77–84, 320–25.

4. On American society at the time of the Revolutionary War, see Gordon S. Wood, *The Radicalism of the American Revolution* (New York: Knopf, 1992), pp. 11–92.

5. On Whig Republicanism and the Founders, see Bernard Bailyn, *The Ideological Origins of the American Revolution* (Cambridge, Mass.: Belknap Press, 1967); Forrest McDonald, *Novus Ordo Seclorum: The Intellectual Origins of the Constitution* (Lawrence: University Press of Kansas, 1985); and Gordon S. Wood, *The Creation of the American Republic, 1776–1787* (New York: Norton, 1969).

6. See Wilson, *Congressional Government,* pp. 57–98; and James Bryce, *The American Commonwealth* (New York: Macmillan, 1911), I: 126–43.

7. On the late nineteenth-century Speakership, see Ronald M. Peters Jr., *The American Speakership: The Office in Historical Perspective* (Baltimore: Johns Hopkins University Press, 1990), pp. 52–91.

8. On the importance of the parties in late nineteenth-century American politics, see Joel H. Silbey, *The American Political Nation, 1838–1893* (Stanford, Calif.: Stanford University Press, 1991).

9. See James L. Sundquist, *The Decline and Resurgence of Congress* (Washington, D.C.: Brookings Institution, 1981), pp. 162–68,

10. On Progressive ideology, see Richard Hofstader, *The Age of Reform: From Bryan to FDR* (New York: Knopf, 1955), pp. 131–212.

11. On Theodore Roosevelt's and Woodrow Wilson's conception of the presidency, see Jeffrey K. Tulis, *The Rhetorical Presidency* (Princeton: Princeton University Press, 1987), pp. 95–144.

12. See Sundquist, *The Decline and Resurgence of Congress,* pp. 37–60; and Steven Skowronek, *Building a New American State: The Expansion of National*

Administrative Capacities, 1877–1920 (New York: Cambridge University Press, 1982).

13. On the decline of Parliament in twentieth-century Britain, see R.H.S. Crossman's Introduction to Walter Bagehot, *The English Constitution* (London, Fontana, 1963), pp. 1–57; and John P. Mackintosh, *The British Cabinet,* 3rd ed. (London: Stevens & Sons, 1977).

14. On the fall of Cannon, see Sundquist, *The Decline and Resurgence of Congress,* pp. 168–76; and Peters, *The American Speakership,* pp. 75–87.

15. On the impact of the Progressives' reforms on the party system, see Walter Dean Burnham, *The Current Crisis in American Politics* (New York: Oxford University Press, 1982); and Michael E. McGerr, *The Decline of Popular Politics: The American North, 1896–1928* (New York: Oxford University Press, 1986).

16. Sundquist, *The Decline and Resurgence of Congress,* pp. 155–95.

17. Theodore J. Lowi, *The End of Liberalism: The Second Republic of the United States,* 2nd ed. (New York: Norton, 1979); and Levi, *The Personal President: Power Invested, Promise Unfulfilled* (Ithaca, N.Y.: Cornell University Press, 1985).

18. See Hugh Heclo, "Issue Networks and the Executive Establishment," in *The New American Political System,* ed. Anthony King (Washington, D.C.: American Enterprise Institute, 1979), pp. 87–124.

19. See Morris P. Fiorina, *Congress: Keystone of the Washington Establishment,* 2nd ed. (New Haven: Yale University Press, 1989), pp. 37–47.

20. Sundquist, *The Decline and Resurgence of Congress,* pp. 91–126.

21. See Arthur M. Schlesinger Jr., *The Imperial Presidency* (New York: Popular Library, 1973); and Barbara Kellerman and Ryan J. Barilleaux, *The President as World Leader* (New York: St. Martin's Press, 1991).

22. On Congress's long-standing defense of racial segregation, see Robert Mann, *The Walls of Jericho: Lyndon Johnson, Hubert Humphrey, Richard Russell and the Struggle for Civil Rights* (New York, Harcourt Brace, 1996); and Gilbert C. Fite, *Richard B. Russell Jr., Senator from Georgia* (Chapel Hill: University of North Carolina Press, 1991).

23. On the Tonkin Gulf Resolution and Vietnam, see Sundquist, *The Decline and Resurgence of Congress,* pp. 120–26; Schlesinger, *The Imperial Presidency,* pp. 177–204; and Kellerman and Barilleaux, *The President as World Leader,* pp. 104–26.

24. On Nixon's use of impoundments, see Sundquist, *The Decline and Resurgence of Congress,* pp. 201–9; and Schlesinger, *The Imperial Presidency,* pp. 229–34.

25. On Cambodia and the War Powers Act, see Sundquist, *The Decline and Resurgence of Congress,* pp. 238–314; and Robert A. Katzmann, "War Powers: Toward a New Accommodation," in *A Question of Balance: The President, the Congress, and Foreign Policy,* ed. Thomas E. Mann (Washington, D.C.: Brookings Institution, 1990), pp. 35–69.

26. On the budget act, see Sundquist, *The Decline and Resurgence of Congress,* pp. 209–37; and Aaron Wildavsky, *The New Politics of the Budget Process* (Glenview, Il.: Scott Foresman, 1988), pp. 142–49.

27. Sundquist, *The Decline and Resurgence of Congress,* pp. 273–314; and Thomas M. Franck and Edward Weisband, *Foreign Policy by Congress* (New York: Oxford University Press, 1979).

28. Sundquist, *The Decline and Resurgence of Congress,* pp. 344–66; and Lawrence C. Dodd and Richard L. Schott, *Congress and the Administrative State* (New York: John Wiley, 1979).

29. On the impact of the 1970s rules changes, see Sundquist, *The Decline and Resurgence of Congress,* pp. 367–414; Samuel C. Patterson, "The Semi-Sovereign Congress," in King, ed., *The New American Political System,* pp. 125–77; and Lawrence C. Dodd and Bruce C. Oppenheimer, "Maintaining Order in the House: The Struggle for Institutional Equilibrium," in *Congress Reconsidered,* 5th ed., ed. Lawrence C. Dodd and Bruce C. Oppenheimer (Washington, D.C.: CQ Press, 1993), pp. 41–66.

30. On congressional elections during the 1970s and 1980s, see David Mayhew, *Congress: The Electoral Connection* (New Haven: Yale University Press, 1974); Fiorina, *Congress;* Gary C. Jacobson, *The Politics of Congressional Elections,* 2nd ed. (Boston: Little, Brown, 1987); and Jacobson, *The Electoral Origins of Divided Government* (Boulder, Colo.: Westview Press, 1990); and Thomas E. Mann, *Unsafe at Any Margin: Interpreting Congressional Elections* (Washington, D.C.: American Enterprise Institute, 1978).

31. On change in the Senate during the 1970s, see Barbara Sinclair, *The Transformation of the U.S. Senate* (Baltimore: Johns Hopkins University Press, 1989); and Norman J. Ornstein, Robert L. Peabody, and David W. Rohde, "The U.S. Senate in an Era of Change," in Dodd and Oppenheimer, eds., *Congress Reconsidered,* pp. 13–40.

32. On the rise of partisanship and more assertive party leadership in the House during the 1980s see Barbara Sinclair, *Legislators, Leaders, and Lawmaking: The U.S. House of Representatives in the Postreform Era* (Baltimore: Johns Hopkins University Press, 1995).

33. On Speaker Wright, see John M. Barry, *The Ambition and the Power* (New York: Viking Press, 1989). See also John B. Bader, *Taking the Initiative: Leadership Agendas in Congress and the "Contract with America"* (Washington, D.C.: Georgetown University Press, 1996), pp. 50–53; and John H. Aldrich and David W. Rohde, "A Tale of Two Speakers: A Comparison of Policy Making in the 100th and 104th Congresses," paper presented at the annual meeting of the American Political Science Association, San Francisco, 29 August–1 September 1996.

34. On the increasing hostility of the House Republicans toward the Democratic leadership during the 1980s, see William F. Connelly Jr. and John J. Pitney Jr., *Congress' Permanent Minority: Republicans in the U.S. House,* (Lanham, Md.: Rowman and Littlefield, 1994), pp. 69–91; and Douglas L. Koopman, *Hostile Takeover: The House Republican Party, 1980–1995* (Lanham, Md.: Rowman and Littlefield, 1996), pp. 31–59.

35. On Gingrich's campaign to undermine Wright, see Barry, *The Ambition and the Power,* pp. 212–52 and 362–72; and Dan Balz and Ronald Brownstein, *Storming the Gates: Protest Politics and the Republican Revival* (Boston: Little, Brown, 1996), pp. 113–30.

36. On Wright's fall, see Barry, *The Ambition and the Power,* pp. 716–63; and Peters, *The American Speakership,* pp. 264–86.

37. On the "therapeutic Speakership," see Peters, *American Speakership,* p. 13.

38. On the founding of the COS, see Dick Williams, *Newt! Leader of the Second American Revolution* (Marietta, Ga.: Longstreet Press, 1995), pp. 98–110.

39. On the Gingrich-Madigan race, see Koopman, *Hostile Takeover,* pp. 11–29.

40. On GOPAC, see Balz and Brownstein, *Storming the Gates,* pp. 143–46.

41. On Gingrich's strategy for taking over the House, see Connelly and Pitney, *Congress' Permanent Minority,* pp. 153–73.

42. Richard Fenno first noticed this tendency while observing members of Congress in their districts during the 1970s. See Richard F. Fenno Jr., "If, as Ralph Nader Says, Congress Is the 'Broken Branch,' How Come We Love Our Congressman So Much?" in *Congress in Change: Evolution and Reform,* ed. Norman J. Ornstein (New York: Praeger, 1975), pp. 277–87; and Fenno, *Home Style: House Members in Their Districts* (Boston: Little, Brown, 1978).

43. On the bank scandal, see C. Lawrence Evans and Walter J. Oleszek, *Congress under Fire: Reform Politics and the Republican Majority* (Boston: Houghton Mifflin, 1997), pp. 35–42.

44. Connelly and Pitney, *Congress' Permanent Minority,* pp. 153–73.

45. See John R. Hibbing and Elizabeth Theiss-Morse, *Congress as Public Enemy* (New York: Cambridge University Press, 1995). For a critique of Hibbing and Theiss-Morse, see Mark D. Watts, "Framing Congress: Media Coverage of the U.S. Congress and Its Impact on Public Opinion," Ph.D. dissertation, University of Minnesota, 1997.

46. On the impact of talk radio, see Balz and Brownstein, *Storming the Gates,* pp. 163–89.

47. On the effect of the Thomas-Hill hearings on the confirmation process, see Stephen L. Carter, *The Confirmation Mess* (New York: Basic Books, 1994).

48. Hibbing and Theiss-Morse, *Congress as Public Enemy,* pp. 22–105.

49. On the term limits movement, see Gerald Benjamin and Michael J. Malbin, eds., *Limiting Legislative Terms* (Washington, D.C.: CQ Press, 1992).

50. See Balz and Brownstein, *Storming the Gates,* pp. 159–202.

51. On Weber's concept of "charismatic leadership," see Max Weber, "The Sociology of Charismatic Authority," in *From Max Weber: Essays in Sociology,* ed. H.H. Gerth and C. Wright Mills (London: Routledge and Kegan Paul, 1970), pp. 245–64.

52. See Hibbing and Theiss-Morse, *Congress as Public Enemy,* pp. 125–62.

Notes to Chapter 2

1. On Clinton's 1992 campaign, see Charles O. Jones, "Campaigning to Govern: The Clinton Style," in *The Clinton Presidency: First Appraisals,* ed. Colin Campbell and Bert A. Rockman (Chatham, N.J.: Chatham House, 1996), pp. 15–50; Paul J. Quirk and Jon K. Dalager, "The Election: A 'New Democrat' and a New Kind of Presidential Campaign," in *The Elections of 1992,* ed. Michael Nelson (Washington, D.C.: CQ Press, 1993), pp. 57–88; and Nicol C. Rae, *Southern Democrats* (New York: Oxford University Press, 1994), pp. 128–50.

2. On Clinton's problems with the Democratic Congress during his first year, see Barbara Sinclair, "Trying to Govern Positively in a Negative Era: Clinton and the 103rd Congress," in Campbell and Rockman, eds., *Clinton Presidency,* pp. 89–125.

3. On the failure of the Clinton health-care plan, see Theda Skocpol, *Boo-*

merang: Health Care Reform and the Turn Against Government (New York: Norton, 1996).

4. On the problematic passage of the crime bill, see Dan Balz and Ronald Brownstein, *Storming the Gates: Protest Politics and the Republican Revival* (Boston: Little, Brown, 1996), pp. 91–94.

5. On the failure of the Democratic majority in the 103rd Congress to accomplish significant institutional reform, see C. Lawrence Evans and Walter J. Oleszek, *Congress under Fire: Reform Politics and the Republican Majority* (Boston: Houghton Mifflin, 1997), pp. 48–82.

6. See John R. Hibbing and Eric Tiritilli, "Public Disapproval of Congress Can Be Dangerous to Majority Party Candidates: The Case of 1994," paper presented at the annual meeting of the Midwest Political Science Association, Chicago, 10–12 April 1997.

7. Interview with Congressman Lindsey Graham, 11 July 1996.

8. Interview with Congressman Walter Jones, 23 April 1996.

9. Interview with Congressman Ed Whitfield, 31 July 1996.

10. Interview with Congressman Bill Martini, 23 July 1996.

11. Interview with Congressman Mark Souder, 21 February 1996.

12. Interview with Congressman Joe Scarborough, 28 May 1996.

13. Interview with Congressman Van Hilleary, 18 July 1996.

14. Interview with Congressman Bob Barr, 18 June 1996.

15. Interview with Congressman Jon Fox, 16 July 1996.

16. Barr interview.

17. Newt Gingrich, *To Renew America* (New York: HarperCollins, 1995), p. 71.

18. See William F. Connelly Jr. and John J. Pitney Jr., *Congress' Permanent Minority: Republicans in the U.S. House* (Lanham, Md.: Rowman and Littlefield, 1994), pp. 77–79.

19. Interview with Congressman David Dreier, 6 June 1996.

20. Interview with Congressman Steve Gunderson, 9 July 1996.

21. See Gary C. Jacobson, *The Electoral Origins of Divided Government* (Boulder, Colo.: Westview Press, 1990).

22. Interview with Congressman Bob Walker, 29 July 1996.

23. Dick Williams, *Newt! Leader of the Second American Revolution* (Marrietta, Ga.: Longstreet Press, 1995), p. 146. On GOPAC, see also Balz and Brownstein, *Storming the Gates,* pp. 145–46; and E.J. Dionne, *They Only Look Dead: Why Progressives Will Dominate the Next Political Era* (New York: Simon and Schuster, 1996), pp. 213–14.

24. Williams, *Newt!* p. 146.

25. Balz and Brownstein, *Storming the Gates,* p. 145.

26. Interview with Congressman J.D. Hayworth, 1 August 1996.

27. See Dionne, *They Only Look Dead,* pp. 211–14. It was the financial relationships between the various elements of Gingrich's personal network—GOPAC, the foundation, and the college course—that would lead to the plethora of Democratic allegations of impropriety and ethics violations against Gingrich during the 104th Congress.

28. See James G. Gimpel, *Legislating the Revolution: The Contract with America in Its First 100 Days* (Boston: Allyn and Bacon, 1996), pp. 9–11.

29. Williams, *Newt!* p. 146.

30. Fox interview.

31. See Gary C. Jacobson, *The Politics of Congressional Elections,* 2nd ed. (Boston: Little, Brown, 1987); and Thomas E. Mann, *Unsafe at Any Margin: Interpreting Congressional Elections* (Washington, D.C.: American Enterprise Institute, 1978).

32. Gingrich, *To Renew America,* p. 112.

33. Ibid.

34. On the genesis of the Contract, see Gimpel, *Legislating the Revolution,* pp. 4–8 and 16–21; John B. Bader, *Taking the Initiative: Leadership Agendas in Congress and the "Contract with America"* (Washington, D.C.: Georgetown University Press, 1996), pp. 171–206; Balz and Brownstein, *Storming the Gates,* pp. 37–43; and Elizabeth Drew, *Showdown: The Struggle between the Gingrich Congress and the Clinton White House* (New York: Simon and Schuster, 1996), pp. 27–34.

35. Gunderson interview.

36. On the process of selecting issues for inclusion in the Contract, see Bader, *Taking the Initiative,* pp. 185–190.

37. Ibid.; and Balz and Brownstein, *Storming the Gates,* pp. 39–43.

38. The five freshman nonsigners were Sam Brownback (Kans.); Jim Bunn (Ore.); Tom Coburn (Okla.); Ray LaHood (Il.); and Jim Longley (Me.). See Gimpel, *Legislating the Revolution,* p. 8.

39. Souder interview.

40. Interview with Congressman Dick Chrysler, 6 March 1996.

41. Hayworth interview.

42. Gimpel, *Legislating the Revolution,* pp. 15–30; Harold W. Stanley, "The Parties, the President, and the 1994 Midterm Elections," in Campbell and Rockman, eds., *The Clinton Presidency,* pp. 188–211; Gary Jacobson, "The 1994 House Elections in Perspective," in *Midterm: The Elections of 1994 in Context,* ed. Philip A. Klinker (Boulder, Colo.: Westview Press, 1996), pp. 1–20; and Clyde Wilcox, *The Latest American Revolution? The 1994 Elections and Their Implications for Governance* (New York: St. Martin's Press, 1995), pp. 7–26.

43. Scarborough interview.

44. Interview with Congressman David Funderburk, 28 March 1996.

45. Interview with Congressman Steve LaTourette, 10 July 1996.

46. Barr Interview.

47. Interview with Congressman "Doc" Hastings, 12 July 1996.

48. Chrysler interview.

49. Interview with Congressman J.C. Watts, 2 May 1996.

50. Interview with Congressman Mark Neumann, 16 May 1996.

51. Interview with Congressman Gil Gutknecht, 29 February 1996.

52. This is not to imply that Republicans were unwilling to exploit a similar advantage when they controlled the congressional redistricting process. Unfortunately for the GOP, however, this was the case in only a handful of states in the early 1980s.

53. See Michael Barone and Grant Ujifusa with Richard E. Cohen, *The Almanac of American Politics, 1996* (Washington, D.C.: National Journal, 1995), p. 91.

54. See also Kevin A. Hill, "Does the Creation of Majority Black Districts Aid Republicans? An Analysis of the 1992 Congressional Elections in Eight Southern States," *Journal of Politics* 57 (1995): 384–401.

55. Jones interview.

56. See Hill, "Creation of Majority Black Districts."

57. Interview with Congressman Mark Foley, 30 April 1994.

58. Graham interview.

59. Interview with Congressman Bob Ehrlich, 23 April 1996.

60. Gutknecht interview.

61. Interview with Congressman Ray LaHood, 26 July 1996.

62. Interview with Congressman Tom M. Davis, 14 May 1996.

63. Interview with Congressman George Radanovich, 31 May 1996.

64. Interview with Congressman Brian Bilbray, 27 June 1996.

65. Neumann interview. Congressman Neumann first ran in 1992, and again in a 1993 special election, which he lost narrowly.

66. Interview with Congressman Mark Sanford, 12 June 1996.

67. Watts interview.

68. Hayworth Interview.

69. Davis interview.

70. Gutknecht interview.

71. Neumann interview.

72. Scarborough interview.

73. Sanford interview.

74. Ibid.

75. Scarborough interview.

76. Souder interview.

77. Sanford interview.

78. Scarborough interview.

79. Souder interview.

80. See Norman J. Ornstein, Thomas E. Mann, and Michael J. Malbin, *Vital Statistics on Congress: 1995–1996* (Washington, D.C.: American Enterprise Institute, 1996), p. 52.

81. See Jacobson, "1994 House Elections"; and David E. Rosenbaum, "GOP Unleashes Its New Weapon: Winning Candidates," *New York Times,* 13 November 1994, p. E1.

Notes to Chapter 3

1. On the 100–day target, see James G. Gimpel, *Legislating the Revolution: The Contract with America Its First 100 Days* (Boston: Allyn and Bacon, 1996), p. 29.

2. On Gingrich's speakership, see Ronald M. Peters Jr., "The Republican Speakership," paper presented at the 1996 annual meeting of the American Political cal Science Association, San Francisco, 29 August–1 September 1996.

3. On Gingrich's reforms of the committee system, see C. Lawrence Evans and Walter J. Oleszek, *Congress under Fire: Reform Politics and the Republican Majority* (Boston: Houghton Mifflin, 1997), pp. 91–100; Gimpel, *Legislating the Revolution,* pp. 33–38; and Elizabeth Drew, *Showdown: The Struggle between the Gingrich Congress and the Clinton White House* (New York: Simon and Schuster, 1996), pp. 23–43. See also John H. Aldrich and David W. Rohde, "Balance

of Power: Republican Party Leadership and the Committee System in the 104th Congress," paper presented at the 1997 annual meeting of the Midwest Political Science Association, Chicago, 10–13 April 1997.

4. Interview with Congressman David Dreier, 6 June 1996.

5. Drew, *Showdown,* pp. 35–39.

6. Dreier interview.

7. Adam Clymer, "Gingrich Moves Quickly to Put Stamp on House," *New York Times,* 17 November 1994, p. A1. See also Evans and Oleszeck, *Congress Under Fire,* p. 88, and Gimpel, *Legislating the Revolution,* pp. 38–40.

8. Interview with Congressman Mark Souder, 21 February 1996.

9. On these changes see Evans and Oleszeck, *Congress under Fire,* pp. 91–93, and Gimpel, *Legislating the Revolution,* pp. 38–40.

10. Souder interview. Tom Delay of Texas held the third-ranking House leadership position of Majority Whip, after defeating Gingrich's close ally Bob Walker of Pennsylvania. John Boehner of Ohio was elected chair of the House Republican Conference (the number-four position), and Christopher Cox of California was chair of the House Republican Policy Committee.

11. Interview with Congressman Mark Foley, 30 April 1996.

12. Interview with Congressman Bob Livingston, 19 July 1996. In fact the seventy-three freshmen constituted almost a third (32 percent) of the House Republican Conference.

13. Interview with Congressman Bob Walker, 29 July 1996.

14. Livingston interview.

15. Interview with Congressman Zach Wamp, 17 July 1996.

16. Those ten freshman members had an average winning percentage of 51.2 in 1994. In 1996, nine of them ran for reelection and only one, Jim Bunn of Oregon, was defeated.

17. Interview with Congressman Steve Gunderson, 9 July 1996.

18. Freshman member interview, "off-the-record" remarks.

19. Interview with Congressman Ray LaHood, 25 July 1997.

20. Interview with Congressman Mark Neumann, 14 May 1996.

21. Walker interview.

22. Livingston interview.

23. Interview with Congressman Clay Shaw, 10 July 1996.

24. Interview with Congressman Bob Ehrlich, 23 April 1996.

25. See Adam Clymer, "With Political Discipline, It Works Like Parliament," *New York Times,* 6 August 1995, sec. 4, p. 6.

26. On the opening-day reforms, see Evans and Oleszek, *Congress under Fire,* pp. 105–9; and Gimpel, *Legislating the Revolution,* pp. 38–40.

27. Wamp interview.

28. Ehrlich interview.

29. On the Republican changes in floor procedures, see Evans and Oleszek, *Congress under Fire,* pp. 101–5, and 135–42.

30. The nonpartisan observers Evans and Oleszek concluded that overall the Republicans had created a more open floor process in the 104th Congress: "Definitional disputes aside, the floor amendment process in the Republican House has been generally more open than during the years leading up to the 104th Congress." Ibid., p. 139.

31. On the passage of the balanced budget amendment, see Gimpel, *Legislating the Revolution,* pp. 42–49; and Drew, *Showdown,* pp. 121–24.

32. On the "crown jewel" remark, see Eric Pianin, "GOP Claims Accord on Tax Cut,"*Washington Post,* 4 April 1995, p. A1.

33. On the Republican defeat on missile systems, see Gimpel, *Legislating the Revolution,* pp. 67–78.

34. Ibid., p. 98.

35. Interview with Congressman J.C. Watts, 2 May 1996.

36. Interview with Congressman Walter Jones, 23 April 1996.

37. Interview with Congressman Van Hilleary, 18 July 1996.

38. Ehrlich interview.

39. On the term limits proposals, see Gimpel, *Legislating the Revolution,* pp. 95–104, and Evans and Oleszek, *Congress under Fire,* pp. 144–46.

40. Interview with Congressman Joe Scarborough, 28 May 1996.

41. Interview with Congressman Mark Sanford, 12 June 1996.

42. Interview with Congressman Gil Gutknecht, 29 February 1996.

43. Interview with Congressman Jon Fox, 16 July 1996.

44. Jones interview.

45. Foley interview.

46. Interview with Congressman Brian Bilbray, 27 June 1996.

47. Souder interview.

48. Interview with Congressman Ed Whitfield, 31 July 1996.

49. Foley interview.

50. Jones interview.

51. Interview with Congressman Tom Campbell, 1 August 1996.

52. LaTourette interview.

53. Bilbray interview.

54. Interview with Congressman Bill Martini, 10 July 1996.

55. LaTourette interview. ISTEA (Intermodal Surface Transportation Efficiency Act) is the legislation authorizing funding of federal road and rail projects including the National Highway System.

56. Interview with Congressman Richard "Doc" Hastings, 12 July 1996.

57. Interview with Congressman Bob Barr, 18 June 1996.

58. Interview with Congressman David McIntosh, 18 July 1996.

59. Interview with Congressman Tom Davis, 14 May 1996.

60. Barr interview.

61. Scarborough interview.

62. Hilleary interview.

63. Interview with Congressman David Funderburk, 28 March 1996.

64. Shaw interview.

65. Gunderson interview.

66. Interview with Congressman Lee Hamilton, 26 July 1996.

67. Freshman member interview, "off-the-record" remarks.

68. Gutknecht interview.

69. Freshman member interview, "off-the-record" remarks.

70. Watts interview.

71. Campbell interview.

72. Neumann interview.

73. Martini interview.
74. LaTourette interview.
75. Walker interview.

Notes to Chapter 4

1. Newt Gingrich, *To Renew America* (New York: HarperCollins, 1995), p. 87.

2. On Reagan and the advent of "supply-side" economics, see Martin Anderson, *Revolution: The Reagan Legacy* (Stanford, Calif.: Hoover Institution Press, 1990), pp. 140–63.

3. On "Reaganomics" and the deficit, see Joseph White and Aaron Wildavsky, *The Deficit and the Public Interest: The Search for Responsible Budgeting in the 1980s* (Berkeley: University of California Press, 1991), pp. 95–204.

4. On Stockman, see William Greider, *The Education of David Stockman and Other Americans* (New York: Dutton, 1982); and David A. Stockman, *The Triumph of Politics: How the Reagan Revolution Failed* (New York: Harper & Row, 1986).

5. See White and Wildavsky, *The Deficit and the Public Interest,* pp. 383–529.

6. On the House Republican revolt against Bush's 1990 budget deal, see Dan Balz and Ronald Brownstein, *Storming the Gates: Protest Politics and the Republican Revival* (Boston: Little, Brown, 1996), pp. 130–40.

7. Interview with Congressman Joe Scarborough, 28 May 1996.

8. Interview with Congresswoman Sue Kelly, 30 May 1996.

9. Interview with Congressman Dick Chrysler, 6 March 1996.

10. Interview with Congressman Richard "Doc" Hastings, 12 July 1996.

11. Interview with Congressman Jon Fox, 16 July 1996.

12. Interview with Congressman Ed Whitfield, 31 July 1996.

13. Interview with Congressman Ray LaHood, 25 July 1996.

14. Interview with Congressman David McIntosh, 18 July 1996.

15. The line-item veto law was immediately challenged in federal court as an unconstitutional violation of the separation of powers by a number of members of Congress led by Democratic Congressman David Skaggs of Colorado and veteran Democratic Senator Robert Byrd of West Virginia. U.S. District Court Judge Thomas P. Jackson found in their favor on 10 April 1997, but the Clinton administration immediately appealed the decision to the Supreme Court. The Supreme Court's 7–2 decision on 26 June 1997 did not rule on the merits of the issue but rejected the case on the grounds that the president had not yet used the veto and thus the members of Congress lacked standing to sue. See Andrew Taylor, "Judge Voids Line-Item Veto Law; Backers Look to High Court," *Congressional Quarterly Weekly Report,* 12 April 1997, pp. 833–37; and Robert Pear, "Court Allows Clinton the Line-Item Veto," *New York Times,* 27 June 1997, p. A17.

16. Elizabeth Drew, *Showdown: The Struggle between the Gingrich Congress and the Clinton White House* (New York: Simon and Schuster, 1996), p. 121.

17. Dick Williams, *Newt! Leader of the Second American Revolution* (Marietta, Ga.: Longstreet Press, 1995), p. 211.

18. Ibid., pp. 212–13.

19. Drew, *Showdown,* pp. 208–9; and Eric Pianin, "House GOP Plan Seeks

$1.4 Trillion in Savings," *Washington Post,* 11 May 1995, p. A1.

20. Drew, *Showdown,* pp. 208–9.

21. Michael Wines, "A Gingrich Budget Gain," *New York Times,* 24 June 1995, p. 1.

22. Michael Wines, "GOP Leadership Announces Deal on Tax Reduction," *New York Times,* 23 June 1997, p. A1.

23. Barbara Sinclair, *Unorthodox Lawmaking: New Legislative Processes in the U.S. Congress* (Washington, D.C.: CQ Press, 1997), p. 176.

24. Charles Murray, *Losing Ground: American Social Policy, 1950–1980* (New York: Basic Books, 1984).

25. On the House welfare plan, see James G. Gimpel, *Legislating the Revolution: The Contract with America in Its First 100 Days* (Boston: Allyn and Bacon, 1996), pp. 79–94.

26. On the Senate welfare bill, see Drew, *Showdown,* p. 315.

27. "Reconciliation: Highlights of the Conference Report," *Congressional Quarterly Weekly Report,* 18 November 1995, pp. 3513–15.

28. David Maraniss and Michael Weisskopf, *Tell Newt to Shut Up!* (New York: Touchstone, 1996), pp. 128–29.

29. See ibid., p. 131; and Drew, *Showdown,* p. 204.

30. On the Republican strategizing over Medicare, see Maraniss and Weisskopf, *"Tell Newt to Shut Up!"* pp. 128–33; and Robin Toner, "GOP Medicare Effort Avoids Deadly Detail," *New York Times,* 2 August 1995, p. A1.

31. Maraniss and Weisskopf, *Tell Newt to Shut Up!* pp. 138–45.

32. See Todd S. Purdom, "Clinton Joins Rally on Medicare's Birthday," *New York Times,* 26 July 1995, p. A16.

33. Maraniss and Weisskopf, *Tell Newt to Shut Up!* pp. 142–45.

34. See Jerry Gray, "In House, Spending Bills Open Way to Make Policy," *New York Times,* 19 July 1995, p. A10.

35. Drew, *Showdown,* p. 256.

36. On DeLay and his opposition to environmental regulations, see Maraniss and Weisskopf, *Tell Newt to Shut Up!* pp. 11–21.

37. John H. Cushman Jr., "GOP Plan for Environment Is Facing a Big Test in Congress," *New York Times,* 17 July 1995, p. A1; and "House Bill Would Block New EPA Pollution Rules," *New York Times,* 17 July 1995, p. A18.

38. On the Istook amendment, antiabortion, and other appropriations riders, see Drew, *Showdown,* pp. 256–72.

39. Ibid., p. 260.

40. LaHood interview.

41. Interview with Congressman E. Clay Shaw, 10 July 1996.

42. Clinton's rhetoric of national unity in the wake of a catastrophe that killed 167 federal government employees contrasted with the harsh partisanship and antigovernment tone of some of the congressional Republicans over the preceding three months. The president, moreover, used the opportunity to attack the extreme right-wing militia movement that had produced the bombers but also had some rhetorical and organizational ties to a handful of Republican members of Congress. On the political impact of the Oklahoma bombing, see Drew, *Showdown,* pp. 195–202.

43. George Hagar, "Budget Battle Came Sooner Than Either Side Expected,"

Congressional Quarterly Weekly Report, 18 November 1995, pp. 3503–09.

44. Alissa J. Rubin, *Congressional Quarterly Weekly Report,* 18 November 1995, p. 3512.

45. Alissa J. Rubin, "Reality of Tough Job Ahead Dampens Joy Over Deal," *Congressional Quarterly Weekly Report,* 25 November 1995, pp. 3597–99.

46. George Hager, "Harsh Rhetoric on Budget Spells a Dismal Outlook," *Congressional Quarterly Weekly Report,* 9 December 1995, p. 3721.

47. George Hager and Alissa J. Rubin, "As Budget Talks Break Down, Finger-Pointing Escalates," *Congressional Quarterly Weekly Report,* 16 December 1995, pp. 3789–92.

48. On Rubin, see Andrew Taylor, "Rubin's Footwork Frustrates GOP," *Congressional Quarterly Weekly Report,* 16 December 1995, p. 3793. On the erosion of public support for the Republicans during the shutdown, see Maraniss and Weisskopf, *Tell Newt to Shut Up!* pp. 170–77.

49. See Jackie Koszcuk, " 'Train Wreck' Engineered by GOP ... Batters Party and House Speaker," *Congressional Quarterly Weekly Report,* 18 November 1995, pp. 3506–07.

50. Marannis and Weisskopf, *Tell Newt to Shut Up!* pp. 179–203.

51. See Adam Clymer, "73 GOP Freshmen at the Fore," *New York Times,* 21 December 1995, p. A1.

52. David E. Rosenbaum, "GOP Rebellion Scuttles Accord on Budget Talks," *New York Times,* 21 December 1995, p. A1.

53. George Hagar, "A Battered GOP Calls Workers Back to Job," *Congressional Quarterly Weekly Report,* 6 January 1996, pp. 53–57.

54. Alissa J. Rubin, "GOP Backs Down, Votes to Raise Debt Limit," *Congressional Quarterly Weekly Report,* 30 March 1996, p. 871.

55. George Hagar, "Congress, Clinton Yield Enough to Close the Book on Fiscal '96," *Congressional Quarterly Weekly Report,* 27 April 1996, pp. 1155–57.

56. See, for example, Jackie Calmes, "Militancy of the GOP Freshmen Leaves Gingrich Little Room to Compromise," *Wall Street Journal,* 22 December 1995, p. A3; and David Bowermaster, "Meet the Mavericks," *US News & World Report,* 25 December 1995/1 January 1996, pp. 53–55.

57. Interview with Congressman Tom Davis, 14 May 1996.

58. On Congressman Neumann's background and passionate commitment to a balanced budget see also Jeffrey Goldberg, "Adventures of a Republican Revolutionary," *New York Times Sunday Magazine,* 3 November 1996, p. 42.

59. Interview with Congressman Bob Livingston, 18 July 1996.

60. On the Neumann affair, see also C. Lawrence Evans and Walter J. Oleszek, *Congress under Fire: Reform Politics and the Republican Majority* (Boston: Houghton Mifflin, 1997), p. 126.

61. Interview with Congressman Mark Neumann, 16 May 1996.

62. Scarborough interview.

63. Interview with Congressman J.D. Hayworth, 1 August 1996.

64. Chrysler interview.

65. Interview with Congressman Van Hilleary, 18 July 1996.

66. Interview with Congressman George Radanovich, 31 May 1996.

67. Interview with Congressman Bob Ehrlich, 23 April 1996.

68. Interview with Congressman Walter Jones, 23 April 1996.

69. Interview with Congressman J.C. Watts, 2 May 1996.

70. Whitfield interview.

71. Hayworth interview.

72. Interview with Congressman Steve LaTourette, 10 July 1996.

73. Davis interview.

74. Interview with Congressman Zach Wamp, 17 July 1996.

75. McIntosh interview.

76. Ibid.

77. Interview with Congressman David Funderburk, 28 March 1996.

78. Freshman interview, 12 June 1996. Anonymity requested.

79. Interview with Congressman Gil Gutknecht, 29 February 1996.

80. Ibid.

81. Livingston interview.

82. McIntosh interview.

83. Wamp interview.

84. Interview with Congressman Brian Bilbray, 27 June 1996.

85. See Drew, *Showdown,* pp. 266–67.

86. See *Congressional Quarterly Weekly Report,* 13 January 1996, pp. 104–5. The twelve freshmen dissidents were Bob Barr (Ga.); Steve Chabot (Ohio); Helen Chenoweth (Idaho); Greg Ganske (Iowa); Lindsey Graham (S.C.); John Hostettler (Ind.); Steve Largent (Okla.); Mark Sanford (S.C.); John Shadegg (Ariz.); Linda Smith (Wash.); Mark Souder (Ind.); Todd Tiahrt (Kans.). All were reelected in the 1996 congressional elections.

87. See Jackie Koszczuk, "GOP Faces Campaign Year Adrift in Roiled Waters," *Congressional Quarterly Weekly Report,* 20 January 1996, pp. 139–41.

88. Interview with Congressman Mark Souder, 21 February 1996.

89. Interview with Congressman Bob Barr, 18 June 1996.

90. Interview with Congressman Lindsey Graham, 11 July 1996.

91. Neumann interview.

92. Scarborough interview.

93. Gutknecht interview.

94. Republican freshman's "off-the-record" remarks, 30 April 1996.

95. Souder interview.

96. Interview with Congressman Bill Martini, 23 July 1996.

Notes to Chapter 5

1. "Off-the-record" remarks.

2. The Republicans secured a 52–48 majority in the Senate in the 1994 elections. Senator Richard Shelby of Alabama switched parties the day after the election, to bring the Republican total to fifty-three.

3. Interview with Senator Bill Frist, 24 July 1996.

4. Interview with David Ayres, chief of staff to Senator John Ashcroft, 29 May 1996.

5. Interview with Tony Fratto, communications director for Senator Rick Santorum, 19 July 1996.

6. Interview with Senator James Inhofe, 10 July 1996.

7. Interview with Senator Craig Thomas, 13 May 1996.

8. Interview with Senator Rod Grams, 29 July 1996.

9. Interview with Senator Jon Kyl, 14 June 1996.

10. Interview with Laurel Pressler, chief of staff to Senator Mike DeWine, 7 August 1996.

11. Interview with Alex Pratt, press secretary to Senator Fred Thompson, 3 May 1996.

12. Grams interview.

13. Fratto interview.

14. Frist interview.

15. The one limitation on the Senate filibuster is that it cannot be used to block legislation pertaining to the annual budget (i.e., reconciliation or appropriations bills).

16. Interview with Senator Thad Cochran, 27 July 1996. Senator Cochran also served in the U.S. House from 1972 to 1978.

17. William S. White, *Citadel: The Story of the U.S. Senate* (New York: Harper & Brothers, 1956).

18. Donald R. Matthews, *U.S. Senators and Their World* (New York: Vintage Books, 1960), pp. 92–117.

19. See Nicol C. Rae, *Southern Democrats* (New York: Oxford University Press, 1994), pp. 96–99. On the Senate in the 1950s, see also Barbara Sinclair, *The Transformation of the U.S. Senate* (Baltimore: Johns Hopkins University Press, 1989), pp. 8–29.

20. Sinclair, *Transformation of the U.S. Senate,* pp. 30–50.

21. Barbara Sinclair, *Unorthodox Lawmaking: New Legislative Processes in the U.S. Congress* (Washington, D.C.: CQ Press, 1997), p. 76. On change in the Senate and the emergence of a new norm of behavior, see also Sinclair, *Transformation of the U.S. Senate,* pp. 60–102.

22. See Christopher J. Bailey, *The Republican Party in the U.S. Senate, 1974–1984: Party Change and Institutional Development* (Manchester: Manchester University Press, 1988).

23. Sinclair, *Unorthodox Lawmaking,* p. 77.

24. Kyl interview.

25. Inhofe interview.

26. Pressler interview.

27. Kyl interview.

28. Grams interview.

29. Thomas interview.

30. Ayres interview.

31. Fratto interview.

32. Inhofe interview.

33. Frist interview.

34. Fratto interview.

35. Grams interview.

36. Kyl interview.

37. Ayres interview.

38. Pratt interview.

39. Inhofe interview.

40. Grams interview.

41. Fratto interview.

42. Thomas interview.

43. See Elizabeth Drew, *Showdown: The Struggle between the Gingrich Congress and the Clinton White House* (Washington, D.C.: Simon and Schuster, 1996), p. 18; and Helen Dewar, "Daschle, Lott Anointed by Senate Peers," *Washington Post,* 3 December 1994, p. A1.

44. The Senate was distinctly less enthusiastic than the House about term limitations, but under pressure from the freshmen, Majority Leader and GOP presidential candidate Dole attempted to bring a constitutional amendment to the Senate floor for a vote in April 1996. Democratic senators did not want to expose themselves electorally by allowing a vote on the measure, however, and an attempted cloture motion failed 58–42 (or two votes short of the sixty required to close debate) with all fifty-three Senate Republicans voting in favor. See David S. Cloud, "Term Limits Stall in Senate; GOP Blames Democrats," *Congressional Quarterly Weekly Report,* 27 April 1996, pp. 1153–54.

45. Cochran interview.

46. Inhofe interview.

47. Kyl interview.

48. Grams interview.

49. Fratto interview.

50. Interview with Will Feltus, staff director of the Senate Republican Conference in the 104th Congress, 6 August 1996.

51. Inhofe interview.

52. Thomas interview.

53. Grams interview.

54. Inhofe interview.

55. Ayres interview.

56. Pressler interview.

57. On the first "fly-around," see Mary Jacoby, "Have Chartered Plane, Will Travel: Senate GOP Freshmen Take to the Air in Class's First Field Trip," *Roll Call,* 22 January 1996, p. A1.

58. Inhofe interview.

59. Fratto interview.

60. Ayres interview.

61. Grams interview.

62. See C. Lawrence Evans and Walter J. Oleszek, *Congress under Fire: Reform Politics and the Republican Majority* (Boston: Houghton Mifflin, 1997), pp. 152–56.

63. Feltus interview.

64. Fratto interview.

65. Evans and Oleszek, *Congress under Fire,* pp. 153–54.

66. Kyl interview.

67. Evans and Oleszek, *Congress under Fire,* p. 155.

68. Cochran interview. In the spirit of the new rules, Senator Cochran announced that he would give up the position of Conference chair, after serving for six years, at the end of the 104th Congress, even though the new rules that came into effect in January 1997 did not apply term limitations retroactively.

69. See Kenneth Cooper and Helen Dewar, "100 Days Down but Senate to Go for Most 'Contract' Items," *Washington Post,* 9 April 1995, p. A6.

70. Fratto interview.

71. Thomas interview.

72. Ayres interview.

73. On the Gramm-Dole rivalry, see Drew, *Showdown,* pp. 77–79.

74. Sinclair, *Unorthodox Lawmaking,* pp. 183–84.

75. David E. Rosenbaum, "Senate Panel Offers Budget That Balances," *New York Times,* 10 May 1995, p. A1.

76. See David E. Rosenbaum, "Gramm Proposal for Deep Tax Cut Killed by Senate," *New York Times,* 24 May 1995, p. A1; and Drew, *Showdown,* pp. 211–12.

77. Eric Pianin, "Senate Passes Balanced Budget Plan; Sharp Program Reductions Are Endorsed in 57–42 Vote," *Washington Post,* 26 May 1995, p. A1. Republican ranks in the Senate had been further augmented by the party switch of Colorado Senator Ben Nighthorse Campbell in March 1995.

78. Michael Wines, "GOP Leadership Announces Deal on Tax Reduction," *New York Times,* 23 June 1995, p. A1.

79. Drew, *Showdown,* pp. 239–42; and Michael Wines, "A Gingrich Budget Gain," *New York Times,* 24 June 1995, p. 1.

80. Ibid., pp. 279–83.

81. Sinclair, *Unorthodox Lawmaking,* pp. 190–91.

82. The Byrd Rule was named after veteran Democratic Senator Robert C. Byrd of West Virginia, who devised it during the budget battles of the 1980s.

83. Sinclair, *Unorthodox Lawmaking,* pp. 199–201.

84. Alissa J. Rubin, "Congress Readies Budget Bill for President's Veto Pen," *Congressional Quarterly Weekly Report,* 18 November 1995, p. 3512.

85. David S. Cloud, "Dole Gambles on Budget Crisis," *Congressional Quarterly Weekly Report,* 6 January 1996, p. 54; and David Maraniss and Michael Weisskopf, *Tell Newt to Shut Up!* (New York: Simon and Schuster, 1996), pp. 188–200.

86. Inhofe interview.

87. Grams interview.

88. Ayres interview.

89. Thomas interview.

90. Kyl interview.

91. Thomas interview.

92. Fratto interview.

93. Pratt interview. Ms. Pratt had earlier worked as press secretary to Republican Congressman Stephen Horn of California.

94. Frist interview. The Foster nomination became controversial because it emerged during his confirmation hearings that Dr. Foster had performed abortions at one point in his career. The nomination was finally withdrawn after the failure of two attempts to end a Republican filibuster on the Senate floor. See Francis X. Clines, "Clinton's Choice for Top Doctor Is Rebuffed by a Vote in Senate," *New York Times,* 23 June 1995, p. A1.

95. Thomas interview.

96. Cochran interview.

Notes to Chapter 6

1. Interview with Congressman Mark Sanford, 12 June 1996.

2. Exceptions were allowed for gifts valued at less than $10, and gifts from relatives and close friends, although the latter would require approval from the Senate Ethics Committee if the value was greater than $250. See Adam Clymer, "Senate Votes 98–0 for Strict Limits on Lobbyist Gifts," *New York Times,* 29 July 1995, p. 1.

3. See Jonathan D. Salant, "House Votes to Toughen Gift Restrictions," *Congressional Quarterly Weekly Report,* 18 November 1995, pp. 3516–19.

4. See Jonathan D. Salant, "Bill Would Open Windows on Lobbying Efforts," *Congressional Quarterly Weekly Report,* 2 December 1995, pp. 3631–33.

5. Ibid., p. 3631.

6. See Donna Cassata, "Bipartisan Overhaul Measure Meets an Unsurprising End," *Congressional Quarterly Weekly Report,* 29 June 1996, pp. 1856–58.

7. On Linda Smith and her impact, see Graeme Browning, "The Cage Rattler," *National Journal,* 27 January 1996, p. 28; Michael Lind, "Me and Mrs. Smith," *New Republic,* 5 February 1996, pp. 16–18; Erika Niedowski, "Rep. Linda Smith: Washington Freshman Steps on Toes as She Crusades for Change," *The Hill,* 13 March 1996, p. 28.

8. Interview with Congressman Bob Livingston, 19 July 1996.

9. Interview with Congressman David Dreier, 6 June 1996.

10. Interview with Congressman Bob Walker, 29 July 1996.

11. On the Hoekstra task force, see Timothy J. Burger and Benjamin Sheffner, "House Task Force Warns of GOP 'Division' on Campaign Reform," *Roll Call,* 26 February 1996, p. 1.

12. Michael Weisskopf, "PAC Cash Infusion, Push for Reform Collide in House GOP," *Washington Post,* 8 June 1996, p. A8.

13. See Adam Clymer, "Contract with America Includes Cash Bonuses," *New York Times,* 18 February 1996, p. 4E.

14. Weisskopf, "PAC Cash Infusion."

15. Jackie Koszcuk, "House Set to Vote on Overhaul, but Issue Appears Dead," *Congressional Quarterly Weekly Report,* 13 July 1996, p. 1949; and Donna Cassata, " 'Reform Week': Divisions on Display," *Congressional Quarterly Weekly Report,* 20 July 1996, p. 2022.

16. Cassata, "Reform Week."

17. Jackie Koszcuk, "House Rejects Democratic, Republican Overhauls," *Congressional Quarterly Weekly Report,* 27 July 1996, p. 2095.

18. On the vote, see *Congressional Quarterly Weekly Report,* 27 July 1996, pp. 2144–45.

19. Interview with Congressman Christopher Shays, 31 July 1996.

20. Richard S. Dunham, "The House Freshmen," *Business Week,* 29 January 1996, pp. 24–32.

21. On the labor effort, see Juliana Gruenwald and Robert Marshall Wells, "At Odds with Some Workers, AFL–CIO Takes Aim at GOP," *Congressional Quarterly Weekly Report,* 13 April 1997, pp. 993–98; and Elizabeth Drew, *What-*

ever It Takes: The Real Struggle for Political Power in America (New York: Viking Press, 1997), pp. 69–78.

22. See Gary Jacobson, "The 105th Congress: Unprecedented and Unsurprising," in Michael Nelson, ed., *The Elections of 1996,* (Washington, D.C.: CQ Press, 1997), pp. 143–66.

23. Shays interview.

24. Interview with Congressman J.D. Hayworth, 1 August 1996. At one point, an AFL–CIO ad was running fifty times a day on television stations in Congressman Hayworth's Arizona district. See Marjorie Randon Hershey, "The Congressional Elections," in Gerald M. Pomper, ed., *The Election of 1996: Reports and Interpretations,* (Chatham, N.J.: Chatham House, Inc., 1997), pp. 205–39.

25. See Jackie Koszczuk, "Democrats' Resurgence Fueled by Pragmatism," *Congressional Quarterly Weekly Report,* 4 May 1996, pp. 1205–10.

26. See Jackie Koszczuk, "Gingrich's Woes May Damage Rank and File, GOP Agenda," *Congressional Quarterly Weekly Report,* 9 December 1995, pp. 3703–5.

27. See Jackie Koszczuk, "Democrats Push to Expand Gingrich Investigation," *Congressional Quarterly Weekly Report,* 16 December 1995, pp. 378–384; and Koszczuk, "Widened Probe Keeps Speaker in Spotlight," *Congressional Quarterly Weekly Report,* 28 September 1996, pp. 2733–34.

28. See Drew, *Whatever It Takes,* pp. 69–78; and James W. Ceaser and Andrew E. Busch, *Losing to Win: The 1996 Elections and American Politics* (Lanham, Mass.: Rowman and Littlefield, 1997), pp. 121–27.

29. Richard E. Cohen, "Off-Balance," *National Journal,* 23 March 1996; and Marcia Gelbart, "Power in House Flows to Point Man Dick Armey," *The Hill,* 20 March 1996, p. 1.

30. See Jason DeParle, "Newt's Endgame," *New York Times Magazine,* 28 January 1996, p. 34.

31. On Gingrich's fund-raising prowess, see Craig Karmin, "Gingrich Nets GOP $3.2M in One Month," *The Hill,* 20 March 1996, p. 1; and Linda Killian, "Newt's Foley," *Weekly Standard,* 15 April 1996, pp. 18–19.

32. On Ganske, see Michael Weisskopf, "Some GOP Hopefuls Seek an Anti-Gingrich Vaccine," *Washington Post,* 22 June 1996, p. A1; and Drew, *Whatever It Takes,* pp. 65–66.

33. Michael Wines, "Democrats See Votes Hitting at Gingrich," *New York Times,* 1 August 1996, p. A16; and Jennifer Bradley, "Study Shows GOP House Party Line Votes Slipping from Last Year's Level," *Roll Call,* 22 July 1996, p. 3.

34. See Jonathan D. Salant, "House Republicans Stray from 'Contract' Terms," *Congressional Quarterly Weekly Report,* 6 July 1996, pp. 1929–33.

35. See Michael Wines, "Fervor of Freshmen Wanes as Re-Election Time Nears," *New York Times,* 24 March 1996, p. 1; Christopher Georges, "Backbone of the GOP Agenda May Be Crumbling under the Strain of Freshman Re-Election Races," *Wall Street Journal,* 1 March 1996, p. A16; and Jackie Koszczuk, "House GOP Freshmen Soften Their Edges," *Congressional Quarterly Weekly Report,* 3 February 1996, pp. 280–81.

36. Interview with Congressman George Radanovich, 31 May 1996.

37. Ibid. On the task forces, see also Mary Jacoby, "House GOP Freshmen 'Taking Control' with New Task Forces to Shape Agenda," *Roll Call,* 18 March 1996, p. 12.

38. On Congressman Neumann, see Jeffrey Goldberg, "Adventures of a Republican Revolutionary," *New York Times Magazine,* 3 November 1996, p. 42.

39. Interview with Congressman Bob Ehrlich, 23 April 1996.

40. Interview with Congressman Brian Bilbray, 27 June 1996.

41. Interview with Congressman Joe Scarborough, 28 May 1996.

42. Interview with Congressman J.C. Watts, 2 May 1996.

43. See Janet Hook, "GOP Freshmen Keep Pork on Reelection Menu," *Los Angeles Times, Washington Edition,* 1 July 1996, p. A1; and Andrew Taylor, "GOP Pet Projects Give Boost to Shaky Incumbents," *Congressional Quarterly Weekly Report,* 3 August 1966, pp. 2169–73.

44. See Dan Morgan, "GOP Hill Revolution Yields to Compromise," *Washington Post,* 15 April 1996, p. A1.

45. Interview with Congressman Steve LaTourette, 10 July 1996.

46. On DeLay and Republican fund-raising efforts, see David Maraniss and Michael Weisskopf, "Speaker and His Directors Make the Cash Flow Right," *Washington Post,* 27 November 1995, p. A1; and Maraniss and Weisskopf, *Tell Newt to Shut Up* (New York: Touchstone, 1996), pp. 110–27.

47. Clymer, "Contract with America Includes Cash Bonuses," p. 4E.

48. Maraniss and Weisskopf, "Speaker and the Directors Make Cash Flow Light," p. A9.

49. Figures from Anthony Corrado, "Financing the 1996 Elections," in *The Election of 1996,* Pomper, ed., p. 162. On the freshmen's fund-raising prowess, see also Susan B. Garland, "Feeding Frenzy at the Money Trough," *Business Week,* 29 January 1996, p. 29; and Benjamin Sheffner, "Vulnerable GOP Frosh Rake in Cash," *Roll Call,* 8 February 1996, p. 11.

50. Buchanan had no public support from any Republican member of Congress, while Forbes had been endorsed only by Ohio House freshman Frank Cremeans.

51. On the 1996 Republican nominating campaign, see Ceaser and Busch, *Losing to Win,* pp. 57–87; William G. Mayer, "The Presidential Nominations," in *The Election of 1996,* Pomper, ed., pp. 21–76; and Harold W. Stanley, "The Nominations: Republican Doldrums, Democratic Revival," in Nelson, ed., *The Elections of 1996,* pp. 14–43.

52. See Jackie Koszczuk, "Democrats' Resurgence Fueled by Pragmatism," *Congressional Quarterly Weekly Report,* 4 May 1996, pp. 1205–10.

53. Jackie Koszczuk and Jonathan Weisman, "Election-Year Gridlock Grips the Capitol," *Congressional Quarterly Weekly Report,* 11 May 1996, pp. 1275–79.

54. See Adam Clymer, "House Approves Repeal of the Ban on Assault Guns," *New York Times,* 23 March 1996, p. 1; and Drew, *Whatever It Takes,* p. 43. The repeal passed 239–173 with forty-two Republicans voting in opposition, including seven freshmen: Campbell (Calif.); Bilbray (Calif.); Ganske (Iowa); Frelinghuysen (N.J.); Martini (N.J.); Fox (Pa.); and Davis (Va.).

55. The House, in an unusual alliance of conservative anti-federal-government Republicans (including most of the freshman class) and Democratic civil libertarians, supported an amendment authored by Georgia Republican freshman Bob Barr that stripped the bill of provisions to expand the FBI's wiretapping authority over suspected terrorists, bar fund raising in the United States by foreign terrorist groups, and ease deportation of suspected alien terrorists. See Holly Edelson,

"House Strips New Powers from Terrorism Bill," *Congressional Quarterly Weekly Report,* 16 March 1996, pp. 702–5; and Ronald Brownstein, "Dole's Juggling of Agendas Faces GOP Opposition," *Los Angeles Times,* 18 March 1996, p. A3.

56. See Eric Pianin, "House Narrowly Passes Balanced Budget Plan," *Washington Post,* 13 June 1997, p. A6.

57. Sanford interview.

58. Jackie Koszczuk and Jonathan Weisman, "GOP Bending on Raise in Minimum Wage," *Congressional Quarterly Weekly Report,* 20 April 1996, p. 1047.

59. On the Farm bill, see David Hosansky, "House Easily Clears Rewrite of Decades-Old Farm Laws," *Congressional Quarterly Weekly Report,* 30 March 1996, pp. 874–75. On the Telecom bill, see Dan Carney, "Congress Fires Its First Shot in the Information Revolution," *Congressional Quarterly Weekly Report,* 3 February 1996, pp. 289–94.

60. See, for example, Charles E. Cook, "Lack of Leadership, Followership Produces House GOP Paralysis," *Roll Call,* 11 March 1996, p. 6; Kevin Phillips, "Why This Congress Must Be Considered the Worst in a Half-Century," *Los Angeles Times,* 4 February 1996, p. M1; Fred Barnes, "Maximum Meltdown," *Weekly Standard,* 29 April 1996, pp. 11–12; and Garry Wills, "What Happened to the Revolution," *New York Review of Books,* 6 June 1996, pp. 11–16.

61. See Marcia Gelbart, "Gingrich Redefines Role as Speaker," *The Hill,* 28 February 1996; and Jackie Koszczuk, "With Humor and Firm Hand, Armey Rules the House," *Congressional Quarterly Weekly Report,* 2 March 1996, pp. 523–28.

62. See Robert D. Novak, "Seeking a GOP Leader," *Washington Post,* 14 March 1996, p. A27.

63. Interview with Congressman David McIntosh, 18 July 1996.

64. Interview with Congressman Funderburk, 28 March 1996.

65. Interview with Congressman Ray LaHood, 25 July 1996.

66. Ibid.

67. Interview with Congressman Tom Campbell, 1 August 1996.

68. LaTourette interview.

69. See Jackie Koszczuk, "Dole Leaves Senate Behind to Hit Campaign Trail," *Congressional Quarterly Weekly Report,* 18 May 1996, pp. 1357–60.

70. Dole was particularly frustrated when the Democrats prevented him from getting credit for a reduction in the federal gasoline tax by persistently attaching their amendment on the minimum wage to the legislation. See Koszczuk and Weisman, "Election-Year Gridlock Grips the Capitol," pp. 1275–79.

71. On Lott, see Donna Cassata, "In Senate Balancing Act, Lott Finds His Footing," *Congressional Quarterly Weekly Report,* 27 July 1996, pp. 2091–94.

72. Interview with Congressman Lindsey Graham, 11 July 1996.

73. Interview with David Ayres, chief of staff to Senator John Ashcroft, 19 May 1996.

74. On the congressional leadership's decision to put their own interests ahead of Dole's, see Drew, *Whatever It Takes,* pp. 89–100.

75. On the flurry of compromise legislation at the end of the 104th Congress, see Helen Dewar and Eric Pianin, "Choosing Pragmatism over Partisanship," *Washington Post National Weekly Edition,* 12–18 August 1996, p. 12; and Adam Clymer, "Clinton and Congress: Partnership of Self-Interest," *New York Times,* 2 October 1996, p. A1.

76. On the welfare bill, see Jeffrey L. Katz, "After 60 Years, Most Control Is Passing to States," *Congressional Quarterly Weekly Report,* 3 August 1996, pp. 2190–96.

77. On the politics of the welfare bill, see Drew, *Whatever It Takes*; and Jeffrey L. Katz, "Welfare Showdown Looms as GOP Readies Plan," *Congressional Quarterly Weekly Report,* 27 July 1997, pp. 2115–19.

78. Alissa J. Rubin, "Congress Clears Wage Increase with Tax Breaks for Business," *Congressional Quarterly Weekly Report,* 3 August 1996, pp. 2175–77.

79. On the health insurance bill, see Steve Langdon, "Kennedy, Kassebaum Steer Insurance Bill to Safety," *Congressional Quarterly Weekly Report,* 3 August 1996, pp. 2197–2200.

80. Freshman Senator Spencer Abraham of Michigan and freshman House members Sam Brownback of Kansas and Dick Chrysler of Michigan played a major role in derailing the legal immigration restrictions, reflecting a lack of consensus among freshman Republicans and the GOP as whole over the immigration issue. See Holly Idelson, "Economic Anxieties Bring Debate on Immigration to a Boil," *Congressional Quarterly Weekly Report,* 16 March 1996, pp. 697–701.

81. On the immigration bill, see Dan Carney, "As the White House Calls Shots, Illegal Alien Bill Clears," *Congressional Quarterly Weekly Report,* 5 October 1996, pp. 2864–66.

82. On the safe drinking-water legislation, see David Hosansky, "Drinking Water Bill Clears; Clinton Expected to Sign," *Congressional Quarterly Weekly Report,* 3 August 1996, pp. 2179–80.

83. George Hagar, "Harmony Born of Pressure Speeds Spending Wrap-Up," *Congressional Quarterly Weekly Report,* 5 October 1996, pp. 2842–44.

84. On the bill outlawing partial-birth abortions, see Elizabeth Palmer, "Late-term Procedure Bill Heads to Clinton for Expected Veto," *Congressional Quarterly Weekly Report,* 30 March 1996, pp. 885–86. On DOMA, see Dan Carney, "GOP Bill Restricting Gay Unions Clears . . . but Does Not Yield Political Dividends," *Congressional Quarterly Weekly Report,* 14 September 1996, pp. 2598–99.

85. On the minimal presence of the GOP Congress at the San Diego convention, see Carroll J. Doherty, "At the Convention, New Contractors," *Congressional Quarterly Weekly Report,* 17 August 1996, p. 2308; and Drew, *Whatever It Takes,* pp. 104–29.

86. See Jacobson, "The 105th Congress," in Nelson, ed., *The Elections of 1996,* pp. 151–54.

87. Ibid.

88. Two freshmen, Wes Cooley (Ore.) and Enid Greene (Utah), were retiring under a cloud of scandal. Sam Brownback (Kans.) was running for the U.S. Senate seat vacated by Bob Dole.

89. On labor's drive, see Jonathan Salant, "Finances Take Priority in This Year's Races," *Congressional Quarterly Weekly Report,* 26 October 1996, pp. 3081–84; Francis X. Clines, "Political Force: Labor, Thanks to New Leader," *New York Times,* 29 October 1996; and Jacobson, "The 105th Congress," in Nelson, ed., *The Elections of 1996,* p. 157.

90. See Adam Clymer, "Labor Flexes Its Financial Muscle to Raise Stakes in a Michigan Congressional Battle," and Steven Greenhouse, "Pro-Labor Republicans Feel Betrayed by Union Effort," *New York Times,* 31 October 1996, p. A16;

and Gary Younge, "In Michigan, Big Labor Tries to Win Back What It Lost," *Washington Post National Weekly Edition*, 14–20 October 1996, p. 12.

91. See Corrado, "Financing the 1996 Elections," in Pomper, ed., *The Election of 1996*, p. 161.

92. Ibid., p. 152.

93. On Barbour, see David Grann, "The Barbour of the Hill," *Weekly Standard*, 2 December 1996, pp. 10–12.

94. Corrado, "Financing the 1996 Elections," in Pomper, ed., *The Election of 1996*, pp. 162–64; Jonathan Weisman, "Republicans Battle Unions on Hill and on Airwaves," *Congressional Quarterly Weekly Report*, 10 August 1996, pp. 2250–52; and Richard W. Stevenson, "A Campaign to Build Influence: Business Groups Try to Forge a Unified Political Front," *New York Times*, 29 October 1996, p. C1. On the role of the Christian Coalition in the 1996 congressional elections, see also Drew, *Whatever It Takes*, pp. 22–28; and Dan Balz and Ronald Brownstein, "God's Fixer," *Washington Post Magazine*, 28 January 1996, p. 8.

95. John E. Yang, "It's Hard to Have Coattails If You're Hanging by a Thread," *Washington Post National Weekly Edition*, 21–27 October 1996, p. 12.

96. Editorial, "Saving the GOP from Dole-Kemp '96," *Weekly Standard*, 21 October 1996, p. 11.

97. Drew, *Whatever It Takes*, pp. 153–74.

98. Elizabeth Drew, who followed the battle for the House closely, is convinced that the fund-raising fracas and the late Republican advertising blitz against a "blank check" for Clinton saved the House for the GOP. See Ibid., pp. 197–228; and Ceaser and Busch, *Losing to Win*, pp. 121–27.

99. From Michael Barone and Grant Ujifusa, *The Almanac of American Politics 1998* (Washington, D.C.: National Journal, 1997).

100. Jonathan D. Salant, "Million-Dollar Campaigns Proliferate in 105th," *Congressional Quarterly Weekly Report*, 21 December 1996, pp. 3448–51.

101. Rhodes Cook, "Actual District Votes Belie Ideal of Bipartisanship," *Congressional Quarterly Weekly Report*, 12 April 1997, pp. 859–62.

102. See Ceaser and Busch, *Losing to Win*, pp. 140–41; and Adam Clymer, "Voters Dividing Almost Evenly in House Races, Survey Finds," *New York Times*, 6 November 1997, p. A17.

103. Ceaser and Busch, *Losing to Win*, pp. 136–42. On the "Clinton Republicans," see also Dan Balz and David Broder, "The Clinton Republicans," *Washington Post National Weekly Edition*, 14–20 October 1996, p. 11.

104. Rhodes Cook, "Thinnest of Margins Shows Country's Great Divide," *Congressional Quarterly Weekly Report*, 15 February 1996, pp. 441–44.

105. See Rhodes Cook, "Freshman Job Security No Comfort for GOP," *Congressional Quarterly Weekly Report*, 22 February 1997, p. 510. Gary Jacobson's data suggest that the AFL–CIO spending may have had a significant impact in suppressing Republican freshman reelection margins; see Jacobson, in "The 105th Congress," Nelson, ed., *The Elections of 1996*, pp. 155–59.

106. Data from Ceaser and Busch, *Losing to Win*, p. 140.

107. See Helen Dewar and Eric Pianin, "A Switch in Time That May Have Saved the GOP," *Washington Post National Weekly Edition*, 7–13 October 1996, p. 9; Andrew Taylor, "GOP's New Willingness to Compromise Brings Party Modest Success," *Congressional Quarterly Weekly Report*, 14 December 1996, p.

3371; and Christopher Georges and Jackie Calmes, "How the GOP Staged Its Comeback in Congress," *Wall Street Journal,* 7 November 1996, p. A16.

108. Interestingly, the Senate freshmen, most of whom were not before the voters in 1996, maintained an average party unity score of 94 percent in 1996. See Rebecca Carr, "GOP's Election-Year Worries Cooled Partisan Rancor," *Congressional Quarterly Weekly Report,* 21 December 1996, pp. 3432–35; and Jonathan D. Salant, "Some Republicans Turned Away from Leadership," *Congressional Quarterly Weekly Report,* 7 December 1996, pp. 3352–54.

Notes to Chapter 7

1. Interview with Congressman Mark Neumann, 16 May 1996. Neuman campaigned hard for reelection and won narrowly in a very difficult district that was easily carried by President Clinton. In 1997 he announced his intention to run for the U.S. Senate seat of Democratic Senator Russell Feingold of Wisconsin in 1998.

2. Interview with Congressman Joe Scarborough, 28 May 1996.

3. Interview with Congressman Steve LaTourette, 10 July 1996.

4. Interview with Congressman J.C. Watts, 2 May 1996.

5. Interview with Congressman Van Hilleary, 10 July 1996.

6. Interview with Senator Jon Kyl, 14 June 1996.

7. Interview with Congressman David McIntosh, 18 July 1996.

8. Interview with Congressman Lindsey Graham, 11 July 1996.

9. Interview with Congressman George Radanovich, 31 May 1996.

10. Interview with Congressman Bob Barr, 18 June 1996.

11. Interview with Congressman Ed Whitfield, 31 July 1996.

12. Interview with Senator Bill Frist, 24 July 1996.

13. See Byron E. Shafer, "The Notion of an Electoral Order: The Structure of Electoral Politics at the Accession of George Bush," in *The End of Realignment? Interpreting American Electoral Eras,* ed. Byron E. Shafer (Madison: University of Wisconsin Press, 1991), pp. 37–84.

14. See Nicol C. Rae, "Intra-Party Conflict in an Evolving Electoral Order: American Party Factionalism 1946–52 and 1990–96." Paper presented at the 1996 annual meeting of the American Political Science Association, San Francisco, 29 August–1 September 1996.

15. For a full discussion of this recent American electoral phenomenon of "losing to win," see James W. Ceaser and Andrew E. Busch, *Losing to Win: The 1996 Election and American Politics* (Lanham, Md.: Rowman and Littlefield, 1997), pp. 1–26.

16. On the rebellious conservative sophomores, see Jerry Gray, " 'Bad Boys' among the House Republicans Make a Point," *New York Times,* 22 March 1997, p. 8; and Matthew Rees, "Rebel for a Day," *Weekly Standard,* 4 August 1997, pp. 14–16.

17. See John R. Hibbing and Elizabeth Theiss-Morse, *Congress as Public Enemy: Public Attitudes toward American Political Institutions* (New York: Cambridge University Press, 1995), pp. 41–61; and *The Gallup Poll Monthly,* October 1996, pp. 27–66.

Bibliography

Interviews

David Ayres, chief of staff to Senator John Ashcroft, 29 May 1996.
Congressman Bob Barr, 18 June 1996.
Congressman Brian Bilbray, 27 June 1996.
Congressman Tom Campbell, 1 August 1996.
Congressman Dick Chrysler, 6 March 1996.
Senator Thad Cochran, 27 July 1996.
Congressman Tom Davis, 14 May 1996.
Congressman David Dreier, 6 June 1996.
Congressman Bob Ehrlich, 23 April 1996.
Will Feltus, staff director, Senate Republican Conference, 6 August 1996.
Congressman Mark Foley, 30 April 1996.
Congressman Jon Fox, 16 July 1996.
Tony Fratto, communications director for Senator Rick Santorum, 19 July 1996.
Senator Bill Frist, 24 July 1996.
Congressman David Funderburk, 28 March 1996.
Congressman Lindsey Graham, 11 July 1996.
Senator Rod Grams, 29 July 1996.
Congressman Steve Gunderson, 9 July 1996.
Congressman Gil Gutknecht, 29 February 1996.
Congressman Lee Hamilton, 26 July 1996.
Congressman Richard "Doc" Hastings, 12 July 1996.
Congressman J.D. Hayworth, 1 August 1996.
Congressman Van Hilleary, 18 July 1996.
Senator James Inhofe, 10 July 1996.
Congressman Walter Jones, 23 April 1996
Congresswoman Sue Kelly, 30 May 1996.
Senator Jon Kyl, 14 June 1996.
Congressman Ray LaHood, 25 July 1996.
Congressman Steve LaTourette, 10 July 1996.
Congressman Bob Livingston, 19 July 1996.
Congressman Bill Martini, 23 July 1996.
Congressman David McIntosh, 18 July 1996.

Congressman Mark Neumann, 16 May 1996.
Alex Pratt, press secretary to Senator Fred Thompson, 3 May 1996.
Laurel Pressler, chief of staff to Senator Mike DeWine, 7 August 1996.
Congressman George P. Radanovich, 31 May 1996.
Congressman Mark Sanford, 12 June 1996.
Congressman Joe Scarborough, 28 May 1996.
Congressman E. Clay Shaw, 10 July 1996.
Congressman Christopher Shays, 31 July 1996.
Congressman Mark Souder, 21 February 1996.
Senator Craig Thomas, 13 May 1996.
Congressman Bob Walker, 29 July 1996.
Congressman Zach Wamp, 17 July 1996.
Congressman J.C. Watts, 2 May 1996.
Congressman Ed Whitfield, 31 July 1996.

Newspapers and Periodicals

Business Week
Congressional Quarterly Weekly Report
Los Angeles Times
National Journal
New Republic
New York Review of Books
New York Times
Roll Call
The Hill
U.S. News and World Report
Wall Street Journal
Washington Post
Washington Post National Weekly Edition
Washington Times
Weekly Standard

Books and Articles

Aldrich, John H., and David W. Rohde. "A Tale of Two Speakers: A Comparison of Policy Making in the 100th and 104th Congresses." Paper presented at the annual meeting of the American Political Science Association, San Francisco, 29 August–1 September 1996.
———. "Balance of Power: Republican Party Leadership and the Committee System in the 104th Congress." Paper presented at the annual meeting of the Midwest Political Science Association, Chicago, 10–13 April 1997.
Anderson, Martin. *Revolution: The Reagan Legacy.* Stanford, Calif.: Hoover Institution Press, 1990.
Bader, John B. *Taking the Initiative: Leadership Agendas in Congress and the "Contract with America."* Washington, D.C.: Georgetown University Press, 1996.

Bailey, Christopher J. *The Republican Party in the U.S. Senate, 1974–1984: Party Change and Institutional Development.* Manchester: Manchester University Press, 1988.

Bailyn, Bernard. *The Ideological Origins of the American Revolution.* Cambridge, Mass.: Belknap Press, 1967.

Balz, Dan, and Ronald Brownstein. *Storming the Gates: Protest Politics and the Republican Revival.* Boston: Little, Brown, 1996.

Barone, Michael, and Grant Ujifusa, with Richard E. Cohen. *The Almanac of American Politics, 1996.* Washington, D.C.: National Journal, 1995.

———. *The Almanac of American Politics, 1998.* Washington, D.C.: National Journal, 1997.

Barry, John M. *The Ambition and the Power.* New York: Viking Press, 1989.

Benjamin, Gerald, and Michael J. Malbin, eds.. *Limiting Legislative Terms,.* Washington, D.C.: CQ Press, 1992.

Bryce, James. *The American Commonwealth.* Vol. 1. New York: Macmillan, 1911.

Burnham, Walter Dean. *The Current Crisis in American Politics.* New York: Oxford University Press, 1982.

Carter, Stephen L. *The Confirmation Mess.* New York: Basic Books, 1994.

Ceaser, James W., and Andrew E. Busch. *Losing to Win: The 1996 Elections and American Politics.* Lanham, Md.: Rowman and Littlefield, 1997.

Connelly, William F. Jr., and John J. Pitney Jr. *Congress' Permanent Minority: Republicans in the U.S. House.* Lanham, Md.: Rowman and Littlefield, 1994.

Corrado, Anthony. "Financing the 1996 Elections." Pp. 135–71 in *The Election of 1996,* ed. Gerald M. Pomper. Chatham, N.J.: Chatham House, 1997.

Crossman, R.H.S. Introduction to Walter Bagehot, *The English Constitution.* London: Fontana, 1963.

Dionne, E.J. Jr. *They Only Look Dead: Why Progressives Will Dominate the Next Political Era.* New York: Simon and Schuster, 1996.

Dodd, Lawrence C., and Bruce C. Oppenheimer, eds. "Maintaining Order in the House: The Struggle for Institutional Equilibrium." Pp. 41–88 in *Congress Reconsidered,* 5th ed. Washington, D.C.: CQ Press, 1993.

Dodd, Lawrence C., and Richard L. Schott. *Congress and the Administrative State.* New York: Wiley, 1979.

Drew, Elizabeth. *Showdown: The Struggle between the Gingrich Congress and the Clinton White House.* New York: Simon and Schuster, 1996.

———. *Whatever It Takes: The Real Struggle for Political Power in America.* New York: Viking Press, 1997.

Evans, C. Lawrence, and Walter J. Oleszek. *Congress under Fire: Reform Politics and the Republican Majority.* Boston: Houghton Mifflin, 1997.

Fenno, Richard F. Jr. "If, as Ralph Nader Says, Congress Is the 'Broken Branch,' How Come We Love Our Congressman So Much?" Pp. 227–87 in *Congress in Change: Evolution and Reform,* ed. Norman J. Ornstein. New York: Praeger, 1975.

———. *Home Style: House Members in Their Districts.* Boston: Little, Brown, 1978.

Fiorina, Morris P. *Congress: Keystone of the Washington Establishment,* 2nd ed. New Haven: Yale University Press, 1989.

Fite, Gilbert C. *Richard B. Russell Jr., Senator from Georgia.* Chapel Hill: University of North Carolina Press, 1991.

Franck, Thomas M., and Edward Weisband. *Foreign Policy by Congress.* New York: Oxford University Press, 1979.

Gimpel, James G. *Legislating the Revolution: The Contract with America in Its First 100 Days.* Boston: Allyn and Bacon, 1996.

Gingrich, Newt. *To Renew America.* New York: HarperCollins, 1995.

Greider, William. *The Education of David Stockman and Other Americans.* New York: Dutton, 1982.

Harris, Fred. R. *In Defense of Congress.* New York: St. Martin's Press, 1995.

Heclo, Hugh. "Issue Networks and the Executive Establishment." Pp. 87–124 in *The New American Political System,* ed. Anthony King. Washington, D.C.: American Enterprise Institute, 1979.

Hershey, Marjorie Randon. "The Congressional Elections." Pp. 205–39 in *The Election of 1996: Reports and Interpretations,* ed. Gerald M. Pomper. Chatham, N.J.: Chatham House, 1997.

Hibbing, John R., and Elizabeth Theiss-Morse. *Congress as Public Enemy.* New York: Cambridge University Press, 1995.

Hibbing, John R., and Eric Tiritilli. "Public Disapproval of Congress Can Be Dangerous to Majority Party Candidates: The Case of 1994." Paper presented at the annual meeting of the Midwest Political Science Association, Chicago, 10–12 April 1997.

Hill, Kevin A. "Does the Creation of Majority Black Districts Aid Republicans? An Analysis of the 1992 Congressional Elections in Eight Southern States." *Journal of Politics* 57 (1995): 384–401.

Hofstader, Richard. *The Age of Reform: From Bryan to FDR.* New York: Knopf, 1955.

Jacobson, Gary C. *The Politics of Congressional Elections.* 2nd ed. Boston: Little, Brown, 1987.

———. *The Electoral Origins of Divided Government.* Boulder, Colo.: Westview Press, 1990.

———. "The 1994 House Elections in Perspective." Pp. 1–20 in *Midterm: The Elections of 1994 in Context,* ed. Philip A. Klinker. Boulder, Colo.: Westview Press, 1996.

———. "The 105th Congress: Unprecedented and Unsurprising." Pp. 143–66 in *The Elections of 1996,* ed. Michael Nelson. Washington, D.C.: CQ Press, 1997.

Jones, Charles O. "Campaigning to Govern: The Clinton Style." Pp. 35–69 in *The Clinton Presidency: First Appraisals,* ed. Colin Campbell and Bert A. Rockman. Chatham, N.J.: Chatham House, 1996.

Katzmann, Robert A. "War Powers: Toward a New Accommodation." Pp. 35–69 in *A Question of Balance: The President, the Congress, and Foreign Policy,* ed. Thomas E. Mann. Washington, D.C.: Brookings Institution, 1990.

Kellerman Barbara, and Ryan J. Barilleaux. *The President as World Leader.* New York: St. Martin's Press, 1991.

Koopman, Douglas L. *Hostile Takeover: The House Republican Party, 1980–1995.* Lanham, Md.: Rowman and Littlefield, 1996.

Lowi, Theodore J. *The End of Liberalism: The Second Republic of the United States.* 2nd ed. New York: Norton, 1979.

———. *The Personal President: Power Invested, Promise Unfulfilled.* Ithaca, N.Y.: Cornell University Press, 1985.

Mackintosh, John P. *The British Cabinet.* 3rd ed. London: Stevens and Sons, 1977.

Mann, Robert. *The Walls of Jericho: Lyndon Johnson, Hubert Humphrey, Richard Russell and the Struggle for Civil Rights.* New York: Harcourt Brace, 1996.

Mann, Thomas E. *Unsafe at Any Margin: Interpreting Congressional Elections.* Washington, D.C.: American Enterprise Institute, 1978.

Maraniss, David, and Michael Weisskopf. *Tell Newt to Shut Up!* New York: Touchstone, 1996.

Matthews, Donald R. *U.S. Senators and Their World.* New York: Vintage Books, 1960.

Mayer, William G. "The Presidential Nominations." Pp. 21–76 in *The Election of 1996,* ed. Gerald M. Pomper. Chatham, N.J.: Chatham House, 1997.

Mayhew, David. *Congress: The Electoral Connection.* New Haven: Yale University Press, 1974.

McDonald, Forrest. *Novus Ordo Seclorum: The Intellectual Origins of the Constitution.* Lawrence: University Press of Kansas, 1985.

McGerr, Michael E. *The Decline of Popular Politics: The American North, 1896–1928.* New York: Oxford University Press, 1986.

Murray, Charles. *Losing Ground: American Social Policy, 1950–1980.* New York: Basic Books, 1984.

Ornstein, Norman J., Thomas E. Mann, and Michael J. Malbin. *Vital Statistics on Congress: 1995–1996.* Washington, D.C.: American Enterprise Institute, 1996.

Ornstein, Norman J., Robert L. Peabody, and David W. Rohde. "The U.S. Senate in an Era of Change." Pp. 13–40 in *Congress Reconsidered,* 5th ed., ed. Lawrence C. Dodd and Bruce C. Oppenheimer. Washington, D.C.: CQ Press, 1993.

Patterson, Samuel C. "The Semi-Sovereign Congress." Pp. 125–77 in *The New American Political System,* ed. Anthony King. Washington, D.C.: American Enterprise Institute, 1978.

Peters, Ronald M. Jr. *The American Speakership: The Office in Historical Perspective.* Baltimore: Johns Hopkins University Press, 1990.

———. "The Republican Speakership." Paper presented at the annual meeting of the American Political Science Association, San Francisco, 29 August–1 September 1996.

Quirk, Paul J., and Jon K. Dalager. "The Election: A 'New Democrat' and a New Kind of Presidential Campaign." Pp. 57–88 in *The Elections of 1992,* ed. Michael Nelson. Washington, D.C.: CQ Press, 1993.

Rae, Nicol C. *Southern Democrats.* New York: Oxford University Press, 1994.

———. "Intra-Party Conflict in an Evolving Electoral Order: American Party Factionalism 1946–52 and 1990–96." Paper presented at the annual meeting of the American Political Science Association, San Francisco, 29 August–1 September 1996.

Schlesinger, Arthur M. Jr. *The Imperial Presidency.* New York: Popular Library, 1973.

Shafer, Byron E., ed. "The Notion of an Electoral Order: The Structure of Electoral Politics at the Accession of George Bush." Pp. 37–84 in *The End of Realignment? Interpreting American Electoral Eras.* Madison, WI: University of Wisconsin Press, 1991.

Silbey, Joel H. *The American Political Nation, 1838–1893*. Stanford, Calif.: Stanford University Press, 1991.

Sinclair, Barbara. *The Transformation of the U.S. Senate*. Baltimore: Johns Hopkins University Press, 1989.

———. *Legislators, Leaders, and Lawmaking: The U.S. House of Representatives in the Postreform Era*. Baltimore: Johns Hopkins University Press, 1995.

———. "Trying to Govern Positively in a Negative Era: Clinton and the 103rd Congress." Pp. 88–125 in *The Clinton Presidency: First Appraisals,* ed. Colin Campbell and Bert A. Rockman. Chatham, N.J.: Chatham House, 1996.

———. *Unorthodox Lawmaking: New Legislative Processes in the U.S. Congress*. Washington, D.C.: CQ Press, 1997.

Skocpol, Theda. *Boomerang: Health Care Reform and the Turn Against Government*. New York: Norton, 1996.

Skowronek, Steven. *Building a New American State: The Expansion of National Administrative Capacities, 1877–1920*. New York: Cambridge University Press, 1982.

Stanley, Harold W. "The Parties, the President, and the 1994 Midterm Elections." Pp. 188–211 in *The Clinton Presidency: First Appraisals,* ed. Colin Campbell and Bert A. Rockman. Chatham, N.J.: Chatham House, 1996.

———. "The Nominations: Republican Doldrums, Democratic Revival." Pp. 14–43 in *The Elections of 1996,* ed. Michael Nelson. Washington, D.C.: CQ Press, 1997.

Stockman, David A. *The Triumph of Politics: How the Reagan Revolution Failed*. New York: Harper and Row, 1986.

Sundquist, James L. *The Decline and Resurgence of Congress*. Washington, D.C.: Brookings Institution, 1981.

Tulis, Jeffrey K. *The Rhetorical Presidency*. Princeton: Princeton University Press, 1987.

Watts, Mark D. "Framing Congress: Media Coverage of the U.S. Congress and Its Impact on Public Opinion." Ph.D. dissertation, University of Minnesota, 1997.

Weber, Max. "The Sociology of Charismatic Authority." Pp. 245–64 in *From Max Weber: Essays in Sociology,* ed. H.H. Gerth and C. Wright Mills. London: Routledge and Kegan Paul, 1970.

White, Joseph, and Aaron Wildavsky. *The Deficit and the Public Interest: The Search for Responsible Budgeting in the 1980s*. Berkeley: University of California Press, 1991.

White, William S. *Citadel: The Story of the U.S. Senate*. New York: Harper and Brothers, 1956.

Wilcox, Clyde *The Latest American Revolution? The 1994 Elections and Their Implications for Governance*. New York: St. Martin's Press, 1995.

Wildavsky, Aaron. *The New Politics of the Budget Process*. Glenview, Il.: Scott Foresman, 1988.

Williams, Dick. *Newt! Leader of the Second American Revolution*. Marietta, GA: Longstreet Press, 1995.

Wilson, Woodrow. *Congressional Government,* Baltimore: Johns Hopkins University Press, 1981.

Wood, Gordon S. *The Creation of the American Republic, 1776–1787*. New York: Norton, 1969.

Index

Nicol C. Rae is currently associate professor of political science at Florida International University. His previous publications include *The Decline and Fall of the Liberal Republicans* (1989), *Southern Democrats* (1994), and, with Tim Hames, *Governing America* (1996).